Divorcing Again?

Lifeboat to Happiness

*Insights and Tips from Over
700 Adults and Their Kids*

HELEN SMITH BARNET, Ph.D.

Divorcing Again? Lifeboat to Happiness: Insights and Tips
from over 700 Adults and Their Children
Copyright © 2025 Helen Smith Barnet, Ph.D.

Produced and printed by Stillwater River Publications. All rights reserved. Written and produced in the United States of America. This book may not be reproduced or sold in any form without the expressed, written permission of the author and publisher.

Book examples are composite cases. The project identified each case profile, including its demographic features and overall divorce process. Then, each account was written with particulars from non-participants given to me by other professionals and friends that matched the situation. The resulting stories read like individual interviews but are about fictional people, blending many people's stories. Identifying characteristics, including names, have been altered to ensure privacy and protect identities. Any resemblance to an actual person living or dead, locations, or events is coincidental.

No book can substitute for in-person professional advice. If expert assistance or counseling is needed, the services of a competent professional should be sought.

Visit our website at **www.StillwaterPress.com** for more information.

First Stillwater River Publications Edition.

ISBN: 978-1-965733-57-8

Library of Congress Control Number: 2025907972

1 2 3 4 5 6 7 8 9 10

Text and charts by Helen Smith Barnet, Ph.D.
Cover and interior book design by Matthew St. Jean.
Cover assets by Natali Snailcat (water), jozefmicic (boat and people),
and Pakon (sky) / Adobe Stock.
Published by Stillwater River Publications, West Warwick, RI, USA.

Publisher's Cataloging-in-Publication
(Provided by Cassidy Cataloguing Services, Inc.)
Names: Barnet, Helen Smith, author.
Title: Divorcing again? : lifeboat to happiness : insights and tips from over 700 adults and their children / Helen Smith Barnet, Ph.D.
Description: First Stillwater River Publications edition. | West Warwick, RI, USA : Stillwater River Publications, [2025]
Identifiers: LCCN: 2025907972 | ISBN: 9781965733578
Subjects: LCSH: Divorce--Social aspects. | Divorce--Psychological aspects. | Remarriage. | Divorce--Anecdotes. | LCGFT: Self-help publications. | Anecdotes.
Classification: LCC HQ814 .B37 2025 | DDC: 306.89--dc23

The views and opinions expressed in this book are solely those of the author and do not necessarily reflect the views and opinions of the publisher.

TO MY TWO FAVORITE MEN:
My husband Stephen and
My son Bradford

Contents

Figures / Tables		*vii*
Chapter 1	Your Divorce Guide	1
Chapter 2	How Are Remarriages Different?	8
Chapter 3	How Are Remarriage Divorces Different?	19
Chapter 4	Mono-remarriage Pitfalls: Challenges When *Only the Man* Is Rewed	32
Chapter 5	Uni-remarriage Pitfalls: Challenges When *Only the Wife* Is Rewed	48
Chapter 6	Bi-remarriage Pitfalls: Challenges When *Both* Are Rewed	59
Chapter 7	Solving Early Tasks: Counselors, Lawyers, Children & Money	68
Chapter 8	Uprooted: Spousal Issues, Social Changes, and Relocating	96
Chapter 9	Weathering the Storm	116
Chapter 10	First-year Postdivorce Transition	149
Chapter 11	Second-Timers—Three Years Later	178
Chapter 12	Mono-Redivorce: What to Expect When Only *He* Is Redivorcing	196
Chapter 13	Uni-redivorce: What to Expect When Only *She* Is Redivorcing	213
Chapter 14	Bi-redivorce: What to Expect When *Both* Are Redivorcing	228
Chapter 15	How Will My Children React? How Can I Help Them?	243
Chapter 16	Project Design	279

Appendix: Progressive Muscle Relaxation (PMR) (Modified version Norelli et al., 2023; designed originally by Jacobson, 1929)	*282*
Notes	*284*
Glossary	*286*
References	*290*
Topic Index	*298*
About the Author	*300*

Figures / Tables

Figure 3-1: Redivorcers with easier, same, or harder second divorce than first	22
Figure 3-2: Adults in each group who described their ex-spouse as honest, dependable, sincere, and loyal	30
Table 7-1: Household budget	89
Figure 8-1: Social difficulties for men and women	98
Figure 9-1: Men and women with an increase in four emotions	119
Figure 9-2: High stress during each stage for men and women	124
Figure 9-3: Men and women with each health and work problem	137
Figure 9-4: Men and women with each relief reaction	144
Figure 10-1: Good adjustment on four indexes during the first year post-divorce	153
Figure 10-2: Men and women with each relative happiness level	155
Figure 10-3: First year romantic relationships	160
Figure 10-4: Men and women with each ex-spouse attitude	165
Figure 10-5: Men and women with each marital review level	167
Figure 10-6: Men and women who described their ex-spouse as dependable, honest, loyal, and sincere	175
Figure 11-1: Men and women who are reasonably satisfied in each area of their lives	180
Figure 11-2: Men and women with good, so-so, poor, or no relationship with their second ex	188

Figure 11-3: Third year romantic relationships for
second-time men and women 191
Figure 12-1: Mean stress for each stage and overall for
mono-redivorced men and women 203
Figure 13-1: Mean stress for each stage and overall for
uni-redivorced men and women 220
Figure 14-1: Mean stress for each stage and overall for
bi-redivorced men and women 234
Figure 15-1: First- and second-marriage children with
negative, positive, ambivalent, and indifferent
reactions to a redivorce. 254
Figure 15-2: Children in each age group with each
negative emotional reaction 258
Figure 15-3: Children in each age group with each
parent-child relationship change 259
Figure 15-4: Children with each behavior problem in
each age group 264
Figure 15-5: Children with each positive or indifferent
reaction in each age group 269

Quizzes

Quiz #1: First versus second divorce 19
Quiz #2: Marital complaints and family background 32
Quiz #3: Difficulties 68
Quiz #4: Social difficulties 96
Quiz #5: Stress, trauma, and relief 116
Quiz #6: Transition 149
Quiz #7: Three-year follow-up 178
Quiz #8: Children's reactions 243

Divorcing Again?

CHAPTER 1

Your Divorce Guide

Divorced again?
Am I doing something wrong?
Am I capable of being happily married?
Why is this happening... again?

Divorce is a multi-year challenge filled with turmoil and ongoing adjustments. A breakup of a second marriage, however, is not a repeat of a first divorce. How it affects you and how others react to it are unique. You have figured this out. That is why my book is in your hands.

That understanding—that the end of a remarriage is different—sets *Divorcing Again?* apart from other divorce books. It is your roadmap and lifeboat through your journey. Based on my groundbreaking research, it provides the information you need to understand this relatively new path, how your spouse and children will respond, and your steps to get through your upheaval and into a happy life.

Many remarriages include one spouse who has had a previous marriage and one for whom it is a first. If you are a once-wed partner in this situation, this guide is for you, too. As you may already suspect, your marriage and breakup are different from your second-time spouse's and different from your friend's traditional-first, where both are leaving a first union. More than one third of this book speaks directly to you about how to navigate your distinct path.

As a psychologist, I have been researching family breakups for more than thirty years, starting with my doctoral dissertation on adult divorce stress and adjustment. Back then, divorce was increasing rapidly, but little was known about it, especially the adult process. With numerous friends, family, and clients getting a divorce at the time, I wanted to better understand these separations and how to make them easier.

The current research began about ten years later. As I watched so many who divorced once now doing it again, I wondered: *Why was this happening again? How could I help families get through their ordeal?* To explore this trend, I conducted a series of studies, including a follow-up. As my research started before the legalization of same-sex marriages, the men and women in this study were exiting opposite-sex marriages. Likewise, in this book, marriage and divorce refer to opposite-sex couples. At last count, 722 adults have joined one of the first four inquiries reported in this book. In two of these, 333 parents described a child's reactions to their recent split as well as their own.

Soon after I began this investigation, I noticed that the breakup of a remarriage was different from the more common divorce, where both are ending a first marriage. Then, I discovered three other facts.

Fact 1: *Remarriage and redivorce are becoming common.* Starting about ten years ago, one in four weddings was a remarriage for the bride and/or the groom. Because second unions are more unstable than first ones, redivorce has increased rapidly in recent years, even among older couples.[1] So if you are in or ending a rewed, you are part of a modern trend.

Fact 2: *Remarriages take three forms.* Each of these marital types has unique characteristics and fault lines. When these couples split, the process and challenges are often dissimilar.

Therefore, I will discuss each of these remarriage and divorce experiences separately and focus on how they are similar and how they are not.

In some marriages, the husband is remarried, but his wife is only in her first. Some male celebrities and four United States Presidents are part of this set. This includes Ronald Reagan and Donald Trump.

In his late thirties, President Reagan's eight-year marriage to Jane Wyman ended. Four years later, he married Nancy Davis, a first-time bride ten years his junior. The couple was happily married for about five decades until he died at age 93.

President Trump is in his third marriage and second remarriage to a first-time bride. His current spouse, Melania Knauss, wed him in her mid-thirties and is about 24 years his junior. When he entered the White House, they had been married for about twelve years, fewer years than his first union to Ivana Zelnickova, but longer than his second to Marla Maples.

In a second group, the wife is rewed, but her husband is only in his first. President Trump's first marriage was an example of this. His original wife was divorced when he met her in his twenties. At 24, Ivana left her first of four husbands, an Austrian skier named Alfred Winklmayr. Four years later, she and Donald Trump wed, but divorced fifteen years after that. For the third or largest remarriage set, the couple is wed following the divorce of both partners. Celebrity marriages are often dual remarriages.

Fact 3: For both first- and second-timers, *the end of a remarriage is a learning opportunity and, for many, the path to a better life.* A successful divorce is a lemonade experience—bitter at the start, but ends with personal growth, a better understanding of how to achieve a happy partnership, and redirection.

How to Use the Book

This book contains general and specific information not only on how remarriages get into trouble, but also, and more importantly, how to successfully navigate the three versions of the redivorce process. For an overview, read the book in chronological order. You can also hopscotch through the book, stopping to read areas that interest you. You may want to start with the section dealing with your top issue so you can solve it first and then read the other parts.

Most chapters incorporate special features to help you understand the material and make the best choices. As an aid, many sections start with a quiz. Completing each of these prior to reading the rest of the chapter will help you grasp the upcoming material.

Especially if you like numbers, you will want to take a close look at the graphs. These will help you quickly see and find the major results from the study.

Recommendations pepper discussions. All these ideas are quick solutions and easy to apply. Everyone is an individual, so find ones that work best for you. You may want to buy a notebook in which to write notes as you read. In your journal, you can write your favorite tips, record your reactions on worksheets, and list relevant resources. Alternatively, you can put these in your note section of your cell phone.

Composite examples are added to clarify the material. They are called composites because they combine several stories. These are often fictional dialogues between two friends talking about their journey. Others emphasize redivorce rules. Although there are many cases, the book primarily uses nine couples. The section below gives a synopsis of these. Many of their children's reactions appear in Chapter 15.

When you read the longer versions of these stories, you will be able to "see" how a person's past often foretells his/her future. Your past, however, does not have to predict your destiny. You can learn from others' solutions to redirect and improve your journey. Use your divorce as an opportunity to take a closer look at yourself, ditch ineffective habits, and develop new, more effective ways of relating to a partner. With increased self-knowledge and the information in this book, you can choose your new direction, make yourself and your family happier, and advance to a better, more fulfilling life.

So, sit down, put your feet up, and let me show you how to get back to happy. We will get through this together. I'll be by your side the whole way through until you're smiling again.

Synopsis of Nine Couples

Type 1: Mono-remarriages have a once-married wife and a twice-married husband.

1. JANET & STANLEY

At 24, Janet, a dental hygienist, married Stanley, a 31-year-old plumber. Eight years later, Janet divorced Stanley when their daughter Lilly was almost seven and his first-marriage son was in high school. When they split, he blamed the divorce primarily on her parents' hostility, while she blamed it primarily on financial strain from his first-marriage obligations.

2. GRACE & WILLIAM

Grace, a hairdresser, and William, a salesman, began their six-year marriage when she was 23 and he was 32. They had three sons, one from his first marriage, Lane, and two from theirs, Mark and Steve. Soon after they married, William lost his job and could not find another one for four months. On his next job, he was frequently away from home for at least three days at a time.

Lonely and worried that he might leave her, Grace left him for someone new.

3. Louise & John

Louise, a late-twenties florist, was married for six years to John, an early thirties supermarket manager. They had one son from his first union, Cody. John's mother and son were openly hostile toward Louise and took every opportunity to undermine their marriage. His mom even shouted at the wedding rehearsal, "Do you have to marry that woman?" Eventually, John left the marriage via an affair.

Type 2: Uni-remarriages have a once-married husband and a second-married wife.

1. Scarlett & Elvis

On their wedding day, Elvis was an early-thirties bus driver, while his bride, Scarlett, was in her late twenties. When they divorced, she went on welfare. They had two daughters, Sunny from her first marriage and Elle from the recent one. Scarlett left Elvis because she was fed up with his partying, drinking, and abuse.

2. Bolta & Carter

When Carter, an artist, wed Bolta, a real estate appraiser, they were both in their late twenties. They had a son, Max, from her first marriage, but no children from this one. Max considered Carter his emotional Dad. Carter complained that she never made a commitment to the marriage or supported his artistic goals and, as a result, they grew apart. Bolta resented that she was the major breadwinner. Carter married Madeline several years later.

3. Savannah & Pug

In their mid-thirties, Pug was an architect, while Savannah was a bank teller with an eleven-year-old daughter, Princess, from a prior relationship. They had a brief, rebound marriage.

With very different lifestyles and values, they bickered over many things, even how to put on the toilet paper. Pug didn't get along with his stepdaughter, felt like an outsider, and didn't feel close to Savannah. He divorced Savannah and then had a brief love relationship with another woman.

Type 3: Bi-remarriages have a remarried wife and a remarried husband.

1. Desirée & Saul

Desirée, a teacher's aide, married Saul, a construction worker. When they married, she was 29 and he was 32. They had Lois from her first marriage, Peter from his first marriage, and their mutual son, Tucker. Their seven-year marriage ended when she left Saul. She complained that he favored Peter over their other children and her. He countered that she treated Peter with disdain.

2. Cheyenne & Ralph

A mid-thirties couple, Ralph and Cheyenne were high school teachers with a daughter, Rose, from his first marriage, and Lilac from theirs. Ralph ran off with the next-door neighbor, Sabrina.

3. Beth & Nickolas

Beth, a veterinarian, and Nickolas, an accountant, were briefly married in their late thirties. She had two daughters, Sarah, 12, and Ann, 7. He had a boy and a girl, Bret, 14, and Carol, 13. They blamed problems with the three older children for their breakup. Sarah got into trouble at school for breaking rules, failed several courses, and fought with her mother, stepsiblings, and stepfather. His children didn't like Beth or her children either. The divorce decision was mutual.

CHAPTER 2

How Are Remarriages Different?

BETH AND NICKOLAS'S WEDDING

Nickolas looked over his shoulder, turned, and smiled broadly at Beth as she walked slowly toward him on the sweltering July morning. Beth, just thirty-eight, smiled and winked back at her thirty-nine-year-old fiancé. She wore an off-white, casual summer dress with a large, yellow sash at the waist, purchased the day before in Walmart. In her hands, she carried a small bunch of freshly picked, yellow sunflowers and white daisies wrapped together with string and taken from their backyard that morning. Beside Nickolas stood their minister from the Unitarian Church; Nickolas's best friend, Luke; Beth's best friend Molly; and the couple's four children. Nickolas, Luke, and his son Bret wore white slacks and navy blazers. Outfitted in short, printed summer dresses, Molly and their three daughters each carried one long-stemmed sunflower.

Several neighbors and about a half-dozen friends attended, but their parents and siblings were absent. They lived too far away to make the last-minute ceremony. The couple decided to get married on the spur of the moment, several months after they met at a church social. They were thankful that their minister agreed to perform the ceremony on the local beach that Saturday morning, with less than a two-week notice. Right after the vows,

Beth and Nickolas updated their Facebook status from divorced to married and added an iPhone photo.

The wedding party and attendees celebrated with a reception at their favorite restaurant, Jack's Seaside Grill. In lieu of a wedding photographer, guests were asked to take photos and upload them to the couple's Facebook page. Friends and neighbors were happy for the couple but puzzled by the suddenness of the wedding. By 3 pm, the group had dispersed, and Nickolas, Beth, and Beth's daughters returned to their home.

Family and friends who didn't attend, called throughout the afternoon and evening to give their congratulations and learn more about the event and their plans. Perhaps the couple would go to Ogunquit, Maine for a delayed honeymoon in late August, but they weren't sure. By Monday, the two were back to their old routines, as if nothing had happened over the weekend. That evening, Beth joked about how different their recent marriage had been from her large, well-planned, and expensive first one fifteen years ago.

Two years later, Nickolas and Beth divorced. When they split up neither had any idea how their brief engagement and quick marriage affected their marital preparation, marriage commitment, and social support. They also did not understand how the lack of these three important issues destroyed their marriage.

Fragile Start

The distinction between a first and second ceremony is striking, especially among the rich. The Queen of England and her palace staff planned a large, splashy wedding for Charles, Prince of Wales, to his first wife, Lady Diana Spencer, but hosted a small, discreet wedding to his second, divorcée Camilla Parker Bowles. Even if Prince Charles' remarriage hadn't been scandalous, it still would have been a quiet event since it was a second. First and second marriage rituals aren't the same in less affluent families, either.

You can almost always distinguish a first or later wedding. When you see a young woman in a white dress, you suspect that this is her first. If the couple is older with child attendees, you presume that this is a rewed. Typically, the first is deemed important, well attended, and carefully implemented, but the remarriage is not.

Few, unfortunately, understand how these practices lead to differences in social support, marital preparation, commitment, and harmony. Fewer still understand how these customs promote first-marriage success, but second-marriage failure. If, however, you read the rest of this chapter, you will understand these important rules and relationships. Then, you can apply these rules and up your chances of having a solid remarriage or an easier second divorce.

More Grounds for Conflict

First-marriage couples usually marry by their early thirties, are about the same age, have roughly the same amount of education, and share similar religious, political, and socio-economic outlooks. Remarried couples have less in common than first-timers. Husbands are often a decade or more older than their wives. Sooner or later, this can be a problem. The wife may be 35 and wants to start a family, but he's 45 and feels too old to do so. Or he's 62 and wants to retire and move to Florida, but she is only 48, likes working, and doesn't want to move away from her family and friends. Now add on political, social, and religious differences, which are standard with remarried partners. So, these couples often have a lot to argue about, have a hard time finding workable compromises, and, thus, are more likely to be dissatisfied with their relationship and divorce than once-wed adults.

As a rule, redivorcing adults are older than first-timers. As you mature, your pocketbook, personality, physical appearance, and marriageability change. You earn more, and your financial assets increase. You become calmer, more outgoing, and more conscientious. After age 40, women have a harder time finding someone new than their husband, and are, thus, less willing to initiate the divorce. All of these affect the breakup process in first and second divorces.

A divorce is easier if you initiate it, can easily recouple, and have more income to fund your costs. It is easier if you have greater stress tolerance, are sociable, so you have more friends, or are conscientious. Conscientious individuals face their problems sooner and are more adept at solving them. Depending on how all these add up, you may or may not be in better stead the second time.

Motivations & Marriage Glue

First and remarriage decisions are unalike. Typically, first-timers consider a marriage a lifetime choice and wed because they're in love and want to start a family. When marital troubles crop up, they often spend a long time trying to correct marital unhappiness, compromise, or simply live with the dysfunction. If, however, problems persist, some will choose to divorce, so they can find happiness with someone else. Within three or four years postdivorce, almost everyone walks down the aisle again.

In contrast, a remarriage is normally based on companionship, finances, or other practical needs. Jackie Kennedy once joked, "The first time you marry for love, the second for money, and the third for companionship." [1]

For many, remarriages are conditional contracts, which expire if problems occur rather than "until death do us part." Having divorced once, they are rapid to recognize their problems and want to correct them either by trying harder, living apart, or getting a swift divorce.

Until lately, second failed marriages were on average shorter than first ones.[2] Today, this is no longer true, at least on paper. Second marriages are likely to be as long as first ones, on average eight years.[3] Hopefully, this trend reflects positive changes, but not necessarily. Instead, second-timers may still want to exit rapidly. For practical reasons, they may immediately separate, but take more time to get a legal divorce. Divorce is expensive, and most do not want to remarry.

One redivorced man sent me a questionnaire from Texas with a note. "I had no idea that I was divorced. Would you please send me a copy of my divorce decree?" Ostensibly, he no longer wanted to live with his wife. Instead of getting a divorce, he moved to the Southwest, leaving her behind. A year or two later, she filed for the dissolution without notifying him, although she and her lawyer had his address and put it on the divorce decree.

As such, the motivations for entering and exiting first and second marriages usually differ. These differences, in turn, can cause a remarriage to be relatively unstable and, if it fails, lead to a different ungluing.

Marriage Importance, Preparation, Commitment, and Social Support

First Weddings: Big and Bold

The average first-time couple garners marriage preparation, commitment, and high social support for their wedding and marriage. Once engaged, you tell as many people as possible, starting with your parents and siblings. An engagement is a more committed social obligation than simply dating or cohabitation. It begins with a public notice and pledge, the engagement ring.

Traditional marriages are a series of well-planned events. Customarily, the bride's parents host and play a key role in the activities. The groom's family plays an important, but secondary role. These rituals foster the couple's marital preparation. To plan and prepare for a traditional event, couples are engaged for six to twelve months. During a long betrothal, twosomes grow closer as they learn more about each other and learn ways to resolve differences.

During the service, the bride wears a white dress—a tradition started by Queen Victoria. The wedding party includes many and wears coordinating attire. Flowers are lavish. Because of this pageantry, most consider the first wedding and marriage important. Friends and relatives make every effort to attend and send a nice gift. Twosomes now have a lot of social support. In turn, this backing promotes a happier, more durable marriage. The more people who attend your wedding, the less likely you will divorce. These ceremonies promote dedication, too. If you say you're going to do something in a large, public format, you increase your faithfulness and marital luck. After the wedding and reception, most couples go on a honeymoon. This next step gives the couple time to be alone, extends their marital celebration, and increases their odds of being happily married. [4]

REMARRIAGE WEDDINGS: HO-HUM AFFAIRS

From start to finish, the typical remarriage process is different in ways that undermine your relationship. Couples usually tell as few people as possible about their upcoming nuptials. Children tend to hear first, followed by their friends and ex-spouses. Parents and other relatives are apt to be the last to know.

Remarrying pairs, like Nickolas and Beth, choose to wed quickly. Marriages after a brief courtship are likely to be unhappy and fail. ***Individuals in this study, who entered their second marriage soon after their first, had the shortest remarriages.*** Why is this so?

Brief courtships skip important traditional steps. Steps, which give you a chance to get to know your partner, to establish ways to resolve differences, get past the rebound period, or, if warranted, break up. Quick marriages don't allow family and friends time to get to know the two of you well enough to support your marriage. This is a big mistake. If they develop a solid relationship with the two of you, they will not only back your marriage, but also encourage others to accept and support it, too. Social backing of your marriage strengthens it.

By tradition, remarrying couples plan, host, and announce an informal service. They distribute handwritten invitations, send e-mails, phone, or tell invitees in person. A maid of honor and a best man are usually the only attendees. Floral arrangements are simple; a bridal bouquet is customarily the only one. The bride's attire is often modest and a non-white dress or suit. Few are invited, and fewer still come. In response to the informal plans, many consider a remarriage unimportant. So, they will not make much of an effort to attend a second wedding. Receptions are a small, informal affair at a local restaurant, social hall, or home. By design, the second marriage is defined as unimportant and excludes many who came to the first marriage.

Most guests do not send a present, either. If they do, the gift is almost always modest and not as nice or as expensive as a first one. Remarried couples seldom go on a honeymoon. This is another mistake. As pointed out earlier, couples who go on a honeymoon, even an inexpensive one, are less apt to divorce.

Couples who abide by the standard, second engagement process and nuptials devalue their marriage. When they do, they receive little help and encouragement to keep their commitment intact. If the remarriage falters, neither can expect as much emotional and financial aid as they did during their first divorce. With little or no social backing, they can feel rejected, isolated, and lonely. This split is now even more painful than the first. Why allow this to happen?

Challenges

THE PUSH AND PULL OF CHILDREN

A first marriage almost always begins with few complications, a set of clear roles and expectations, and good social support. Couples rarely have children to interfere with it. This is especially true for college-educated, non-minority pairs, or those from the middle or upper class.[5] Marriage for most is a prelude and first step toward starting a family. Once born, children help cement the relationship with lifetime obligations to raise them.

Not so with remarried couples. Prior marriage children—his, hers, or theirs—and the lack of clear remarriage rules, start a remarriage out with a list of pre-existing problems to solve, more potential interference, and low social backing.

Rewed couples rightfully want their children to accept and support their new marriage like the family in the TV series, "The Brady Bunch," instead of like the children in the films, "Step Brothers" or "Daddy's Home." Social norms, legal obligations, and relationships in stepfamilies, however, are unclear, vary from state to state, and are complicated.

Remarriages include at least one remarried partner. If you are a sole remarried spouse, then your spouse gets an instant family, including any children from your first marriage, and your ex-spouse. If the reverse is true, you get an instant family. If you are both remarried, you have two sets of ex-spouses and maybe minor or adult children from both previous marriages. On top of this, you both gain your spouse's birth relatives. Your pool of relatives expands further as ex-spouse(s) remarry, have more children and stepchildren, and add more relations. Eventually, you have a large cast of people who can interfere in and undermine your marriage.

Many children dislike their parents' remarriage. Their

reactions depend on their age. Minors, especially teens, have a hard time accepting their parents' remarriage. Adult ones resent a parental rewed, if they feel disinherited or alienated from you.

Former spouses can threaten a new family emotionally or financially if there are prior marriage minor children. A former spouse may have an emotional bond with either the new husband or wife, even if he or she initiated the first divorce or is remarried. When so, this lingering attachment can cause a chronic upheaval or undercurrent in a remarriage. Integrating two families may be a major challenge or undertaking.

As documented later, children conceived in first and second marriages are different. In a first, they're usually from this relationship, want their mom and dad to stay together, and are upset by their parents' divorce. In a second, children are from this or a past union. Prior-marriage children usually undermine a remarriage. If the pair separates, they rarely try to reunite the couple. Rather, they celebrate the split and help their parents thru the ordeal. Children from the marriage do not want their parents to divorce and want their parents to reunite, even years postdivorce. Simply, children are more varied in their responses to a second divorce.

Musical Chairs

Finding a second spouse is often like musical chairs, where good partner choices are limited and quickly vanish. Many divorced people have great personalities. When they rewed, they establish happy marriages like President Ronald Reagan.

From a probability point of view, however, divorced adults are more likely to be hard to live with than others. They are more likely to be disagreeable, dissatisfied, anxious, unhappy, hostile, impulsive, or lack conscientiousness. Although it isn't clear to what extent these character differences are the cause or the consequence of marital splits, they are well-documented and can lead to future relationship problems.[6]

THE PARENT TRAP

Parents often pass on their marital quality and stability to the next generation. Adults who grow up in cohesive, warm homes often are happily married men and women. Adults raised in divorced parental homes have a higher chance of divorcing. Likewise, those from unhappy, intact two-parent homes tend to form unhappy marriages, but rarely divorce unless their spouse initiates it.

Part of modeling your parents' relationship is copying how they related. Parents also pass on their socio-economic status, which in turn, affects marital quality. It is easier to be happily married if you have more education, a better job, and, as a result, a higher income. Those with divorced parents tend to drop out of school earlier, have lower incomes, and then, divorce due to financial strain.

Thus, the pool of available partners for divorced adults includes more from divorced parental homes, with problematic traits, and with lower financial resources than the first time. Singles who marry a divorced person often have an insecure attachment style and a lower chance of being happily married.[7] Divorced adults, thus, have a smaller chance of finding someone with whom they can be happily wed. So, achieving a happy second marriage is often about changing, improving your income, and finding a low-risk mate.

Important Things Remarriage Couples Often Fail to Do
- Select a partner who is a close match in age, background, and lifestyle.

- Make sure both partners are committed to the marriage.
- Long engagement/adequate marital preparation
- Socialize as a couple with friends and family before they wed.
- Finalize and announce the wedding months before the date.
- Make the wedding as special and as large as a first.
- Include parents, stepchildren, and siblings in wedding events.
- Take a honeymoon.

Things to Remember about How Remarriages Are Different:

- On average, remarried couples have less social support, less marital preparation, less commitment, and more problems to tackle than first-marriage couples. Many of these reflect marriage rituals.
- Children's roles and responses in first and second marriages and divorces differ.
- First- and second-marriage couples differ on demographic and non-demographic traits. These affect the stability of the marriage and the breakup process.
- Divorced people are apt to have or marry someone with divorce-prone traits.
- You can reduce your risk for remarriage problems by avoiding these pitfalls.

CHAPTER 3

How Are Remarriage Divorces Different?

Many chapters begin with a quiz. These are the questions I asked to obtain the information presented in the chapter. Completing each quiz before reading the material should help you understand the section.

Quiz #1: First versus Second Divorce

Q1. Compared with your first divorce, how difficult was your second divorce?
1. ___ Much easier
2. ___ Easier
3. ___ Same
4. ___ Harder
5. ___ Much harder

Q2. How stressful was your life when each of the following occurred? Please use a scale of 0 (no stress at all) to 4 (very heavy stress) to answer this question.
1. Before the decision   0 1 2 3 4
2. Divorce decision   0 1 2 3 4
3. Separation   0 1 2 3 4
4. Filing   0 1 2 3 4

5. Divorce decree   0 1 2 3 4
6. Now   0 1 2 3 4

Q3. Compared with before the divorce, are you now?
1. ___ Much less happy
2. ___ Less happy
3. ___ About as happy
4. ___ Happier
5. ___ Much happier

Q4. How often do you go over what happened during your recent marriage?
1. ___ All the time
2. ___ Frequently
3. ___ Sometimes
4. ___ Rarely
5. ___ Never

Q6. Which of the following adjectives describe your ex-spouse? (Check all that apply).
1. ___ Dependable
2. ___ Honest
3. ___ Loyal
4. ___ Sincere

Carter's Erased Marriage

Carter pushed the last of thirty paintings into his old, green van and drove off to the weekend art fair. With the help of several of his students, Carter set up his booth. Tom, his most talented art student, pitched a tent in the assigned space. The other students unloaded the van and placed the paintings where Carter directed. Madeline, his wife, would arrive after she dropped off their two youngsters at her sister's house.

No exhibit was successful without Madeline. Of the two, he was the better artist, but she was the promoter. Sociable, she could strike up a lively conversation with anyone. She would make a sale or talk a newspaper reporter into running a piece on one or both. Madeline made sure that the local weekly paper highlighted his work.

Carter's paintings were arranged in sections: early ones drawn in his mid-twenties, a second group painted in his late twenties and early thirties when he was married to Bolta, and his most recent works in a third section. During this last stage, Carter was a teacher at Baldwin High and married to his second wife, Madeline. Waiting for the show to open, Tom turned to Carter and made small talk. "It's really interesting to see your artwork in chronological order," Tom observed.

"I like doing that," Carter responded. "It is fun to see how my art and life have evolved."

"What was going on when you did those dark paintings in the middle?" Tom asked.

"I call that my blue period, Tom. I was getting a divorce from my first wife, Bolta. I hope those sell today."

"Wow. I didn't know you were married before. Thought you and your wife had been together forever."

"Feels like it. I really don't consider my time with Bolta a real marriage. Bolta had a son Max, who lived with us, but we never had any children ourselves. We were never close like I am with Madeline. My marriage to Madeline is my only real marriage."

"How did the two of you meet?" Tom asked.

"I was sketching the Tower in Narragansett, Rhode Island on Memorial Day weekend. Madeline came over to me and started criticizing it."

"Really?"

"Yeah, she asked me to add color, people, and sunlight. Normally, I would have been irritated and told her off, but I instantly liked her. Next thing I knew, we were traveling every weekend to sketch a different Rhode Island site. In July, we worked side-by-side every day."

"Sounds like fun," Tom interjected.

"By the end of the summer, I asked her to marry me. She said yes, but insisted that I get a full-time job and wait a year before we tied the knot. Baldwin High needed another art teacher. I applied and got the job using her as a reference. The following Memorial Day, we wed in Narragansett. The rest is history, a happy history."

"Whatever happened to your first wife? Did she remarry?"

"Her son says that she is happy, loves her job, and has lots of friends and a partner. She has ruled out a third marriage. Doesn't want to do that again," said Carter.

Second Divorce

Second Versus First Divorce Difficulty

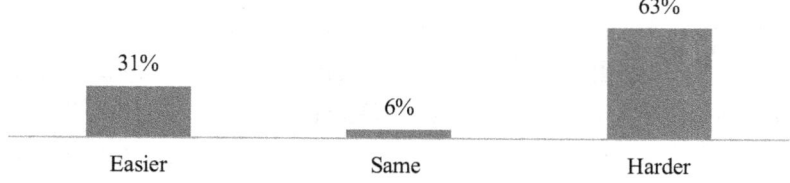

Figure 3-1: Redivorcers with easier, same, or harder second divorce than first. Note: Adults included 361 (women 215).

Nearly two-thirds said they had a tougher time with their second divorce than their first one. Why did most say this? Almost everyone else came to the opposite conclusion. Who were they?

Erased Marriages

In some respects, a second divorce is a rerun of a first, but in other respects it is not. In both, you and your spouse usually exit with health problems like insomnia and emotional distress such as shaken self-esteem, doubts about your lovability, and diminished confidence in your ability to be happily married. To protect your self-respect, you almost always blame someone else, probably your former partner. Oftentimes, you even blame your ex-spouse for the decision to get married. However, your second split is harder to explain, more discouraging and humiliating, and most people will not treat you with the same empathy and support.

After the first breakup, almost everyone remarries within four years. Before you do, you often decide that you will succeed the next time because you are determined not to make the same mistake again. To ensure this, you proceed in one of two ways.

You usually decide you married the wrong type of person—your first spouse is a mismatch. This solution is ideal because it presumes that you are fine, including being loveable, and do not have to change except to make a better marital choice next time. After you come to this conclusion, you single out one or two of your first partner's traits, annoying habits, or his or her occupation so you can find someone with the opposite characteristics.[1] If your first husband is a dependent musician, you might choose a self-reliant engineer. If your first wife is a dark-haired, stay-at-home mom, you may look for a blonde career woman. By doing this, you devalue your first spouse and first marriage.

Sometimes, you go even further and emotionally erase it. You call the first union a pretend marriage. It is a starter marriage, an impulsive mistake, or a "mulligan" that allows you a free do over.

But with the failure of the second marriage, the question now is "Why did I divorce, *again*?" This is a tougher question. This time, a satisfactory answer requires that you not only blame the marital end on someone else, but also avoid the stigma and discouragement of a second failure.

After ruminating on this question, adults in my study usually ended up with one of four reactions. The first group was unable to come up with a satisfactory answer, while the other three groups did so either by claiming that the two mistakes were different or by erasing one of their unions.

Reaction 1: *Many decided that if they married again, they would fail again.* They could not dodge the second divorce stigma. They were distrustful of others and/or their decision-making. These adults almost always decided the disgrace and despair of a second divorce was harder than their first, even when they said they handled the second divorce stress and problems better this time than the first. As long as they held this perspective, they did not want to remarry.

Reaction 2: *A few erased their first marriage before they remarried and continued to do so.* They denied that they had failed twice because they had only been emotionally married once. Typically, these men and women deemed their second divorce was harder, but thought they had a path to a solid remarriage because they had made only one mistake.

Reaction 3: *Some claimed their splits were different—they did not make the same mistake twice.* One husband asserted that his first wife's substance abuse and gambling triggered his original divorce, but his subsequent in-laws' disapproval of him led to his second. Further, he argued that her parents did not want their daughter to marry a divorced man and undermined the marriage. His "situation" caused his second divorce. By asserting that he was not making the same mistake again and blaming others, he refused to take responsibility for the breakups. Many women did the same—they had different reasons for each divorce with the second marriage often impacted by a difficult situation. Men and women who pick this choice may consider the first or second divorce easier for reasons other than their social skills, such as the presence or absence of children, who initiated the divorce, or a reasonable versus unreasonable spouse.

Reaction 4: *The remaining adults said their first union was their only real marriage.* They emotionally erased their second marital tie. Unlike most, their second divorce was the easiest. Who were they?

Parents with children from a long, first marriage, but a brief, childless second marriage, often erased their second union and, thus, had easier second breakups. They considered their first relationship their primary or only marital tie because it was the only one that was long and produced children. Moreover, they faulted their teens for their marital woes and subsequent divorce, leaving them feeling personally blameless and relatively unperturbed. In contrast, when describing their earlier split, they lost important, real marriages, had upset youngsters, and suffered first-love heartbreaks.

Second-timers, Nickolas and Beth, had teenagers from long, prior marriages when they wed, but no children from their short marriage. The couple blamed their teens' shenanigans for their rocky relationship. When they decided to split, Beth's oldest daughter was delighted, started studying again in high school so her grades improved, dropped her acting-out, rebellious behaviors, and helped her mom get through the ordeal. Nickolas's children from his prior marriage reacted in the same way. Nickolas and Beth considered this split easier than their firsts.

Another woman in the same situation refused to answer the query for her second divorce. Instead, she filled out the form for her first split. Throughout her answer sheet, she crossed off the word second and wrote in FIRST in large print to emphasize the point. Predictably, she had an easy breakup and an easier second divorce than her first one. She wrote:

> I am answering for my first marriage. My first husband was my only real love and husband. My second marriage doesn't count. It was short and we didn't have any children. We didn't have a true love relationship.

Regardless of what you say, if you're exiting your second marriage, everybody else believes you have made the same mistake twice. As a result, you're almost always in a more difficult social situation the second time.

A first divorce is common, so most people don't criticize this breakup, but instead are empathetic and help you through the process. A second divorce is less common and a repeat act.

When you make the same mistake twice, others blame you for the failures. As they now believe you caused your problems, they may even think you deserve to suffer. They also reason you can handle the breakup by yourself because you have done it before. Thus, in a second divorce, family, friends, and acquaintances are less empathetic, more disapproving of you and your split, and less willing to help you.

Traditional-firsts versus Seconds

In this section, I compare the stress, challenges, emotional reactions, and recovery of the average first-timer divorcing a once-married spouse (traditional-first) and the average second-timer. By doing so, we get a detailed picture of the multi-divorce process and a better understanding of when and how the two differ.

At the start, typical first-timers Frieda and Frank and typical second-timers Sandra and Sawyer are equally distressed. During the divorce, all four have roughly five problems, like upset children or higher costs, but the second-timers have a more difficult social situation than first-time Frieda and her ex-husband. As explained earlier, most people are more accepting and helpful toward a first-timer. Despite this, second-timers like Sawyer are less upset from the decision until the end. They have less stress and only four or one less sign of emotional distress, such as insomnia, weight loss, and anger. Why is this so?

For starters, first-timers are usually young adults, while second-timers are apt to be older and middle-aged. Young adults tend to be more easily upset than middle-agers. Second, first-time couples usually begin their relationship as deeply in love sweethearts. Remarriages are often based on companionship and financial needs. Losing a first romantic love is often harder than losing a friendship. Third, many reweds view their relationship as a conditional contract. They see their union as "until marital problems" occur, rather than "until death do us part" like Frieda and Frank. Fourth, first-timers are more apt to have children from their union than the remarrieds. Fifth, unlike the once-marrieds, the twice-marrieds have been down this path before, know the process, and know they will survive it.

Trust Issues

First-timers like Frieda with a first-time ex-spouse, Frank (traditional-firsts), and second-timers like Sandra and Sawyer have different recovery strengths. Immediately afterwards, second-timers are usually happier and have less marital review than the other two. Typically, both couples are wary, but the multi-marrieds are more so and socially reticent. Twice burned, the multi-divorced trust each other less than the other pair. Men are almost twice as likely to call their first wives honest (52% vs 31%) and dependable (48% vs 27%) than their second.

Trust is an even bigger problem for the wife. She usually distrusts her ex-spouse, especially her second. She is almost three times more likely to call her first husband honest (33% vs 13%) or loyal (21% vs 7%) than her second.

Mistrust makes it hard for second-timers to start over. During the first year afterwards, first-timers like Frieda and Frank are more romantically involved with someone new. Three years later, they have often found new spouses, but the second-timers have usually not. Worse yet, the redivorced seldom trust other potential love partners or their ability to pick a compatible lover.

As a result, behind most multi-divorced, happy façades are individuals who report a harder recovery from their second breakup. For many, the two endings are unalike.

The first usually deals with harsher short-term problems such as stress and emotional reactions. Most first-timers, however, receive empathy and help and end up with solid adjustment within a few years after the divorce. Normally, second-timers are less upset with the process, but suffer more embarrassment and criticism, have little to no help from others, and have more long-term unresolved hurdles with trust, confidence, and re-partnering.

Hybrid First

Singles who marry and then break up with a previously married spouse are called hybrid-firsts. These second partners follow a different breakup journey than singles who marry and break up with another once-married spouse.

Major Research Findings

1. From the decision stage on, traditional-first-timers usually have the highest stress levels, while second-timers usually have the least.
2. Typically, hybrid first-timers have stress levels in between the other two groups.
3. Hybrid first-timer stress is closer to the second-timer experience than the traditional-first-timer one.

Traditional-first versus Hybrid-first

Remarriage breakups are different than first-marriage splits not only for the multi-wed men and women, but also for their once-married, second partners like Louise, who divorced second-timer Stanley in Chapter 4, or Carter, who divorced second-timer Bolta in Chapter 5. *These first-timers are a hybrid group, sometimes reacting like traditional-first ex-couples (both first-timers), but usually reacting more like their redivorced former partners.*

If you are a hybrid-first-timer, you often report short-term divorce reactions like stress and relief that are in between those voiced by your once-married friends who are divorcing another once-married mate, and second-timers like your ex-spouse.

Just after the split, your adjustment is usually a mixed bag. Like other first-timers, you usually get a lot of sympathy and help, and do not have the discouragement of a second mistake. Like a second-timer, you are typically happier than the traditional-first-timer. You are, however, almost as distrusting as your former love and other redivorcers.

Unfortunately, you have probably put up with a lot of disrespect during the marriage. As I will be discussing in the upcoming sections, hybrid-first-timers are often not accorded the same dignity as the traditional first-timer by their spouse and in-laws. If you were disrespected or mistreated in your recent union, you may need counseling to outgrow these problems, refuse to put up with this abuse, and select more respectful and kinder future relationships. With extra help from friends and counseling, you can often make better decisions and heal faster than your former spouse.

Next Step

When you are exiting a remarriage, good advice and emotional support are important to help you work through your grief, reduce your stress, and make the best choices for yourself and family. Good advice, of course, will depend on your situation and divorce subtype.

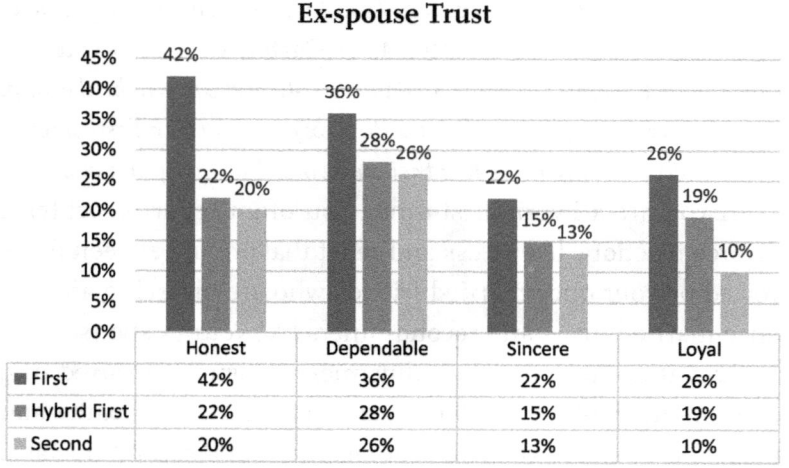

Figure 3-2. Traditional first-, hybrid first-, and second-timers who described their ex-spouse as honest, dependable, sincere, and loyal. Note: Adults: 312 includes traditional first-timers: 90, hybrid first-timers: 94, second-timers: 128.

Graph Take-aways:
1. Traditional first-timers are about twice as likely to trust their ex than second-timers or hybrid-firsts.
2. Hybrid first-timers are slightly more trusting of their exes than second-timers, but much less trusting than traditional first-timers with a once-married ex.

To navigate the breakup of a remarriage, rebuilding confidence and trust are essential tasks that require more emphasis and work in this healing process than during the typical first split. Unlike the traditional-first-timer, a hybrid-first-timer will need to take some of the steps advocated for second-timers, especially steps to increase your trust of others and yourself. You may also need to get rid of other emotional baggage that is getting you into unhealthy relationships.

To do so, use your divorce as an opportunity to learn about yourself, including what you want in life and how to choose more fulfilling relationships. Then, with certainty, you will make sound decisions about your future and, if you choose to look for a new partner, trust your upcoming decisions and trust "the right one." With the right perspective and actions, both first and second timers leaving a remarriage, can resolve these breakup challenges.

Things to Remember about: How are Remarriage Divorces Different?

- Second-timers often receive less empathy, more disapproval, and less help during their divorces than first-timers.
- Many second-timers erase a first union to move on to a second or avoid the twice-divorced stigma and discouragement. Erased marriages are often brief and childless.
- First-timers with once-married ex-spouses usually report more stressful breakups and lower initial non-social adjustment than second-timers or first-timers with second-time ex-spouses.
- Afterwards, second-timers are happier and calmer, but slower to socially heal than traditional-first-timers. They are distrustful and less likely to find a new partner or remarry.
- Due to emotional scars and distrust, most second-timers consider their second divorce harder than their first.
- First-timers leaving redivorced spouses are a hybrid class. Sometimes they behave like first-timers, but usually they react more like a second-timer.

CHAPTER 4

Mono-remarriage Pitfalls: Challenges When *Only the Man* Is Rewed

> This quiz applies to all remarriages and, thus, it's best completed before reading Chapter 4, 5, or 6. Everyone going through the ending of a remarriage, including a once-married spouse, can complete this form. Questions ask why you think you got divorced, who initiated your split, and your and your spouse's family background. Background, divorce initiation, and marital problems are often linked. If you are leaving a mono-remarriage, see if and how these are coupled for you, too.
>
> ## Quiz #2: Marital Complaints and Family Background
>
> ### A. Complaints
>
> **Q1. What caused your divorce? (Check all applicable)**
> 1. ___ Alcohol abuse   ___ mine   ___ spouse's
> 2. ___ Basic unhappiness
> 3. ___ Children—disagreements over/with
>   ___ mine   ___ spouse's

4. ___ Children other issues
(What?) _____
5. ___ Communication
6. ___ Drug abuse   ___ mine   ___ spouse's
7. ___ Emotional abuse
8. ___ Emotional problems
                             ___ mine   ___ spouse's
9. ___ Ex-spouse interference
                             ___ mine   ___ spouse's
10. ___ Financial difficulties
11. ___ Incompatibility
12. ___ Infidelity   ___ mine   ___ spouse's
13. ___ In-laws—conflicts with
                             ___ mine   ___ spouse's
14. ___ Physical abuse of _____ by _____
15. ___ Religious difference
16. ___ Sexual problems/Intimacy
17. ___ Other (What?) _____

B. Divorce Initiation

Q1. Who first left the relationship?
   1. ___ I did   2. ___ Mutual   3. ___ Ex-spouse

Q2. Who first suggested the separation?
   1. ___ I did   2. ___ Mutual   3. ___ Ex-spouse

Q3. Did you or your ex-spouse start the divorce proceedings?
   1. ___ I did   2. ___ Mutual   3. ___ Ex-spouse

Q4. How long did you consider getting a divorce before the final decision? _____

C. Family Marital Background

Q1. Your parents are: (fill in applicable)
    1. ___ Married to each other or living together
    2. ___ Separated since I was ___ age
    3. ___ Divorced when I was ___ age
    4. ___ Mom died when I was ___ age
    5. ___ Dad died when I was ___ age
    6. ___ Mom remarried when I was ___ age
    7. ___ Dad remarried when I was ___ age

Q2. When you were growing up, how would you describe your parents' relationship?
    1. ___ Very poor 2. ___ Poor 3. ___ Average
    4. ___ Good 5. ___ Excellent

Q3. How often was there parental conflict in your childhood home?
    1. ___ Never
    2. ___ Rarely
    3. ___ Sometimes
    4. ___ Fairly often
    5. ___ Very often

Q4. When your recent spouse was 18, her/his parents were: (Check all that apply.)
    1. ___ Married to each other or living together
    2. ___ Separated or divorced
    3. ___ Mom deceased
    4. ___ Dad deceased
    5. ___ Mom remarried
    6. ___ Dad remarried

> **Q5. Your recent spouse's parents' relationship is/was:**
> **(Check all that apply)**
>   1. ___ Very poor   2. ___ Poor   3. ___ Average
>   4. ___ Good   5. ___ Excellent

STANLEY AND NEIL DISCUSS THEIR RECENT SECOND DIVORCES

Stanley is going through a divorce from his second wife. They have a seven-year-old daughter, Lilly, who stays with him several days a week. Stanley also has a teenage son, Bobby, from his first marriage, who spends every other weekend with him. After breakfast one Saturday, when Bobby is staying with his mother, Stanley and Lilly jump into the family car. They head off to the public pool in Sebastian, Florida, where Lilly has been taking swimming lessons for the last couple of months. Bobby is also a swimming enthusiast, and on the Saturdays he's with Stanley, he accompanies Stanley and Lilly to the pool so he can do laps and practice his dives.

When Stanley and Lilly arrive at the pool, Lilly goes to her class, while Stanley sits down on the bleachers next to Neil, another separated dad. Neil and Stanley have become good buddies over the last few months while waiting for their children. The two men are going through a second divorce from their once-married women. In both cases, the wife initiated the divorce. The men started talking about their problems the previous week. They continue the discussion.

"Yo, Neil," Stanley says as he sits down. "How are things?"

"Okay, how about you?" Neil asks.

"Hangin' in there."

"What's going on?" Neil asks.

"Janet just called. She's driving me crazy. No matter what I do she complains."

"What went wrong with you two?" Neil wonders.

"She resented my spending time and money on my oldest child. Her parents didn't like me. They kept meddling."

"My in-laws didn't like me, either," Neil says. "I'm older, married before, and had a kid. Couldn't accept my kid or me."

"We grew up with different values and habits," Stanley says. "That was another problem."

"We had that, too, but worked it out. We also had age issues. I'm twelve years older and I don't want any more kids. She's only thirty-two and does."

"Age wasn't an issue although I'm seven years older," Stanley says. "Janet doesn't want any more kids."

"Sure, we have a few problems, but to bust up our marriage?" Neil says. "I'm so pissed."

"I'm pissed, too. Sometimes, I have to hit something, so I don't hit someone."

"I have a punching bag in my garage. When my wife or someone else gets me angry, I punch the bag until I calm down. Use it almost every day. How's parenting going?" Neil asked.

"Better now that we have a routine down. It's still a lot to handle."

"Are you getting counseling for yourself or your kids?"

"My teenage son from my first, Bobby, is fine. Only Lilly and I are in counseling."

"Has it helped?" Neil asked.

"Some. It helps Lilly and I deal with our anger and upset. We're still both touchy, but we're happier and calmer. This split is harder than my first. I'm more discouraged. I don't trust Janet or any other woman. My counselor is helping me with all this."

"I don't trust women, either. But I don't like living without one." says Neil.

Mono-remarriage Troubles

As a reminder, I call marriages where the husband is the sole remarried partner mono-remarriages. Mono means one. In this case, the man is the remarried spouse. Many of these are stepmother families. This arrangement sets these couples up for a list of troubles and poses a high risk for unhappiness, dissatisfaction, and divorce. When these marriages unwind, couples chalk up their loss primarily to (1) problems with finances and the wife's parents, (2) the wife's infidelity, or (3) the husband's infidelity coupled with problems with his relatives.

MARITAL FAULT LINES

Typically, when these couples wed, the groom is in his early thirties with one or two small children from his former marriage, like Stanley, while his bride is in her twenties, like Janet. Invariably, her parents are unhappy about the marriage and rarely accept him, reasoning that their daughter should have picked a man without children and the other complications that come from being divorced. They worry that he's a bad husband for any woman, much less their daughter. His family's reaction depends on how his prior marriage ended. If his first wife left him, his parents and siblings are likely to welcome his new wife into their family. If he left his first wife to marry his second, then the new wife is apt to be disliked and labeled a "home wrecker."

HOW THE CHILDREN FEEL

The husband's second marriage is an adjustment for his children, and sometimes a harder one than the original divorce. When their dad remarries, children deal with loss, divided loyalties, and change. If their dad's remarriage occurs before his ex-wife's remarriage, which it usually does, the children must accept the permanent loss of their original family. After the separation, some children become closer to their dad. Typically, his remarriage means that they may lose this special relationship and will have to share him with his new wife and perhaps other children. If they like their stepmother, they may feel disloyal toward their mother. The wedding brings other alterations, including who lives in the new home, routines, and further rules. Like everyone else, the children must adjust to them.

How the New Wife Feels—Secondhand Rose

When the husband has children from his first union, his new love must share her marriage with his first family. Typically, she is apprehensive about her relationship with his first wife and children, her stepmother role, and her importance in the new family.

The first wife can easily undermine their new home, especially if the two wives do not get along. The biological mother can interfere and control her relationship with the children. Many children resent the new marriage and their stepmother. If so, she often feels like a failure as a parent and is undermined.

As the second wife, she commonly feels like a "secondhand rose"—she feels second best to his first wife and children, excluded, or haunted with the knowledge that he has done everything before with his first love—his ex.[1] Since his first marriage failed, his current wife may worry that their marriage might end, too. When she is younger than her husband and his ex, she may feel intimidated, have a hard time standing up for what she wants, and as a result, becomes resentful. After the sexual and romantic haze wears off, growing resentment and feelings of exclusion and disrespect may jettison her emotionally out of the marriage.

How the Remarried Man Feels

Often, the man is insecure and in a no-win situation. He almost always carries some emotional baggage from his first to his second marriage. Distrust over money, jealousy, or fears of abandonment may undermine his new relationship, especially if these were issues in his first. If he has children from his first marriage, he rarely has the money, time, or energy to make both families happy. On top of that, he frequently has at least one set of disapproving, hostile parents or in-laws. To escape, he may flee his remarriage. To overcome these issues, wise couples focus their energy on establishing a solid, fulfilling relationship in which the needs of the couple and marriage are paramount. Even though they fulfill their obligations to all their children, they let everyone know that the marriage comes first and insist that others respect it.

> **Children Don't Know Stepmother Beforehand**
> Children often don't get to know their future stepmother before the wedding. When they don't, they're less apt to accept her and the remarriage.[2]

Three Major Grievances

In mono-remarriage, there are three key complaints:

- Financial problems accompanied by conflict with her parents.
- Her infidelity
- His infidelity accompanied by her conflict with stepchildren and his relatives.

How the stepmother and his first-marriage children co-exist is a major issue for almost everyone in this situation. When couples break up, they rarely make this complaint, although this is an almost universal problem. In the first two instances, the wife initiates the divorce. In the third case, the husband is the first to leave the relationship. Who initiates the divorce, and why, almost always affects (1) the breakup process, including the difficulties encountered by each spouse, (2) stress patterns, and (3) the recovery process.

FIRST SUBTYPE: SHE BLAMES FINANCIAL PROBLEMS, WHILE HE BLAMES CONFLICT WITH HER PARENTS

One third of the men fault hostility and interference from her family, but she doesn't think that. For her, the major issues are problems stemming from his first marriage, especially the financial burden. She resents the financial bite the child support takes and sometimes also hates the way his children and ex-spouse intrude on her life with him. Stepchildren are a major issue just below the surface.

When they wed, Janet was a mid-twenties dental hygienist, while Stanley was an early-thirties plumber. They had two children—Bobby, from his first union and eight years old at the start of the remarriage, and Lilly, from their eight-year relationship. Janet depicted her problems:

> The last couple of years, I was miserable and thought about leaving. I couldn't decide. I loved him, but felt unloved and shortchanged. I resented all the money that we sent each month to Stanley's ex. We rarely went out to dinner or took a vacation, except for a rare day trip. Stanley spent Saturdays alone with Bobby, excluding the rest of us. Sunday afternoons, he watched a football game and drank with his friends in the basement, or went off with his buddies, leaving me with the children. Stanley seldom made time or had the money for all of us to have fun together. The final straw was that he

forgot my birthday. When I told him I felt hurt, he shrugged his shoulders. After that, I knew he didn't love me, so why stay?

Financial Upset

Before the marriage, she usually doesn't understand how difficult her life is about to become or how her views about their finances and their life will change. Before the wedding, she considers his paycheck just his and is not upset that he sends child support to his first wife. Once they wed, their paychecks are no longer just his *or* hers, but joint revenue, and when their income is being spent both are spending it. Psychologically and legally, for the first time, she is sending money to his first wife and resents it just like she might resent paying his gambling debts or college loans. Besides, he often does not fully disclose his financial situation until after the wedding. His first-marriage obligations may hurt their lifestyle even more than she envisioned.

> **Second Wife Financially Surprised**
> After the wedding, many wives get two shocks. First, his first-family obligations and their financial situation are worse than has been disclosed to her. Second, she goes from viewing his income as his to theirs. With this shift, she resents how her money is now going to his first wife.

Secondhand Rose

Before, he split his weekends and evenings between his fiancée and his family and friends. As a couple, they rarely socialized with his children on an extended basis. When they did, he took care of them himself. After the marriage, his children regularly stay with the couple on weekends and for several weeks during the summer. Now, taking care of these children is a standard problem for her, not him. Unfairly, he normally expects her to take care of his visiting children.

The once-married, second wife faces a major loss. She isn't the first love or the first wife. Unlike most wives, she can't create a life unencumbered by a prior family. This loss is embedded in the "Secondhand Rose" resentment these second wives often feel.

Parental Disapproval

The second wife's parents seldom support the marriage. Their hostility to him and concern for her are understandable. As the second wife, their daughter faces atypical hazards and missed chances. It isn't just the added burden from his prior marriage. The typical husband who complains about his in-laws is far from the ideal son-in-law. He is often a blue-collar man who lives paycheck to paycheck. Postdivorce, she repeatedly describes her ex-husband as insecure and/or a heavy drinker or drug user, who sometimes physically abuses her. Occasionally, she has a hard time getting out of this relationship because she also has a substance use problem or low self-esteem.

In-law hostility demeans the twosome. Not surprisingly, the husband often feels disrespected and becomes resentful. Remarried men with a remarried wife rarely feel disrespected.

From his perspective, the problem is that his second wife and her parents are unwilling to accept his children. He argues that she knew he had children when she married him. He can't erase these obligations, so she must accommodate them. However, he almost always expects more than that. As a rule, he shoves his first-marriage childcare responsibility on to her—he expects her to take care of them when they visit. Invariably, he fails to understand two things: (1) he needs to continue as the primary parent and disciplinarian and (2) to be a successful stepmother, she needs to ease into her new role over several years.

Second Subtype: Her Infidelity

One-third of the women exit their marriage via an affair. Typically, she is under thirty and comes from a divorced parental home or has parents who disapprove of the marriage. As such, this sometimes overlaps with the first problem situation—finances and in-law issues. When her parents are married, these relationships last on average seven years. If her parents are divorced, the marriage is usually much shorter.

As this is her first marriage, but his second, she may assume that it is his fault and unfixable. She doesn't try to straighten things out or look at her contribution to the mess. Instead, she rushes into a new relationship. She usually has problems with loneliness and feels that she needs a different man immediately instead of a period of independence for self-discovery, development, and redirection before searching for a better match. Her loneliness is often linked to growing up in a divorced parental home. An example is Grace and William.

When the couple met about a year after William's first divorce, he was an early-thirties salesman and Grace was a mid-twenties hairdresser. A year later, they had their first child, Mark. Nine months later, they married. Within a few years, they shared his son, Lane, from his first family and their two youngsters, Mark and Steve. As with his first, this one lasted about six years. Grace recalled their home life:

> Lane visited the family most weekends and several weeks in the summer. He enjoyed visiting with his dad and stepsiblings. William's and my parents accepted the situation and were uncritical. When William lost his job about four years into the marriage, he became unhappy and irritable. Finally, he found another job, but he had to take frequent long sales trips out of state. While William was on the

road, I was lonely and worried that he might leave me as he had left Nan, his first wife. I developed a relationship with a recently divorced friend, Doug. With his prodding, I decided to leave William and filed for a divorce.

> **Loneliness**
> If you are lonely when you aren't in a relationship, you may be at risk for having an affair, jumping from one unhappy relationship to the next, or getting stuck in a bad one.

> **Strained Relationships**
> Strained family relationships with in-laws, ex, or stepchildren undermine remarriages.

THIRD SUBTYPE: HIS INFIDELITY AND HER CONFLICT WITH HIS RELATIVES

One out of three husbands ends the marriage, usually by having an affair. He thinks conflict drove him out of his second marriage and into a new relationship and contends that his affair is the result, not the cause, of his divorce. Louise and John were a typical couple in this situation.

Louise owned a florist shop. She met John when she was in her late-twenties. John was in his early thirties and had divorced his first wife. A supermarket manager, John, had a first-marriage son, Cody. Cody turned eleven at the start of their seven-year marriage. John recalled:

My first wife was my school sweetheart and a stay-at-home mom. After we divorced, I wanted a career woman. If a woman voiced little interest in a career or referred to her recipes as her inheritance, my stomach churned. It felt as if she was scratching a blackboard with her fingernails. Louise was like a breath of fresh air—interesting, fun, and knowledgeable about business and politics. But my family wasn't happy. At our wedding rehearsal, Mom shouted. 'Do you have to marry that woman?' I was in the middle of a war between Louise and my family. Louise felt that they mattered more to me than her. Visits with my son, Cody, were touchy. Cody spent as much time as possible either in his room hiding or alone with me in the den. Eventually, I found a new honey. One day, Louise saw my credit card bill with charges for a hotel room and jewelry. When she confronted me, I admitted that I was cheating, packed a suitcase and a couple of black trash bags, and left.

Frequently, the husband's first wife is his high school or college sweetheart. After his first union, he may decide to marry someone quite different. If his first wife is a stay-at-home mom, he may seek a career woman or vice versa. Regardless, successful remarriages typically have solid incomes and meet the needs of both households. As to why his family dislikes his second wife, two reasons often surface.

First, many second wives are considered "home wreckers." He divorced his first wife to marry her. His ex-wife and children resented and disliked her for breaking up their home. His parents and siblings were surprised and distressed by the situation.

Second, his family and ex-wife may feel uncomfortable with

her and she with them. Her background, values, or lifestyle may differ from his parents' and ex-wife's. While his family and first wife may be Protestant professionals, his second wife may be from a blue-collar, Catholic home and works part time as a hotel clerk. Other times, there is a personality clash, or his new wife is aloof. Regardless of the scenario, she doesn't fit in, like, or get along with his family.

His behavior, parents, first spouse, and children contribute to the dispute. Often, he fails to make his second wife feel special and protected from outside hostility. Until and unless he lets everyone know that his first loyalty is to his second wife, his new love will not be secure and the marriage will falter. Usually, his first-marriage children are adolescents and older than other stepchildren. As a rule, they are upset by his remarriage and have a tough time getting along with her.

The pair often can't figure out how to schedule two careers, private moments as a couple, fun with his first-union children, and leisure activities with their new family. His teens are busy with their activities, so they have less time for family. Sometimes, his parents accuse his new wife of taking him away from his children. Time limitations are a major culprit.

Frequently, he decides that he can only take care of one family. If he meets his first family obligations, his second family often feels shortchanged. His second wife feels unloved and wants to leave. If he doesn't take care of his first family adequately, he is likely to feel stressed, misses his older children, and gets hauled into court by his ex over child support, visitation schedules, and, if she isn't remarried, alimony. He may leave to get out of the mess. One husband said:

> My second marriage didn't allow me to take care of my first-marriage children. I had to leave my second wife to fix this.

> Often, he fails to make his second wife feel special and protected from outside hostility. Until and unless he lets everyone know that his first loyalty is to his second wife, his new love will not be secure and the marriage will falter.

THINGS TO REMEMBER ABOUT MONO-REMARRIAGE:

- At the typical wedding, the groom is in his thirties and has one or two youngsters. Since the new wife is often much younger, the couple soon shares two sets of children, his and theirs.
- Often, women feel second place and excluded, while men feel they are in a no-win dilemma.
- Major grievances include 1) financial problems and conflicts with her parents, 2) her infidelity, and 3) his infidelity and conflicts with his relatives.

CHAPTER 5

Uni-remarriage Pitfalls: Challenges When *Only the Wife* Is Rewed

Quiz #2 below first appears in Chapter 4. If you have not taken it yet, you will want to complete this quiz now so you can best grasp the upcoming material. To understand uni-redivorces, you need to understand this family situation and the three parts to this quiz: family background, divorce initiation, and marital problems. If you are leaving a uni-remarriage, see if you can figure out how these factors are related and impacted your relationship and split.

Quiz #2: Marital Complaints and Family Background

A. Complaints

Q1. What caused your divorce? (Check all applicable)
  1. ___ Alcohol abuse   ___ mine   ___ spouse's
  2. ___ Basic unhappiness
  3. ___ Children—disagreements over/with
      ___ mine   ___ spouse's

4. ___ Children other issues
(What?) _____
5. ___ Communication
6. ___ Drug abuse   ___ mine   ___ spouse's
7. ___ Emotional abuse
8. ___ Emotional problems
                               ___ mine   ___ spouse's
9. ___ Ex-spouse interference
                               ___ mine   ___ spouse's
10. ___ Financial difficulties
11. ___ Incompatibility
12. ___ Infidelity   ___ mine   ___ spouse's
13. ___ In-laws—conflicts with
                               ___ mine   ___ spouse's
14. ___ Physical abuse of _____ by _____
15. ___ Religious difference
16. ___ Sexual problems/Intimacy
17. ___ Other (What?) _____

B. Divorce Initiation

Q1. Who first left the relationship?
    1. ___ I did   2. ___ Mutual   3. ___ Ex-spouse

Q2. Who first suggested the separation?
    1. ___ I did   2. ___ Mutual   3. ___ Ex-spouse

Q3. Did you or your ex-spouse start the divorce proceedings?
    1. ___ I did   2. ___ Mutual   3. ___ Ex-spouse

C. Family Marital Background

Q1. Your parents are: (fill in applicable)
1. ___ Married to each other or living together
2. ___ Separated since I was ___ age
3. ___ Divorced when I was ___ age
4. ___ Mom died when I was ___ age
5. ___ Dad died when I was ___ age
6. ___ Mom remarried when I was ___ age
7. ___ Dad remarried when I was ___ age

Q2. When you were growing up, how would you describe your parents' relationship?
1. ___ Very poor   2. ___ Poor   3. ___ Average
4. ___ Good   5. ___ Excellent

Q3. When your recent spouse was 18, her/his parents were: (Check all that apply.)
1. ___ Married to each other or living together
2. ___ Separated or divorced
3. ___ Mom deceased
4. ___ Dad deceased
5. ___ Mom remarried
6. ___ Dad remarried

Q4. Your recent spouse's parents' relationship is/was: (Check all that apply)
1. ___ Very poor
2. ___ Poor
3. ___ Average
4. ___ Good
5. ___ Excellent

The Hornet's Nest

In couples where the wife is the sole remarried partner, I dubbed uni-remarriage. Uni means one. In this instance, the wife is the one in a second union.

Typically, when they wed, both are in their late twenties to early thirties. As a rule, she has one or two small children, a six-year or shorter first relationship, and two to three years between her marriages. If she has children from a prior relationship, then her new husband has an instant family—her and her youngsters. They do not have the customary year or two to cement their relationship without the stresses of child rearing. Upset children, low marital commitment, and problems from her first marriage are common obstacles to forming a close, new home.

After the wedding, her youngsters may pull away from her. If so, they are angry with her and their stepfather for getting married. They see him as an intruder, who displaces them and their father.

Between her two marriages, her youngsters usually establish "a closeness" with her that makes them feel important. After her second nuptials, that special mom time declines. Instead, she often spends time alone with her new husband. If her oldest helped take care of her younger ones pre-remarriage, she often loses this role and resents her demotion. The marriage dashes the children's hopes that their parents will reunite if she remarries before her ex-husband.

Healthy marriages focus on developing a fulfilling, strong marital bond in which children revolve around the marriage. Certain women do the reverse. Some feel guilty about the impact of the first divorce on their youngsters or they are trying to maintain a positive relationship with them. Others worry that he will desert them, or the marriage will not last. Even if they love each other, she may wonder if she is loveable. Fears of desertion and distrust are common, especially for those with divorced parents or those whose first husband left them.

Instead, she can't keep the peace between her new spouse and children, who resent him. Even if they want a close home, he may continue to feel like an outsider, while her children are so unhappy that the marriage crumbles.

There may be other troubles. Sometimes, her first husband stresses the new family. Co-parenting with him is often difficult. When the children visit their dad, she may worry about them and worry that he is making nasty remarks about her to them. At times, taking the youngsters to see their father or picking them up at the end of the visitation results in an argument or resurrects bad memories. Moreover, some couples are struggling financially. If they occur, substance abuse, financial, or recurring problems from her earlier marriage cause too many problems for a shaky marriage. Irrespective, the husband often feels that he is living in a hornet's nest. Routinely, he feels stung by her displeased children, in-laws, and his queen-bee wife, who often sides with her children over him.

> **Unrealistic Expectations Hurt Remarriages**
> Couples who expect their stepfamily to be close and connected in less than two years undermine their relationship with their unrealistic expectations.

Major Grievances

When these families disintegrate, they usually emphasize one of several major explanations: 1) substance abuse and infidelity, 2) sexual and intimacy problems, or 3) emotional difficulties. Beneath these surface explanations, they often have additional issues, such as a fear of commitment that blocked the family from forming a cohesive unit and led to these troubles.

Substance Abuse and Infidelity

Substance abuse with or without infidelity is a pivotal concern for six out of ten couples. Especially among men, substance abuse is common and an addressable matter with other divorcing couples, too, but usually takes a less central or dominant role. In most of these homes, the husband is the one who overdrinks or takes drugs. However, one out of four women engages in substance abuse also or instead. This women's rate is twice that reported by other couples.

Elvis and Scarlett were recently divorced and in their early thirties. Elvis, a bus driver, grew up with his divorced mother and older sister. Raised by her divorced mother, Scarlett was an only child. This was her second marriage, but Elvis's first. During their five-year marriage, they parented her first-marriage daughter, Sunny, and their daughter, Elle. Scarlett recalled her past:

> Both of my marriages were brief. I married my first husband, Miles, in my early twenties, because I was pregnant with Sunny. Two years into the marriage, we were both miserable. No matter what I did, I couldn't make things right between us. I left with Sunny. Miles was relieved and quickly found a new love. We both considered our marriage a youthful mistake, best forgotten.
>
> Two years later, I married Elvis and had a second daughter. From the start, Elvis behaved like a carefree teenager without any family obligations. Several times a week, he went out with his friends to the local bar, while I stayed home with the kids. Often, he came home drunk and then missed

> work the next day. His partying caused strain on our budget and financial security. When I complained, Elvis became verbally and physically abusive. I alternated between struggling to save my marriage by overlooking things, criticizing him, and wanting to run away. With my family's help, I told him to leave and filed for a divorce.

Often, these couples cite financial problems or disputes for starting marital discontent. Once marital troubles ensue, he frequently drinks more or takes drugs, while she sometimes looks for another man. Nearly sixty percent of the women who grew up in a divorced home cite their husband's alcohol and drug abuse, but only one in three of the women from intact homes makes the same charge. Half the women, who instigate the divorce, blame substance abuse and money.

Typically, he faults the split on her infidelity, friction, and contempt from her parents; has a harsh breakup; and lower recovery. In contrast, she has a somewhat easier split-up and good post-divorce adjustment. Afterwards, she is happier, on an even keel, and relieved, but still mulling over her past from time to time and sometimes haunted by self-doubts.

If they have joint children, co-parenting is difficult. She doesn't respect him, especially if he has an untreated substance abuse problem. When the children are with him, she worries about their welfare. In turn, he resents her distrust.

SEXUAL PROBLEMS

Twice-married women with once-wed husbands are likely and more likely to have sexual problems than other women. If her parents are divorced, then she and her husband are more likely to make this complaint. Why is this so? Women from divorced parental homes often enter their marriages with low commitment and confidence, intimacy fears, low resilience, and low social skills. Often keeping their partner at a distance, they are quick to emotionally overload and when they do, they do not have the resilience tools or social skills to calm themselves or reduce negativity, but instead rapidly and impulsively jump out of the relationship.

Sexual issues are rarely the only trouble. Instead, they tend to be the result of or cause additional complications. And especially with women, it is often the canary in the coalmine— sexual dysfunction is frequently an early warning signal that something is wrong with the relationship.

Typically, medical, intimacy, and emotional reactions are linked to sexual troubles, but the scenario is different for men and women. According to a recent research review by Weir in 2019, a man's sexual dysfunction tends to be caused by inadequate testosterone and, thus, is usually elevated or corrected with medical treatment such as a medication like Viagra. Low confidence, lower self-esteem, and avoidance of intimacy often result from his medical problem and need to be addressed with counseling. Lack of emotional closeness—not a physiological deficit—usually causes a woman's sexual difficulties. Most of the time, she feels distant, unloved, or unappreciated. To regain sexual desire, she commonly needs to regain intimacy.[1]

Despite these gender differences, it is always a good rule to make sure that a medical problem is not causing a sexual dysfunction, especially as we age. And, of course, when one person has a sexual or intimacy concern, the issue quickly becomes a problem for both partners.

Sexual and Intimacy Problems
For most men, sexual dysfunction causes intimacy difficulties, but for most women the reverse happens—lack of intimacy causes sexual problems.

Carter and Bolta's marriage illustrated the couple with physical and emotional intimacy problems. Both recalled unhappy childhoods. Bolta's parents were divorced, while Carter's parents were unhappily married. Wed in their late twenties, the couple had a son Max from Bolta's first marriage living with them. Her story appears in a later chapter titled, Uni-redivorce—What to expect when only she is redivorcing. Carter's story is next.

> Bolta kept one foot out the door from the start—she never made a commitment to our marriage. Because she had the higher, steadier, income, she paid most of the bills, but resented it. An artist, my income depended on how many of my paintings were sold during the month. To make matters worse, I didn't get along with her parents, and she didn't get along with mine. Several years into the marriage, we had many unresolved disputes. When we tried to resolve our issues, Bolta became upset and would not calmly discuss them. She would storm out of the house and drive around for an hour or two. As we became more distant, we had more sexual problems. Finally, she refused to have sex. Bolta suggested the separation and filed for the divorce.

Emotional problems

In this study, once-married men were more likely to blame their ex-wife's emotional problems for the divorce than the twice-married men. Three out of four husbands who want and initiate the divorce assume that their unhappiness is rooted in her personality problems. When so, he thinks that her temperament triggers a long list of marital troubles, including arguments and sexual problems, and, in some instances, her drug use. As proof of her instability, he often points to her impulsive actions, her hostile conduct, and recurring arguments with him about their children and other issues. Conflicts between him and her parents are common. He feels overwhelmed by chaos.

Women who fault emotional issues also cite a long list of problems and chaos—disputes about the children, poor communication, sexual problems, emotional abuse, and sometimes spousal substance abuse. Her finger, however, usually points in the opposite direction—she blames her husband's character, not hers.

Savannah, a mid-thirties bank teller with a junior high daughter, met and married Pug, a mid-thirties architect, soon after her first divorce. When Pug later filed for the divorce, he blamed Savannah's emotional problems for the marriage's failure. Savannah recounts her remarriage:

> Pug and I met just after I separated from my first husband. I was on vacation at Moon Lake, while my daughter was with her dad. Pug and I hit it off instantly. A month later, the three of us were living together. Right after my first divorce, we wed. We both jumped into this marriage impulsively—not thinking through whether the three of us would be happy together. We both concluded that the other one was emotionally unstable and unreasonable. My daughter was angry and didn't get along with Pug. By the end of our first year, Pug and I were bickering about trivia, felt distant, and stopped having sex. We had a major blow-up and split. Pug filed for a divorce.
>
> My daughter was happier and helped me through the mess. I was an emotional wreck and squeaked by financially for the first six months.

Now, I'm okay, glad I have a daughter, and like my job and friends, but I don't want another husband.

THINGS TO REMEMBER ABOUT UNI-REMARRIAGE:
- Customarily, the wife has an under seven-year earlier marriage, several years between marriages, and one or two children from her first marriage.
- Too often, husbands feel excluded rather than a central member of the new family. At the same time, some children are jealous and feel the stepfather is intruding, trying to replace their father, and/or is taking their mother away from them.
- Couples usually blame the divorce on the husband's substance abuse along with infidelity, sexual problems and intimacy, and/or emotional problems.

CHAPTER 6

Bi-remarriage Pitfalls: Challenges When *Both* Are Rewed

Quiz #2 below first appears in Chapter 4. If you have not taken it yet, you will want to complete this quiz now so you can best grasp the upcoming material. To understand bi-redivorces, you need to understand the bi-remarriage family situation and the three parts to this exercise: family background, divorce initiation, and marital problems. If you are leaving a dual remarriage, see if you can figure out how these factors are related and impacted your marriage and divorce.

Quiz #2: Marital Complaints and Family Background

A. Complaints

Q1. What caused your divorce? (Check all applicable)
1. ___ Alcohol abuse   ___ mine   ___ spouse's
2. ___ Basic unhappiness
3. ___ Children—disagreements over/with
                          ___ mine   ___ spouse's
4. ___ Children other issues
(What?) _____
5. ___ Communication

6. ___ Drug abuse   ___ mine   ___ spouse's
7. ___ Emotional abuse
8. ___ Emotional problems
                      ___ mine   ___ spouse's
9. ___ Ex-spouse interference
                      ___ mine   ___ spouse's
10. ___ Financial difficulties
11. ___ Incompatibility
12. ___ Infidelity   ___ mine   ___ spouse's
13. ___ In-laws—conflicts with
                      ___ mine   ___ spouse's
14. ___ Physical abuse of _____ by _____
15. ___ Religious difference
16. ___ Sexual problems/Intimacy
17. ___ Other (What?) _____

B. Divorce Initiation

Q1. Who first left the relationship?
   1. ___ I did   2. ___ Mutual   3. ___ Ex-spouse

Q2. Who first suggested the separation?
   1. ___ I did   2. ___ Mutual   3. ___ Ex-spouse

Q3. Did you or your ex-spouse start the divorce proceedings?
   1. ___ I did   2. ___ Mutual   3. ___ Ex-spouse

C. Family Marital Background

Q1. Your parents are: (fill in applicable)
   1. ___ Married to each other or living together
   2. ___ Separated since I was ___ age

3. ___ Divorced when I was ___ age
4. ___ Mom died when I was ___ age
5. ___ Dad died when I was ___ age
6. ___ Mom remarried when I was ___ age
7. ___ Dad remarried when I was ___ age

Q2. When you were growing up, how would you describe your parents' relationship?
1. ___ Very poor   2. ___ Poor   3. ___ Average
4. ___ Good   5. ___ Excellent

Q3. When your recent spouse was 18, her/his parents were: (Check all that apply.)
1. ___ Married to each other or living together
2. ___ Separated or divorced
3. ___ Mom deceased
4. ___ Dad deceased
5. ___ Mom remarried
6. ___ Dad remarried

Q4. Your recent spouse's parents' relationship is/was: (Check all that apply)
1. ___ Very poor
2. ___ Poor
3. ___ Average
4. ___ Good
5. ___ Excellent

Double Trouble

When both spouses are in a second marriage, I dubbed it a bi-remarriage. Bi means two. In this instance, it means both spouses are remarried. These couples are the largest subgroup in this study. A few met in their twenties after each had exited a brief first marriage. Overall, however, they are older and from longer first marriages. The typical couple in this study had children with other spouses in their twenties, divorced their first spouse in their early thirties, and then remarried in their mid-to-late thirties. By this time, most adults had first-marriage teens.

The newlyweds enter their new relationship on equal footing with "first-marriage baggage," including children, ex-spouses, resentments, and hurts. They often worry that their past marital failures may increase their divorce risk, especially when they have children. Divorce veterans, they are equally familiar with the breakup process and have survival techniques in case this marriage fails, too.

These couples have the highest risk for child complications. Child-allied problems jump from under 30% in families with one remarried spouse to roughly 50% in these homes. Most are blended families with two sets of children and have twice as many stepchildren as other remarriage couples. As they usually have long first marriages, children are older and likely to be from the age group most prone to resent and disrupt a remarriage—adolescents. Verbally articulate and physically as large or larger than their parents, these teens can't be ignored or dismissed. Instead, they often rock the marital boat until it overturns and sinks. That is why so many affluent remarried families send their teens off to boarding school.

To add to their woes, they have an ever-growing number of relatives, who more often than not interfere. As men tend to remarry faster than women, her ex-husband is probably rewed. If so, they are dealing with her ex-husband and his new wife, and stepchildren from the start. The new husband's first wife normally remarries a year or two afterwards. In doing so, his ex-wife adds another stepparent and sometimes another set of children to the total situation. Scheduling child visitations is a logistical nightmare with so many people involved.

Expectedly, the average family complains about in-laws, ex-spouses, disrespect, and physical abuse. An over-39 woman is three times more likely to experience child-linked stress as well as more likely to be physically abused than other women. Physical abuse troubles take many forms— couple violence, child abuse including incest, and fights between the (step) children.

Major Subtypes

Dual remarried couples fall into one of two situations: younger couples with both first and second marriage children and middle-aged couples with two sets of adolescents.

Younger Couples: His, Hers, and Ours

Younger couples who give birth to children in their second marriage usually end up having two, if not three, sets of offspring: his, hers, and/or ours. Invariably, they both exit short, first marriages. First marriages are often an impulsive decision or a shotgun wedding where she got pregnant accidentally. At remarriage, both are in their mid-to-late twenties and about six to seven years younger than the usual, bi-remarried couple. When they split, they often have longer second marriages than the older bi-redivorcers.

When they first wed, they are young with young children. By the time their marriage deteriorates, their sons and daughters are preteens or teens trying to form their own identities and independence. For many, adolescence is a difficult, tumultuous life stage as they struggle to achieve these goals and define their adult life path. Teenage struggles strain most families. In fragile ones, the home cannot withstand years of teenage storms and upheaval. The husband's alcohol or drug use may create additional strain on their household, especially if substance abuse sparks emotional or physical abuse. With these changes, marital conflict escalates and undermines their home.

Young couples are usually more upset during their divorce than middle-aged ones for two reasons. Younger couples often have children in common, but middle-aged couples rarely do. The couple's young age can be an additional risk. Younger couples are more easily upset than middle-aged couples.

Case Example: Desiree Divorced Saul

In their thirties, Desiree, a teacher's aide, and Saul, a construction worker, were splitting after a seven-year marriage. Both grew up in divorced parental homes. Together, they shared three children—a junior high son from his first marriage, Peter; a grade-school daughter from her first union, Lois; and a preschooler from their relationship, Tucker. Feeling guilty about not seeing his first-marriage son, Peter, more, Saul spent more on him than on his other children. Without Desiree's knowledge, Saul sent extra money each month to his first wife to make sure that he had the latest electronic gadgets and enough money to partake in after-school activities and weekend sporting and social events with his friends. Desiree described their arguments about Peter:

> When Peter visited, Saul spent all his time with him. He showered his son with gifts—ignoring the rest of the family. After Peter returned to his mom's home, Saul and I would fight. I accused him of favoritism and neglecting his other children, Lois and Tucker. He accused me of treating his first-marriage son as a second-class member of our family. Stressed by the family circumstances as well as problems at work, Saul drank more and

more. When he drank too much, he was nasty, irritable, and sometimes hit me. Disillusioned and resentful, I wondered if the situation was correctable. If anything, his drinking and his abuse escalated. We were making each other miserable. We were incompatible. Tired of the stress and situation, I suggested the separation and filed for a divorce.

Case Example: Ralph divorced Cheyenne

The younger of two children, Cheyenne grew up in a middle-class neighborhood near several colleges. Her parents co-owned a grocery store where her father managed the operations and her mother was the bookkeeper. Her parents never divorced, but conflict between them was ongoing. In junior high, she dreamed of becoming a teacher. At 18, she attended a local college.

Sophomore year, she met Watson, an aspiring accountant. Within three months, they wed. She married Watson in part to escape the conflict at home. To help him pay his college bills, she dropped out of college to work full time as a secretary. She assumed that as soon as he received his degree and CPA certification, she would go back to school. After he obtained his CPA, however, Watson insisted that she work in his newly established accounting firm. She felt betrayed. She was trapped like her mother, working for her husband. Feeling exploited and enraged, she filed for a divorce.

As the divorce seeker without children from the marriage, she had a relatively easy first disunion. At 23, she divorced Watson, secured a scholarship, and went back to college. By her mid-twenties, she had graduated and started teaching history in the local high school. On the job, she met her next husband ,Ralph, another divorced teacher. Together, they soon shared two children—Lilac from this marriage and Rose from Ralph's first family. Within a couple of years, they started arguing about finances and their children. Unhappy, Ralph began an affair with a neighbor, Sabrina. Ralph and Sabrina ran off together, leaving their spouses without any warning.

> ***Do Both Sets of Children Get Along?***
> Conflict between the two sets of children often undermines the marriage.

Middle-aged Couples: Two Sets of Adolescents

By far, middle-aged couples and their children make up most bi-remarried homes. Normally, they left their first union after eight to ten years, and then three to four years later wed for the second time. When they did, they were in their mid-to-late thirties. Universally, they share two sets of first-marriage adolescents, but do not have children from their remarriage. Troubles with these teens are standard. There are two central issues here: the number and age of the children.

In these households, some teens are so disruptive that they tear the family apart. Although most parents are empathetic with their children's plight, two sets of teenagers can be overwhelming. With so many individuals with legitimate roles in these homes, bad relationships, jealousies, and disputes erupt. Everyone is in unchartered territory and needs to find new household rules; new niches for each; as well as establish rights, clear communication, and respect. Vocabulary may even be a challenge. The family needs to make sure the same words mean the same thing to everybody in the household.

Case Example: Beth and Nickolas

Beth sat quietly as Nickolas recounted their story.

Beth and I were married to others in our twenties and early thirties. We wed when Beth was 38 and I was 39. From the start, we had challenges—difficulties we didn't face in either of our first marriages. The trouble wasn't spousal substance abuse or financial problems that destroyed our first marriages.

The problem was our children. When we wed, Beth's daughters were Sarah, twelve, and Ann, seven, while mine were older: Bret, fourteen, and Carol, thirteen. They were angry that we got married. They fought with each other and us, especially after we wed. Beth's oldest, Sarah, was the biggest problem. She withdrew from her mom, got into trouble at school, and started drinking. She was demanding, delinquent, and spiteful. She rarely did her homework and thus failed several courses. Sarah was suspended for buying beer in the parking lot. For Halloween, she egged the cars in our neighborhood, including my Camry. Ann, the youngest, and I got along. Beth's relationship with mine was worse. I suggested the separation, but Beth quickly agreed. It was a joint decision.

THINGS TO REMEMBER ABOUT BI-REMARRIAGE:
- Bi-remarrieds walk into their marriage on equal footing. They have comparable marriage and divorce knowledge and equal "emotional baggage" from the past.
- In younger couples, children and substance abuse are usually the stressors during the marriages and divorces.
- Middle-aged couples have first-marriage teens, which destabilize the family. Some children don't get along with their stepparent. Others don't get along with their stepsiblings.

CHAPTER 7

Solving Early Tasks: Counselors, Lawyers, Children & Money

The following quiz asks about divorce difficulties and applies to both this chapter and the next one. In this section, clinical and legal choices are reviewed as well as the two factors, children and finances, which up your need for clinical and legal help.

Quiz #3: Difficulties

Q1. What made your divorce difficult?
1. ___ Finding a good lawyer
2. ___ Negotiating the financial settlement
3. ___ Negotiating child custody/parenting plans
4. ___ Communication with lawyer
5. ___ Lower or irregular income
6. ___ Higher expenses
7. ___ Worried my higher income would be used against me like a weapon
8. ___ Difficulty getting job
9. ___ Children upset by divorce
10. ___ Visitations with children

11. ___ Spouse undermines relationship with children
12. ___ Single parent, responsible for everything
13. ___ Part-time parent
14. ___ Worried about children's welfare
15. ___ Spouse involved with someone else
16. ___ Loss of communication with spouse
17. ___ Loss of relationship with spouse
18. ___ Loss or change in social relationships
19. ___ Fear of social rejection
20. ___ Single in a couple's world
21. ___ Criticism of divorce
22. ___ Change of residence
23. ___ Not sure if I wanted the divorce/divorce indecision
24. ___ Not know if spouse wanted a divorce
25. ___ Spousal harassment or violence
26. ___ Finding a good marriage or divorce counselor/therapist
27. ___ Other (what? _____)
28. ___ No problem

Q2. When have you had counseling? (check all that apply)
1. ___ Before your first marriage
2. ___ During your first marriage
3. ___ Between your first and second marriage
4. ___ During your second marriage
5. ___ After your second marriage
6. ___ Never

LOUISE AND HER COUSIN ELVIS DISCUSS THEIR DIVORCE DIFFICULTIES

Louise yawned and slowly drank her morning coffee on the back porch of her parents' Cape Cod beach house. A salty, fishy smell of mid-summer filled the air, as the waves gently rolled in and the sun danced on the Atlantic. Peaceful as this was, Louise was a bit on edge. She was still adjusting to her recent divorce and wondering how her cousin Elvis was coping with his separation from his wife, Scarlett. Both Louise and Elvis were leaving their first marriages, but their respective spouses were breaking up their second. Louise was expecting her cousin Elvis to arrive later that morning with his daughter. The three planned on spending the next week vacationing together.

Twenty minutes later, Elvis's red sports car rolled up. He and his daughter, Elle, bolted out of the vehicle and began the unpacking process—bags, surfboards, and a new volleyball net to replace the dilapidated one in the house. Once unpacked, Elle changed to her new, turquoise bathing suit and dashed to the beach. Elvis grabbed a soda and sat down next to his cousin to relax. They watched Elle and the neighborhood youngsters at play. Elvis turned to Louise.

"Thanks for letting us stay here for the week. It's fun down here with you."

"It is fun being with you, too, Elvis. I appreciate having family around. It's been only six months since my divorce. I still feel awkward doing things without a guy with me, but I'm not ready to date yet either."

"I feel awkward at times as well and need to learn how to do some things. I'm not used to taking care of Elle by myself or cooking."

"Why don't I show you how to make simple stuff like grilled cheese sandwiches?"

"That would be great, Louise. I know how to make coffee,

pour cereal, and grill things out back, but that's it. Thank goodness for McDonald's."

"Is this the first week of your separation, Elvis?"

"Yup. But we haven't figured out very much, except that Elle will probably stay with Scarlett during the week in our current place. I've found a rental condo close to our apartment and work. That was something else. Every time I looked at a place, I had to explain that I was getting a divorce—so humiliating. Everyone was nice about it. But I kept on thinking people would be critical. I'm still embarrassed and upset that Scarlett left me. We can't agree on how to divide the furniture or the rest of our things. We both want the furniture. What do you think?"

"Are you arguing about something special like your grandfather's watch?"

"No."

"Let her have it. Furniture is hard and expensive to move and it has bad memories. You don't want to look at the sofa and start thinking about your bad times. Start with new gear. Let her have that awful stuff in exchange for something better. Maybe she gets the furniture and your older car, while you get the newer one you're driving?"

"We'd both like that. I'll call her later. The condo has a rental furniture plan. They could set that up this week, so it's furnished by the end of the week when I move in. Scarlett wants most of the photos. So do I. What do I do about that?"

"Simple. Scan your favorites or all the photos and make two copies. You each get a copy and if she wants the originals, so what? You can make copies that look like originals."

"Another issue is financial records. We probably could do the same thing with that, too. Maybe she can scan the photos, while I copy our tax returns and other financial things. I have my summer clothes, trophies, and personal junk already in the car. I need to fill up the car one more time with my winter clothes. Then, I'm done."

"That was easy."

"You have really helped, but this hasn't been easy and it's not over. We've been arguing about this for weeks and they're other matters to figure out like child support. Worst part, I don't trust Scarlett; she's sneaky."

"I know how you feel. My ex, John, was shifty and impossible. He put a $5,000 engagement ring for his new fiancée on our debt list so that I would be stuck paying for half. He didn't get away with it. My lawyer caught it. God, was I mad."

"Wow. Good you're rid of him."

"You're probably right. And I'm lucky in other ways. Let's go for a swim. Enough with our problems for now."

"Good idea, Louise. But I need more advice later, especially about how to handle Elle. She is upset. I don't know how to calm her down."

"Carter is coming over later. Why don't we brainstorm with him?"

"Okay."

To Do List

Like most, you will probably struggle with at least several general complications: selecting a divorce counselor, legal disputes, children's issues, finances, social losses, spousal difficulties, and residential move snags. Women usually grapple with five or six specific concerns, such as higher expenses or one more stumbling block than their ex-husbands.

This chapter deals with common initial difficulties like selecting a good divorce counselor, initial financial steps, and legal issues such as child custody. Later chapters will touch on or go into more depth about these issues. Chapter 15, for instance, will look in depth at children's responses.

Self-care: Counseling Choices

Airline safety instructions tell parents to "put the oxygen on your mouth first, then give oxygen to your children." The point is that you must take care of yourself, before you can help anyone else in an emergency. The same is true when you are divorcing. You need to take care of yourself before you can help the rest of your family. The best way to do this is to get the counseling you need fast as well as use the tips in this book. How, then, do you know what type of therapist and therapy form is best for you?

SUPPORT GROUPS

Women's centers, churches, synagogues, and clinicians in private practice routinely lead support groups for divorcing men and women. These groups are essential for anyone with limited emotional support. Although directed by a leader, they are primarily self-help groups that share divorce information and social support. They give you a chance to be with others who are going through the same experience, so you do not feel alone in your grief and troubles.

For many, joining a support group allows you to vent your emotions so you don't "over chat" about your divorce with your children, disapproving adults, or close friends and family. Your children can benefit from a simple age-appropriate explanation of your divorce, but they don't need to hear the details or be your primary source of emotional support. Some neighbors, friends, and family are against your divorce, so they will not be a source of comfort or good advice. Even empathetic friends and family tire of hearing about your troubles and will avoid you if you don't limit your divorce remarks.

Some second-timers, who want their divorce and are in good

shape, join these groups. Other times, you find you need more help and select individual counseling instead or in addition.

> ***Common Reasons for Divorce Counseling***
> - Can't decide whether to get a divorce.
> - Thinking about suicide.
> - Are or were in a physically abusive relationship.
> - Can't control your temper/ Anger Management.
> - Depressed for more than two weeks.
> - Can't get out of bed in the morning.
> - Can't get work done (office or home).
> - Need antidepressants or anti-anxiety medication.
> - Over-drinking or taking drugs.
> - Driving while intoxicated.
> - Hostile divorce.
> - Emotional support.
> - Prevent strong emotions from causing bad decisions.
> - Speed up recovery.
> - Reduce the child's problems with advice and self-healing.
> - Learn better communication skills, including negotiation skills.
> - Improve parenting and co-parenting skills.
> - Resilience training.
> - Intimacy problems.

DIVORCE COACH

Confident individuals, who initiate their second divorce and are in decent emotional shape, often choose a divorce coach. No matter how many times you have been divorced before, each one is different and you will need an objective guide on your path.

Coaches may or may not have a background in law or counseling. So, you will want to ask them about their education to make sure they can provide you with the services you require.

Coaches are not therapists, who delve into and resolve deep emotional issues. Instead, they are mentors. Especially at the beginning, coaches make sure emotional reactions do not interfere with good business decisions, such as how to divide your property or custody. Later, coaching is more of a supportive, structuring, and educational role. Together, you will establish needed support, learn how to communicate effectively with your ex and children, and set and work on realistic goals, including if and how you want to change. Many adults get divorced because they can't communicate effectively. Chances are that you need to improve your communication skills not only to make your current divorce easier, but also to improve your relationships in general. Throughout, your mentor will let you know where you are in the process, keep you on track, and help you take a proactive role. Taking a proactive role ensures that you have a reasonable amount of control over your divorce process and outcome. This reduces your stress, speeds up your recovery, and leads to a better outcome.

CLINICIANS

Most people who do not want a divorce need more than a support group or a divorce coach. If so, you will want to consult a clinician, who will help you handle the stress, grief, anger, and other emotions and troubles common in a divorce. Your primary care doctor is often a good place to get a referral. Online referral systems and state licensing boards can give you names, but they rarely know you or your local mental health community as well as your doctor does. When picking one, make sure yours specializes in divorce counseling and you feel comfortable with her or him. You will achieve more in therapy if you feel that your therapist understands you and can give you good advice for your situation. You have multiple choices: pastoral counselors, social workers, licensed mental health workers, clinical psychologists, and psychiatrists.

Pastoral Counselor

Many clergy provide free or low-cost counseling. If you belong to a religious organization, approach your spiritual leader to see if he or she can provide divorce therapy. If not, ask for a referral to another pastoral counselor or clinician in your area.

Social worker or Licensed Mental Health Worker

Social workers and licensed mental health workers, who specialize in divorce, are trained to deal with grief and other divorce reactions and issues. Typically, they have more clinical training than a coach or pastoral counselor, but not as much as a clinical psychologist or a psychiatrist. Most have a two-year master's degree plus a two-year supervised internship. Some social workers have even more training and hold a doctorate in social work. They tend to be less expensive than psychologists or psychiatrists, practical, and sometimes quite innovative. Many chose their specialty because, at some point in their life, they had the same problems you are facing and have literally "walked in your shoes."

Clinical Psychologist

Clinical psychologists hold a doctoral degree, Ph.D., Psy.D., or Ed.D. They have four or more years of graduate training in psychology, psychological testing, and therapeutic methods as well as two one-year clinical internships, one pre-doctoral and one postdoctoral. Of the choices, psychologists usually know the most about how to deal with emotional and interpersonal problems, including deep-seated ones.

Look for a clinical psychologist who specializes in divorce. Then, ask a lot of questions. What is her/his preferred therapeutic approach? Where are you in your journey? What do you need to work on and in what order? If you have additional issues such as an attention deficit disorder, a substance abuse problem, a sexual dysfunction, a history of physical abuse or trauma, or added stress because you or someone in your family is in the military, make sure the therapist has specialized training in these areas, too.

Many psychologists not only understand emotional problems and how to resolve them, but also are skilled instructors. They can teach you how to reduce your divorce stress, communicate more effectively with your lawyer and family, and handle other practical issues.

If you are having a difficult breakup and/or have additional concerns, an experienced divorce psychologist with expertise in the other areas for which you need help is a good choice.

Psychiatrist/Medical Doctor

Divorcing adults who are suicidal, or need medication to get through a rough patch, almost always select a psychiatrist or family doctor. Psychiatrists are medical doctors who specialize in mental health problems and prescribe antidepressants and anti-anxiety drugs. In most states, other therapists do not have the medical training or the legal right to prescribe. If you need medication, you will need to see a psychiatrist or your family doctor. Many psychiatrists provide psychotherapy. Other psychiatrists and family doctors will prescribe and monitor your drug therapy, but leave counseling to another clinician, like a social worker or a psychologist. So, you will want to ask interviewed medical doctors how they normally treat their divorcing clients.

> **Picture Success**
> Imagine that you have successfully developed an agreement that works for your family. Tell yourself this several times a day as well.
>
> **Win-Win Solution**
> Think cooperatively and flexibly about how to make your settlement a win-win solution. Try to get at least some of your top wants and needs and make sure your ex gets some of what he or she really wants and needs.

Legal Landscape

Four Ways Out

In most states, couples have four ways to reach a divorce settlement:

- one-on-one negotiations or do-it-yourself
- mediation
- collaborative divorce
- litigation

The first three methods are cooperative, streamlined, and cost effective. The fourth, litigation, is usually adversarial, time-consuming, and expensive. Your best choice depends on where the two of you are in your emotional process and your situation. In turn, the method you select may affect your process and adjustment.

DIY Divorce

Of the non-adversarial approaches, the most straightforward is the do-it-yourself style. With this model, you work directly with your spouse to form an agreement with minimal or no help from others. The two of you have total control over your process. You may consult a lawyer or other specialists before finalizing your agreement. Your attorney may review, suggest changes to conform to your state's laws, and file the legal paperwork.

Alternatively, you can go to the court with your agreement and file the papers with the assistance of a court clerk. In some states, you can download forms and instructions. To be successful with this method, you and your partner must want the divorce, communicate easily, be fully informed about all the issues, and have relatively little to decide. You are a good candidate for this if you're childless or briefly married with few joint assets and roughly the same incomes.

Mediation and Collaboration

You may prefer mediation or collaborative divorce. In these methods, you and any hired experts work cooperatively and transparently toward an agreement without litigating the case. In mediation, a neutral party such as a psychologist helps you and your spouse find a solution that best fits the needs and concerns of your family.

A relatively new model is collaborative divorce. An evolving, individualized process, this approach varies to fit your family's needs. Meetings include a series of group conferences with the two of you, a lawyer for each of you, and often a neutral facilitator and neutral financial adviser. You and your spouse hire consultants to provide answers to specific questions or teach you skills. A real estate appraiser may evaluate your home or a child specialist might suggest a parenting plan. A therapist or divorce coach may mentally prepare you for sessions, help you improve your communication and negotiating skills, and support you throughout. You may need assistance staying calm during your meetings. Advocates of collaborative divorce argue that this process has the greatest potential for creative problem solving and can be tailored to handle even the most difficult situations.

In both mediation and collaboration, you proceed through five general steps:

- **Introductory**: The professional(s) explain the process and obtain background information, including areas of agreement and disagreement. If you decide to proceed, you will sign initial papers promising to work cooperatively with your spouse toward a settlement agreement without litigation.
- **Information gathering**: You collect all your necessary monetary information, such as recent tax returns, bank statements, and pension reports. You obtain needed outside appraisals to help you agree on estimates such as the value of your home. Your major danger is that financial disclosures are voluntary and may be inaccurate, unless substantiated.
- **Framing**: Your and your spouse's goals and desired outcomes or interests are explored and determined. For example, you may want to sell your house to pay off debt, while your spouse may want to keep it for sentimental reasons.
- **Negotiating**: You brainstorm for possible options. You and your team will seek to find the best option for everyone in your family.
- **Concluding**: Together, you review, revise, and sign an agreement. This agreement is then filed with the court as an uncontested divorce.

To use these methods, both you and your spouse need to be emotionally prepared to settle and committed to developing a cooperative, transparent solution. Especially in the early stages of a divorce, one of you is usually ready to end the marriage, but the other isn't. When so, you have to wait until both of you are beyond denial and high distress to use either of these approaches. Alternatively, you can hire a therapist to accelerate the slower partner's healing so that you and your spouse are ready to settle. These processes rely on voluntary information and assume that both of you are being honest and open about important information.

Mediation and collaborative divorce have their limitations. If you have a power imbalance where one of you intimidates the other, a history of physical abuse, or one of you has an untreated addiction, you are often more comfortable and successful with collaborative divorce, or litigation, than mediation. In collaborative divorce, experienced professionals can handle many of your issues or refer the problem to another specialist such as a substance abuse counselor.

Litigation is your last choice. You may become tired of waiting for your spouse to be ready to use other methods and want to get it over with. Conflict is high, or you rule out less adversarial approaches. Sometimes, you select lawyers to represent you in court. If you do, they may take a cooperative or an adversarial stance.

LITIGATION

Your last choice is litigation. Litigation with legal representation is expensive. Largely due to cost, you and a large and growing number of individuals often pick the pro se method, where one or both of you represent yourselves. Childless couples with little to dispute can sometimes do this and end up with a fair solution. Sometimes you don't. You may not consider pensions or tax consequences, or know which assets are dividable and which aren't.[1]

Time-consuming and stressful, litigation often inflames your hostility and distrust, increases your upset, and reduces your assets. This undermines your co-parenting, trust, and recovery. Not surprisingly, when you litigate, you're often less satisfied with your outcome.[2] Yet, this may be your best or only realistic choice.

> ***Educate Yourself***
> Learn as much as you can about the legal process, especially mediation and collaborative divorce, and the resources for these in your community.
>
> ***Prepare for Meetings***
> To reduce misunderstandings and ease your process, be ready to listen to your spouse, try to understand his or her point of view even though you don't agree with it, and focus on the future and what is best for your children.

Burned by the Legal Process

Half the time, you end your marriage emotionally and financially burned. You are like William and Grace. You fight viciously over child custody and the financial settlement, resent high legal fees, and have other legal problems. For years, you are in an emotional boxing ring beating each other up. Alternatively, you can circumvent these complications, especially if:

- You don't have minor children from the marriage. Couples who do not have minor children seldom have legal complications.
- Neither of you had an affair. Affairs enrage the wronged spouse.
- The two of you have roughly the same salaries or little to divide.
- You represent yourself during the legal proceedings, ducking legal costs.
- You use cooperative approaches to resolve your legal issues, so you can reach an acceptable and low-cost settlement and file an uncontested divorce.

> **Don't Argue in Front of Your Children**
> To decrease problems with your children, avoid arguing in front of them.

Children's Complications

If you have children from an earlier relationship but none from this one, you run a good chance that your children are relieved. Frequently, first-marriage teens are angry when you remarry and try to undo it. Many succeed. During the uncoupling, these teens drop their obnoxious behavior and rarely cause a problem or add to your stress. They are happier, cheer up your home, pitch in more with chores, and help you through the ordeal. There are, however, exceptions like those who are close to their stepparent.

Beth and Nickolas' blended family is a typical story. Beth's oldest daughter resented the marriage, got into trouble at school, and fought nonstop with her stepsiblings and stepfather. Nickolas's teens didn't like their marriage, stepsiblings, or Beth. When Beth and Nickolas divorced, however, their teens dropped their disruptive behaviors. Beth's youngsters emotionally supported her, while Nickolas's gave him backing as well. They had no problems with their children. Child upset, custody disputes, and financial support discussions didn't happen.

If you have remarriage minors, expect to struggle with child-related issues—upset children, changes in your relationship with them, trouble paying their bills, or maybe custody disputes. These youngsters are usually distressed by the conflict, separation, and marital dissolution. Their tears and misery cast a negative shadow on your home, intensifying your troubles. You almost always worry about their welfare, have higher distress trying to deal with their upset and child-related legal complications, and suffer guilt for putting them through this. You can reduce these troubles by providing your children with:

- A simple divorce explanation without blaming just one of you or giving them false hope that you will reconcile.
- A parenting plan that ensures that both parents will be involved in their everyday lives.
- A simple explanation of how their schedule will change.
- Opportunities to discuss their worries and emotions. Talking about their emotions with you, their other parent, or a counselor can help reduce their worries, anger, misunderstandings, and other common reactions.

STAY FAITHFUL

In addition, you can lessen problems with your children by working cooperatively with your spouse to make your divorce a low conflict, cooperative action. With this aim, don't have an affair before the two of you have decided to end your marriage. If one or both of you have an affair or quickly find someone else, your negotiations will tend to be hostile, prolonged, and costly. Grace's infidelity enraged her husband and made their divorce more difficult. They had a long, expensive battle over the financial settlement and custody details. With ongoing antagonism, co-parenting during and afterwards was tough.

In this study, those with an unfaithful spouse tended to denigrate their spouse. Williams' comments were standard for couples with continuing conflict:

> I had endless problems with our kids. I worried about them. I didn't know how to handle their upset when they were with me yet missed them when they weren't. I suspect that my ex made nasty remarks about me to them. I can't help making

nasty remarks about her either. I'm still angry about her affair.

> **Don't Belittle Your Ex to Your Youngsters.**
> When your children respect and have a good relationship with both of you, they're happier, more confident, and healthier.[3]

Co-parenting

Like many adults, you may decide that your children should spend most of their time with their mom. For moms, this increases obligations and decreases your free time. It limits your ability to increase your income, find a new partner, or rebuild self-esteem.

When so, moms on a limited budget with preschoolers usually have the toughest time. On welfare, Scarlett couldn't afford childcare or pay for interesting opportunities for her children such as after-school athletic, musical, and/or artistic activities. Luckily, her mom stepped in and helped with babysitting and finances.

Other times, you have work schedules that prevent you from doing ordinary parental tasks such as driving your children to extracurricular activities. To quote one mom:

> It's hard being a single parent with less money and most of the childcare responsibilities. My biggest concern is my daughter. She is still upset, although not as much as in the beginning. We can take her to her weekend activities, but she misses going to her ballet lessons Wednesdays after school. Neither of us can take time off to get her there.

At the same time, when children spend the bulk of their time with their mom, fathers have the opposite reaction. You feel locked out of your sons' and daughters' everyday activities. You miss day-to-day opportunities to share your youngsters' lives, whether simply hearing about their school day, playing basketball with them in your backyard, or attending their special events. When parenting roles are reversed, Dad feels overloaded, while Mom misses her youngsters.

Custody Dilemmas

Joint custody arrangements where your children spend roughly the same amount of time with each parent may alleviate some problems. Yet, missing your children on non-custody days and feeling overloaded on others still happens. And many find these plans stressful, complicated, and impractical.

Most parents dislike the ongoing change, added work, and restrictions imposed by complex schedules. Joint custody and co-parenting schedules can increase certain risks. What if you want to move? What if you and your ex want to achieve maximum separation and independence, so you both can pursue new lives? High-conflict mothers and fathers often hate joint parenting. Occasionally, parents are abusive or use their children as pawns and shouldn't have primary or joint custody. Sometimes, your spouse's request for joint custody is insincere. S/he is only suggesting this as a bargaining maneuver to reduce his or her financial obligations.

Many youngsters can't handle or loathe recurrent change. Your children are constantly adapting to a different lifestyle and set of rules, and often don't have things they want because they're at the other house. Many resent this. Relocating fuels parental conflict if you and your ex don't get along. This can be upsetting for everyone. Even under the best circumstances, when you live close by, have similar home rules, and get along, children may be distressed by and balk at frequent residential shifts. Most handicapped and emotionally sensitive children are upset by minor variations in your home and moves.

SOCIAL INVESTIGATION

When you and your partner can't work out custody and child support questions, even after mediation or collaborative attempts, the court will ordinarily order a *Social Investigation*. A child specialist conducts most of these.

Typically, a psychologist spends many hours interviewing, testing, and observing your family. She usually visits your home(s) to determine first-hand your lifestyle and family relations. She is looking for answers to questions like: "Is the home clean, neat, and a safe, healthy environment for your youngsters? How well do you and they relate? Are your children's needs met?" She may even check your refrigerator to see if you have a healthy, well-stocked food supply. On top of that, she often interviews other people like doctors, teachers, or neighbors to get an objective perspective on your situation. Then, she designs and recommends a child-rearing arrangement to the court. This examination often invades your privacy and adds to your family's cost and distress.[4]

> *Home Visit*
> Before the call, tidy up your place. Make sure your refrigerator is clean and well stocked with healthy foods and no alcohol. Relate positively to your youngsters during the visit.

Sweating Your Financial Future

During your divorce, you will be dealing with many financial concerns. Your most common ones include the increased cost of maintaining two homes; new legal, accounting, and counseling fees; lower or irregular income; alimony and child support payments; and the division of assets and debts. You may also worry that your relatively higher or lower income or wealth will hurt you in the process.

Your best approach to monetary complications is preparation. Begin by outlining your current budget. Then, estimate your income and costs after the two of you separate and establish two separate residences.

Especially if you can't cover your future bills, you need to raise your income, cut costs, and/or improve your credit line. Increasing your education or technical training helps increase your income. Consider attending your local community college. These universities have many short certification courses that can land you a new, better-paying career or advance your current one. Wise couples encourage and help each other improve their vocational skills, so you both have higher incomes and can better provide for yourself and your children.

After separating, you may keep on spending and ignore your new financial plight. You spend more of your savings or increase your debt. By procrastinating, you make your problems worse and harder to solve. Instead, slash your expenditures right away. This is a key to managing your divorce successfully. Through diligence, necessity, and ingenuity, two out of three keep their expenses in tight check and run two new households for the same cost as their previous combined one. Daunting as this is, you probably can, too. Your accountant can help you with budgeting or point you toward someone who can. Mediation and collaborative approaches automatically include budgeting advice, along with an overview of your monetary situation. Help with financial management is readily available, including free online courses. If you need assistance, explore your options.

Table 7-1: Monthly Budget	Joint Now	You After Split
Car payments		
Clothing		
Credit card debt		
Day care		
Gasoline, oil		
Groceries, meals		
Healthcare		
Insurance		
Parking, tolls		
Phone, internet		
Rent/Mortgage		
Repairs		
Savings		
Taxes		
Utilities		
Vacations		
Miscellaneous		
Total Estimate		

*Convert annual or quarterly bills into monthly costs.

> **Protect Financial Records**
> Store a copy of your important documents somewhere safe such as in an email to yourself.

INVENTORY

Everyone needs to gather detailed financial information before finalizing a financial settlement and a divorce. Typically, you itemize savings, checking, and retirement accounts. Then you put down ordinary possessions, such as your house, cars, and furniture as well as other items like a business or an injury settlement. Finally, you record debts—your mortgage, car loans, legal and accounting fees to process the divorce, and credit card obligations. Valuations for most of these need documentation. Sometimes, you can download bank statements and other financial information from the Internet.

Like many, you may feel overwhelmed by all the things you must do to obtain your financial information. Start by making a list of the records you need. Then break down complicated tasks into smaller more manageable ones. After you complete a step, cross it off, praise yourself for accomplishing it, and then do the next. You will feel a growing sense of relief as you plough through your assignments. If you can, you may want to hire someone else to help you do this. Other times, you hire an appraiser to estimate a valuation.

CONVERT JOINT ACCOUNTS TO INDIVIDUAL ACCOUNTS

You are normally better off if you convert your joint credit cards, bank accounts, stock holdings, and safe deposit boxes into individual ones long before you make a formal settlement. Sometimes, the issue is gaining control over your finances and credit rating. You are safer with an individual account that you can control. With a joint account, you have partial control and never know what your partner might suddenly do. During a divorce, many otherwise responsible people do not pay their bills on time or make unwise charges. Worse yet, your spouse might empty out your safe deposit box or bank accounts. All of these could hurt you.

Sometimes, the issue is establishing individual credit so you are sure you have it. In the nine community property states, like California, you can get credit based on your household or total family income. In these states, you get a higher credit line while you are living together and can claim joint revenue than later, when you can only use your income. In other states, credit is established by your income, not your household income. In these states, if you are a stay-at-home parent or otherwise unemployed, take a part-time or full-time job so you have the personal earnings to apply for a line of credit. Should this fail, find a bank that will give you a secured credit card—a card secured by your savings or checking account in the same bank. Even a small credit is a start. From there, if you are responsible, you can raise your limit.

IMPROVE CREDIT

Make sure you have good credit in your name, safe from your spouse's actions. In that way, you will be able to rent a desirable place after you separate/divorce, charge purchases, obtain affordable insurance, and increase your eligibility for certain jobs and job promotions. Employers often check credit scores as part of their job-offering decisions. Basic steps to establish good credit are the following:

- Pay off your monthly bills completely and on time.
- Keep your monthly credit card charges to 30% or less of your bankcard limit.
- Use only one or two cards in your name. Your score goes up

as the number of accounts with balances drop. Review your reports several times a year, so you know your rating and can correct any errors. Every year, you are entitled to a free one from Experian, TransUnion, and Equifax. By staggering reports, you can get three free ones annually.
- Hide important personal property in a safe place.
- Protect your joint assets. Either ask your lawyer to do this or do this yourself. Some get so mad that they destroy or spend an asset rather than share it with their spouse.
- Ask your accountant to help you with budgeting, income, and credit scores. Ask how your separation date is defined in your state and how it and your divorce date affect you money-wise. Tax returns, eligibility for your ex's social security, pensions, alimony, and more are date sensitive. In most cases, you need 10 years to qualify for benefits.[5]

Financial Preparation
1. Estimate your current and post-separation budgets.
2. Decrease discretionary spending and debt.
3. Increase work skills and income.
4. Increase cash and savings. An emergency savings account is essential.
5. Make sure you have good credit in your own name.
6. Open individual accounts and, then close joint accounts.
7. List your assets and debts.
8. Photograph your assets to document them and their condition.
9. List and copy important financial records, including your recent tax returns.

Financial Settlement

Typically, you are stressed, but not overwrought during your financial negotiations. If you are bitterly fighting over your settlement, you and your spouse are not cooperatively and flexibly aiming for a win-win solution. Ask a divorce accountant or lawyer to review your situation, suggest alternative plans, and mediate your final plan. You can usually avoid acrimony if the two of you take a business-like approach and tailor your plan to meet the needs of your whole family.

Dollar and Cents Heroes and Heroines

With planning and determination, you can often skillfully tackle a list of financial concerns. Even so, one or two monetary worries can cause moderate strain until the issue is resolved.

Abandoned by her second husband, Coral, a late-thirties Wal-Mart cashier, exited a seven-year, childless marriage. She had a long list of economic challenges: lower household income, higher expenses, trouble selling their home, uprooting to a new neighborhood, and a long, bitter property negotiation. Throughout the split, she had moderately high stress and insomnia, and put on twenty pounds. Afterwards, she was irritable, didn't date, and obsessed on her recent marriage. With the aid of her minister, Coral turned her life around two years later. With his help, she received a scholarship to attend the nursing school at a nearby college. Her church helped her with other costs. Soon, she had new friends, lost weight, and regained an optimistic outlook. She started to date again. When she graduated, she landed a good job at the local hospital and said good-bye to her financial and social woes, permanently.

If you have numerous, ongoing financial troubles, you may be unhappy throughout the dissolution. Most of the time, you can solve these challenges and calm down soon after the divorce. However, sometimes you are upset long after the marriage has ended. When you are perpetually upset, you seldom have a decent income, good budgeting habits, adequate social support, or trouble-free children. Especially if you have substance abuse problems, you can end up with serious health and emotional issues. To turn your life around, you will probably need mental health and vocational counseling, occupational training, and improved budgeting.

Financially Burned

If you're wealthier than your spouse, you will probably worry that your relative wealth will be used against you. You may be afraid that s/he will get a lot of your money and assets. Once in a while, you have the opposite problem—your spouse is richer than you. When so, you may fret that s/he will confront you with monetary threats and/or superior legal representation.

The manager of a medium-sized corporation, Charles, had a high income, but his wife, Carolyn, was a salesclerk and earned a lower salary. Worried about his junior-high daughter, he struggled for many months before he decided to end his marriage. Early on, he was tense and angry. Then, after a quiet six-month separation, he was once more enraged by her demands at their settlement talks. Unable to work cooperatively, they ended up in a court trial. Charles was again upset by the judge's decision. He was bitter that his higher income was used to justify giving his former wife the use of their family home until their daughter was 18, as well as alimony and child support payments. Although he loved his daughter, he couldn't see the ruling as anything other than a financial hit. He couldn't admit that the ruling put the best interest of his daughter first and was a reasonable, workable solution. A wiser couple would have sought counseling for both, so that they could have been calmer during the split and cooperatively worked out a settlement. Instead, they were stuck with a needlessly expensive court decision.

Men who complain primarily about finances may feel disadvantaged and resent any payments, lost equity, or other new costs. By the divorce, you seldom care about your former partner or the ending of your marriage, except to the extent that it hurts you financially or your children. Even if you care about your children, you may be angry that your child support is going to your ex.

You and your wallet are best served by thinking cooperatively with your spouse to find a win-win solution to skirt litigation. Consider automatic payments from your bank account for child support or other costs. That way, you do not have to think about the situation every month or worry about whether the check is late.

Things to Remember about Solving Early Challenges:
- Counseling is an important part of your self-care and supports your recovery.
- Prepare for your financial future before you separate.
- Adults have four legal options to reach a settlement. Try to select a cooperative one.
- A cooperative divorce is especially important if you have minor children from the marriage. Low hostility protects your children and minimizes legal fees and complications.

CHAPTER 8

Uprooted: Spousal Issues, Social Changes, and Relocating

Quiz # 4 Subset: Social Difficulties.

This quiz is part of the Difficulties Quiz found in the prior chapter.

Q1. What family, social, or relocating reactions made your divorce difficult?
 1. ___ Spouse involved with someone else
 2. ___ Divorce indecision
 3. ___ Not know if spouse wanted divorce
 4. ___ Loss of communication with spouse
 5. ___ Spousal harassment
 6. ___ Criticism
 7. ___ Social rejection
 8. ___ Single in a couple's world
 9. ___ Loss of spousal relationship
 10. ___ Loss or change in social relationships
 11. ___ Change of residence
 12. ___ Other (What? _____

Spousal Fires

Runaways

Sometimes, the worst part is feeling scorned. John and Grace had affairs, ran off, and were hostile toward their spouses. Their spurned spouses, Saul and Louise, had excruciating distress when they unearthed the affairs and separated. Mid-divorce, they were depressed and slow to recover. For the first year or two afterwards, they frequently reviewed their pasts, disliked and distrusted their ex-spouses and others, and were overly cautious socially. Slow to reach out for new or existing social relationships, Saul didn't develop new acquaintances, but eventually started dating. Even though Louise had a solid job and a couple of friends, she didn't have children or close family, was cynical, and rarely socialized in the first year afterwards.

If scorned, you normally benefit from therapy and increased socialization with your family and others. Once you heal and become more trustful again, you will probably find another long-term relationship. Carter, who had a painful first divorce, went on to have a happy marriage with Madeline. He met Madeline sketching the Narragansett Towers Memorial Day weekend. Beth and Nickolas continued to be friends. Several years later, they were both re-partnered, but not remarried. Nickolas met Vita, another accountant, at a local convention. Beth met Sam, a widower and college history professor, at a New Year's Day party.

> *Wondering Whether You Should Divorce?*
> Consult a therapist who can help you make the right decision. There are also several books like Kirshenbaum's 1997 book entitled *Too Good to Leave, Too Bad to Stay* that can help you decide.

Social Difficulties

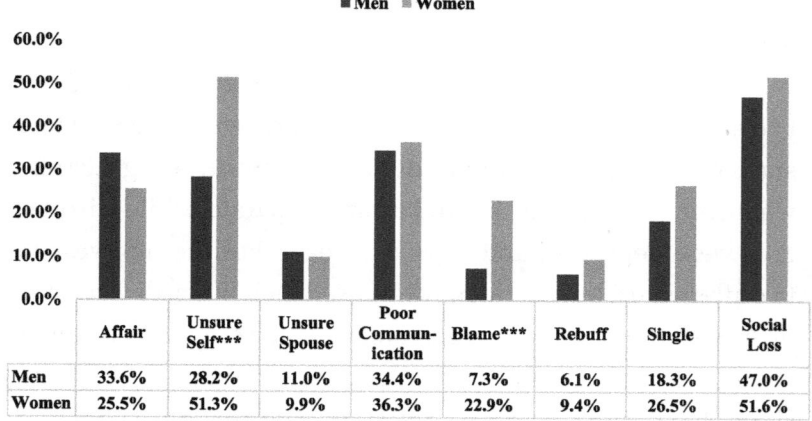

	Affair	Unsure Self***	Unsure Spouse	Poor Communication	Blame***	Rebuff	Single	Social Loss
Men	33.6%	28.2%	11.0%	34.4%	7.3%	6.1%	18.3%	47.0%
Women	25.5%	51.3%	9.9%	36.3%	22.9%	9.4%	26.5%	51.6%

Figure 8-1: Social difficulties for men and women. Note: Strains include spousal affair (affair), indecision (unsure self), unsure spouse wanted divorce (unsure spouse), criticism (blame), rejection (rebuff), dislike single status (single), loss/change spousal or other relationships (social loss). Adults: hybrid first-timers: 97 (women 53) and redivorcers: 289 (women 170). *** $p < .001$.

Graph Takeaways:
1. Women report more indecision and criticism than men.
2. Women's top three: social loss (52%), indecision (51%), and communication (36%).
3. Men's top three: social loss (47%), communication (34%), and infidelity (34%).

Sitting On the Fence

When you ask for a divorce, you usually spend months, if not years, wondering if you should leave. You are the slowest to decide, if you are a once-married woman. Most of the time, you take over a year to mull it over. Half the time, you deliberate for at least two years. Men, especially those who don't instigate the breakup, have the shortest period of indecision, often less than a month or two. Janet's fence sitting put her family into an upsetting multi-year limbo. Ultimately, her ambivalence was a major aggravation per se and propelled the couple to a permanent split. To complicate matters, you may not know whether your spouse wants a divorce, too.

One version of this is the *on-again/off-again* couple. When this happens, your decision to split alternates with reconciliation repeatedly. When you refuse to admit that you want a divorce or you are indecisive, your spouse often doesn't realize that your relationship is over. Throughout the process, your actions and uncertainty prevent your partner from facing and dealing with the marital demise. Eventually, your spouse is rightfully confused, faces late peak anguish, and is on an emotional rollercoaster during the volatile, tumultuous, on-again/off-again breakup.

In her late thirties, Catherine, a pianist, was divorced twice from the same husband, Michael, a pizza restaurant owner. Their marriage represented a small but interesting divorce style in which one spouse didn't emotionally believe, despite two divorces, that the relationship was over.

Michael and Catherine had a volatile, sixteen-year relationship marked by many disputes, many separations, and two divorces. Two months after their first break, Michael's new girlfriend split up with him to marry someone else. Devastated, Michael returned to Catherine, insisted that he only loved her, and begged Catherine to forgive him and marry him again. Soon after they remarried, they started arguing again. Michael left again and redivorced her. Still in love with him and in "wait mode," Catherine did not accept her second divorce. She didn't date or try to create a new life. Concurrently, Michael headed toward a third union with another woman. Certain couples marry and divorce each other several times. After the first, if you were the plaintiff, you may propose remarriage. This occurs when you are jilted by a new love or when your rejected ex-partner finds someone else. You rarely want your ex-partner, but you also don't want anyone else to have him/her. Remarrying your former spouse is usually a mistake, unless you have resolved your marital troubles.

Elizabeth Taylor and Richard Burton had an on-again/off-again relationship. Even after their second divorce and until they died, they cared deeply about each other.[1]

> **Don't Date Your Ex**
> After a divorce, some date their ex again because they remember the good times, but have forgotten the bad or they are lonely. Talk to a therapist before you do this.
>
> **Speak Respectfully Toward Your Ex**
> Don't invade your ex's privacy or harass him or her. Talk to your ex-spouse respectfully even during difficult conversations.

Poor Communication

Like most, you probably faulted communication problems for destroying your marriage. Then, you separate and find that the same bad habits prolong your divorce and continue to fuel hostility, even postdivorce. Now, about a third of the time, miscommunication continues to aggravate you. Here are some well-known tricks to deescalate your arguments and, as a result, improve the quality of your life and adjustment. To work, you need to go out of your way to practice these until they are new, automatic habits.

- Use "I" messages that state how you feel when your ex does something hurtful. This allows you to express your anger in a nonthreatening way that can lead to a constructive solution.

For example, "I feel short-changed when the kids aren't ready on time. I only get to see them on Sundays as is." An alternative comment like "You are so irresponsible and inconsiderate." incites a counterattack and escalates troubles.
- Be respectful. Avoid put-downs or nasty comments or behaviors.
- Improve your listening skills. Try to understand and empathize with your ex's viewpoint even if you don't agree with it. Send cues that you are hearing what he or she is saying by nodding, eye contact, and comments like I hear you. Give your ex a chance to talk without interrupting or countering his/her comments. To make sure you understand, summarize what she/he has said. Ask if your summary is accurate.
- Focus on solving problems, instead of blaming others.
- Offer alternative suggestions, not one solution to a problem.
- Make requests instead of complaints. "Please pay the child support by the first." is more effective than "Your late payments are so irresponsible."
- Stay calm by using calming techniques like deep breathing/ triangle breathing.
- Use standard business techniques to negotiate your settlement and custody routine. Use and stick to an agenda, know what you want, and solve the easiest problem first. Find solutions which best meet everyone's needs in your family.
- Take a business-like, solution-focused approach toward co-parenting.

Deep Breathing[2]
Inhale thru your nose for a count of four, hold for four counts, then exhale thru your mouth for a count of four. To increase the calming effect, clench your fists as you breathe in and relax them as you breathe out. Repeat this for five to ten minutes until you are calm.

Harassment and Violence

Some people harass, threaten, or try to embarrass their former husband or wife. You may leave irritating messages on your ex-spouse's answering machines, send hostile emails or letters, or write derogatory comments about your ex-partner on his/her Facebook page. After his divorce, Saul sent nasty email messages to his ex-wife. In one, he threatened to post nude pictures of her unless she agreed to his demands. Initially, she volleyed back spiteful comments. Later, she deleted his emails without reading them.

Other times, you use friends, neighbors, or your children to keep tabs on your ex's actions. For two years, Elvis pumped his daughter Elle for information about his ex, Scarlett. He asked her about what her mom did evenings and details about male friends or dates. Once Elvis found a new mate, he stopped his meddling. You may pull childish pranks like putting nails in your ex's car tires. Just before they split, William got so mad that he left a dead mouse in his wife's mailbox to upset her.

Some stalkers cause so much turmoil you are on edge from then on. One man in this study came into his wife's office and made such a row that her boss fired her on the spot. If there was physical abuse in your marriage, you may fear for your life or your children's welfare.

> ### *Write, But Do Not Send*
> Writing hostile messages in your journal may get the venom out of your system. But don't send a nasty letter or do or say anything hateful to your ex.

Emergency Preparation

In about a third of the remarriage breakups in this study, physical abuse occurred. Especially if there has already been abuse in your marriage, take standard precautionary steps:

- Work out an exit plan, including how to leave in an emergency. If you're a woman, your local women's center can help you with this.
- Stash an extra set of car and home keys, clothes, and money in a safe spot.
- Locate safe housing such as a women's shelter.
- If you have a child, ask her to go to the neighbors to call 911 if you say a code word.
- Memorize your local domestic abuse hotline or the National Hotline 800-799-7233.
- Report every incident of stalking, harassment, threats, and domestic violence to the police. A recorded history of problems will make getting a protective order easier.
- Join a support group. A support group will bolster your emotional support, increase your knowledge and options, and add friends who can help you in an emergency.
- If physical abuse occurs:
    » Call 911 and ask the police for help.
    » Go to your local hospital for your injuries, get copies of your medical records, and keep them in a safe spot for potential use in court later.
    » Have a friend or relative take photos of your injuries along with the date and details of the incident. Again, put these in a safe place.
    » Go to a safe place with your children.
    » Press charges and get a restraining order against your spouse. Women's centers often have access to pro-bono lawyers who can help you do this.
    » Take precautions to keep safe, even if you have a restraining order.

> **_Warning—Leaving an Abusive Husband Increases Your Danger Level_**
> When you leave an abusive person, you are in the most danger. Don't let your spouse know that and where you are going. Most Women's Centers provide safe housing.

> **_Criticism_**
> Few will criticize you for getting a divorce. If they do, infidelity is usually the issue. Don't beat yourself up about this or allow others to make you feel worse. Infidelity is a common breakup mistake and something in the past you cannot change.
>
> Apologizing and forgiving are private solutions and just between the two of you.

Take Back Your Social Life

CRITICISM

Some people may criticize you for getting a divorce or condemn some aspect of your breakup. Especially for men, this trouble is often the only rough social patch—it stands alone. Different men and women complain about one or more of the other three—single status discomfort, rejection, and societal changes. Typically, high-stressed women resent all four of these.

If you're a woman, you have almost a one-in-four chance of being slammed and upset with harsh criticism. If you're a man, you're somewhat less likely to encounter this. The good news is that if you're upset by criticism, you're unlikely to have any other social troubles.

You may be slammed by disapproval for multiple reasons.

The wife's infidelity is the number one reason for both you and your ex to feel humiliated. Brenda, a 25-year-old cook in the Navy, divorced her second husband, Milton, to marry her new love. Milton, a once-wed, thirties police officer, felt humiliated by his wife's infidelity and rejection as well as the community censure. His family, friends, and neighbors blasted Brenda for having an affair. The marriage was brief—only four years, including a one-year separation. According to Milton:

> Brenda's affair with a Naval officer caused the breakup. For a while before that, we were unhappy and constantly arguing. Even though I knew we brought out the worst in each other and should have separated, the split was traumatic and humiliating. Initially, I was angry, couldn't concentrate at work, and lost weight. Later, however, I was relieved. Of my difficulties, four were the most painful: our families' disapproval, the snickering about Brenda's cheating, becoming single again, and the loss of my relationship with Brenda.

Likewise, Amelia talked about this problem when she recalled her recent marriage:

> Lonely and miserable, I left my second husband, Clinton. I was forty-two, college-educated, and had a good job. I could make it without him. At work, I discovered Flint, who was leaving a remarriage, too. Our six-month affair grew into a new partnership. With my children in tow, I left Clinton and moved in with Flint. Clinton was angry and made a scene as we headed off. My kids were distressed, even though Clinton isn't their dad.

They saw this as one more upheaval and round of unwanted changes in their bumpy childhood. After we moved in with Flint, I was happier, but the disapproval began. Criticism from my kids and others grated. Two months later, Flint and I wed. From our perspective, reasoned love conquered all. My second was easier than my first despite the criticism.

The husband's infidelity is the second reason for criticism. The third is being tagged a "two-time loser." Many people think that you have minor personality problems if you have been divorced once, but if you have been divorced twice, they assume you have severe emotional ones. So, they feel justified to criticize you for getting divorced again and try to "shame you into shaping up." Thus, if you're a second-timer, you're at a high risk for being criticized, although first-timers can have a hard time, too. When John departed to live with another woman, first-timer, Louise felt humiliated.

Regardless, please remember that a divorce is a joint issue, not an individual one. You're only partly at fault and cannot change the past. Once the divorce decision has been made, take care of yourself, avoid those who condemn your divorce, and take an active role in finalizing your divorce. By doing so, you will recover quicker.

Shunned

Occasionally, you feel socially rejected. Men and women who have this problem are different.

If you're a woman who feels ostracized, you probably have a wide variety of other difficulties, which compound your distress. If this sounds like you, contact your local women's center. Here, you will find compassionate counselors who will provide you with support and information. They usually provide free or low-cost counseling, both in individual sessions as well as support groups. Support groups quickly erase feelings of isolation and offer instant new friends. Many women's centers also provide job coaching, short-term safe housing, and may be able to put you in touch with legal aid so you can get a restraining order, if need be.

Typically, men who feel shunned are insecure and drink heavily. Often, you are uncomfortable being single and resentful. If you're in this group, you are not at your best. You can take a new path. Start a daily exercise program and reduce your drinking. A positive next step is joining a divorce support group. Low-cost support groups are available at some churches and synagogues. Many counselors offer group sessions for a reasonable or sliding scale fee.

Enlarge Your Social Circle
1. Volunteering adds to your social circle, confidence, skills, resume, and network.
2. Join a singles social or athletic club. This way, you can befriend other singles and will be around singles like yourself and not feel out of place.
3. Reach out to re-establish friendships with former friends, especially single again ones, and befriend new ones in your community and activities.

Don't Flaunt a New Relationship
This hurts your children and makes your settlement more difficult.

Fish Out of Water

You may feel uncomfortable being single again and socially out of place, especially if you were married for a long time. You may be scared to get close to another lover. Or you are afraid that a new partner will desert you, too. With these fears, you can feel like a fish out of water in "singles' land." Much of the time, you initially lack the outlook, self-confidence, or social skills to navigate the singles world to find someone new. This is resolvable and usually temporary.

Rarely unfaithful, the single-distressed women may or may not initiate the divorce. Like the men, you usually have a traumatic breakup with many complications and little relief. During the first year after, you usually have low recovery with severe strain, strong or ambivalent attitudes toward your ex-husband, and no interest in finding a new partner.

Petunia's first marriage lasted ten years and ended in her late twenties. Two years later, she wed Raymond, a previously married man who, like herself, worked as a sales associate in a local department store. Unlike her, he grew up in a gloomy, intact home—not a divorced parental one like she did. Together, they shared two teens from their first marriages: her teenage daughter and his teenage son. She describes her brief remarriage.

> At the end, we were unhappy, always fighting, and didn't like each other. Having gone through a prior one and recalling my parents' rough marriage and divorce, I ended it quickly. I left and filed for the divorce. The split was tough. I resented being single again, was lonely, and missed Raymond. Financial troubles made things worse initially. My household income collapsed and my bills skyrocketed. My cousin steered me out of my financial mess—she helped me get a higher-paying job and

helped me slash expenses. My first year afterwards was alright, but not great. I was reasonably happy, relieved to be out of an abusive marriage, and financially self-sufficient. I didn't date or do much with friends. Therefore, I was still lonely. A year on, I joined a sports club and a different church. With friends and a new love, my loneliness ended. Three years later, I was happy and rewed.

Most single-distressed men do not want the divorce, are faithful, and are devastated. It doesn't matter whether you move out to a new residence, she packs her bags and leaves, or you both move, you are uncomfortable and upset. You have numerous negative divorce reactions, including one of the signs of intense emotional trauma—weight loss.

Pluto's divorce was much like Petunia's, but not identical. Like Petunia, he left a short second marriage, hated being single, was from a divorced parental home, and had a partner from an intact parental home. Both had social and financial divorce difficulties. Unlike her, Pluto was the abandoned partner. Pluto blamed his divorce primarily on his wife. To quote him,

> My wife's partying and infidelity were the main reasons for our divorce. Emotional abuse and long-standing marital unhappiness were added troubles. My breakup was nerve-wracking and stressful, especially in the beginning before she filed for the annulment. I resented being single again and missed Meg. My household income dropped and barely covered necessities. We fought endlessly about how to divide our stuff, even over our dog, Barker. To me, splitting up our things was a bad reminder that our relationship was over. Because

I was the one trying to keep the marriage together, I insisted that I should get the wedding presents. The first year afterwards, I was miserable, often thought about my past marriage, and hated Meg for deserting me and taking my dog, Barker. Single life doesn't suit me, but neither does marriage. It's been three years since we divorced. I'm living with a new love, Marylou, but I don't want to marry her or anyone else—ever.

Upbringing affects your risk. Adults with happily married parents seldom feel this way. You have close family ties and a network of contemporaries who stand by you through the ups and downs of life. If, however, you grew up with a single parent or in an unhappy two-parent home, you are at a higher risk for single-distress and would be in better stead if you developed closer ties with your family and others to ward off this potential trouble.

Your first solution steps are to join a support group, get counseling, and spend more time with other singles. The quicker you do these, the quicker your distress will dissipate.

Social Losses

Almost half of the men and women have a hard time with all the social shifts caused by the breakup. For some, your trouble is the end of your spousal relationship per se. If so, you often struggle with loneliness, single distress, and may still feel emotionally married. Alternatively, you do not miss your spouse but are coping with other social changes.

Everyone deals with damaged relationships in addition to spousal loss. Most of these are strained or awkward relationships with secondary relationships like neighbors, acquaintances, and non-close in-laws. Handling or replacing these ties is usually unpleasant but relatively easy.

However, about one in three of your social losses includes important non-spousal relationships. Many of your relatives and friends find the acrimony overwhelming and pull away from you, especially in redivorce. Even your close friends and family may tire of hearing about your misery and start avoiding you. Should this happen, stop talking about your divorce with these individuals and instead get your emotional support from other friends, a clinician, or a support group.

Your parents and siblings may initially side with your ex. Over time, they will probably respond to family pressure, drop their in-law ties, and side with you. Staying calm and waiting it out is often your best strategy.

Conversely, you may be close to a child or in-law but lose this relationship partially, suddenly, or eventually. Of these, the loss of your child or your stepchild is almost always the most hurtful. Children, including child-parent changes, are such an important topic that I discuss this later in a separate chapter. Stepchildren are discussed next.

Stepchildren

Some stepparent-stepchild relationships are hostile or distant and short-lived, but for a sizeable group, your relationship is important. Especially when your marriage is long, you spend years helping your stepchildren through thick and thin, rejoice in their achievements, and form deep bonds with them. You give your youngster(s) a "role model" and a "lifetime compass." Both you and they view your relationship as a primary parent-child bond. Then, you divorce and you suddenly lose all contact with your youngster. This is traumatic for both of you.

Many youths view the loss of a stepdad or stepmom as a rerun of their parents' first divorce and first parent loss, and a double whammy. Knowing this, you may not only grieve the end of your tie, but also worry about your youngster's welfare.

Unfortunately, few acknowledge this loss. Many Americans insist that bloodties are the only real family ties. They further argue that bemoaning the loss of a step-relationship is wrong and disrespectful to blood relatives. Now, remorse for mourning blocks grief work. This prolongs pain and delays recovery for you and your stepchild.

Increasingly, divorce experts acknowledge this trouble and encourage their adult and child clients to openly discuss this loss. As common law marriage and remarriage increase, more and more clinicians, lawyers, and courts are recognizing that living arrangements establish family relationships. Certain judges support co-parenting between a stepparent and a parent when the link is important to the stepchild and the stepparent requests the role.[3]

Stepchildren
1. Share your stepchild-loss grief with empathetic others. Don't hide your feelings. If keeping a step-relationship is desired, ask for it in your agreement.
2. If true, reassure a close stepchild that you love him or her and would like to stay in touch. Discuss how you can do this with emails, tweets, phone calls, and visits. But don't promise something unless you are sure you can and will do it.

Relocating

Do you label your address change a financial loss, an embarrassment, a change in your family, the end of arguments, or the start of a happier life? Your perspective, rather than the actual event, determines your distress or lack of anguish and welfare.

For one in four, moving is a major issue. For most, however, moving is just a necessary hassle, which ups costs. As soon as you part, two bills replace every prior one. With two homes, rent or mortgage payments, utility bills, transportation expenses, and general supply fees double. Your lifestyle becomes more modest. Sometimes, you or others in your family resent the changes. Moving can trigger positives, too:

- Reduces arguments.
- Ditches reminders of your marital problems. A fresh start can accelerate recovery.
- Many adults move into condos or apartments with a superintendent, who handles maintenance. This frees you to tackle other tasks or adds to your leisure time.
- Changes in travel time to a job, children's schools, or family. Reductions can add discretionary time and emotional support.
- Increased opportunity to determine your own lifestyle and schedule.

Bolta moved to a new section in town to get a fresh start. Safe from bumping into her ex-husband, Carter, she felt happier and relieved despite moving costs and new aggravations. John eagerly left his place and woes to run into the arms of his new love.

Occasionally, you resent the move. Typically, you don't want the divorce, are upset by a long list of things, and, for women only, are headed toward poor adjustment.

Certain men balk at moving. You are lonely, worried, and downhearted. For William, moving symbolized the breakup of his family, and he resented it. Sometimes, you equate your move with a financial loss. Other times, social *and* financial issues trouble you. Carter not only missed his ex and Max, but also worried about paying his bills without his wife's help.

Wives make similar, but not identical, complaints. You are usually overwhelmed, don't get along with his family, and have an unfaithful husband. Louise not only had a strained bond with her husband's parents and stepson, but was also deserted. Angered, she fought viciously over the finances. After, Louise continued her struggle. Financially strapped women are best to contact a women's center or their house of worship for low-cost counseling, budgeting, and vocational advice.

Feeling overwhelmed by a move is a warning signal that you need to reduce "a list of problems" and get additional emotional support and practical help. Most tasks are best solved little by little. Take the quickest to fix or the most upsetting, break it down into steps, and tackle it one step at a time. Then move on to the next issue. As your list shortens, you should feel better.

For a few, protecting financial rights or trouble selling your home forces you to continue living together long after you have decided to divorce. This entrapment often leads to excruciating pain, unnecessary arguments, and uncomfortable situations. If you're in this nightmare, fix it. Could you rent your home, so you have the means to cover two rentals? Ask your accountant or real estate agent for solutions.

THINGS TO REMEMBER ABOUT SPOUSAL ISSUES, SOCIAL CHANGES, AND RELOCATING:

- Individuals who do not want the divorce voice most of the social, spousal, and residential move complaints.
- At least one-third of the women dealt with social loss (52%), divorce indecision (51%), and spousal communication troubles (36%).
- At least one-third of the men had problems dealing with

social losses (47%), spousal communication (34%), and infidelity (34%).
- For some adults and children, the step relationship is strong and important to both. If so, some judges support co-parenting between a stepparent and a parent when the bond is important to the stepchild and the stepparent requests the role.
- One-third reported physical abuse in the marriage. For families with a history of abuse, the abused person needs to have an emergency exit plan.
- One in four has a difficult residential move. This is a red flag for a woman's recovery.

CHAPTER 9

Weathering the Storm

Quiz # 5: Stress, Trauma, and Relief

Q1. What was the most difficult time in your divorce process?
1. ___ Before the divorce decision
2. ___ Decision
3. ___ Separation
4. ___ Filing for the divorce
5. ___ Divorce decree
6. ___ After the divorce (how long after? _____)

Q2. How stressful was your life when each of the following occurred? Please use a scale of 0 (no stress at all) to 4 (very heavy stress) to answer this question.
1. Before the decision   0 1 2 3 4
2. Divorce decision   0 1 2 3 4
3. Filing   0 1 2 3 4
4. Divorce decree   0 1 2 3 4
5. Now   0 1 2 3 4

Q3. Which of these occurred more often during your divorce process than before? (Please check all apply)
1. ___ More lonely
2. ___ Greater depression

3. ___ Increased drinking
4. ___ Increased smoking
5. ___ Increased use of drugs
6. ___ Memory difficulties
7. ___ Gain of unwanted weight (10 pounds or more)
8. ___ Loss of weight from stress (10 pounds or more)
9. ___ Didn't care about self
10. ___ More sleeping problems
11. ___ More anger toward spouse
12. ___ Harder getting work done
13. ___ Less optimistic
14. ___ More worry
15. ___ Increased health concerns
16. ___ Remorse/ Guilt
17. ___ Failure feelings
18. ___ Poor self-care
19. ___ Other (What? _____)
20. ___ None of the above

Q4. Which of these occurred more often during your divorce process than before? (Please check all applicable)

1. ___ Less lonely
2. ___ Less depression
3. ___ Less drinking
4. ___ Less smoking
5. ___ Less use of drugs
6. ___ Fewer memory difficulties
7. ___ Gain of wanted weight (from reduced stress, 10 pounds or more)

8. __ Loss of unwanted weight (from reduced stress, 10 pounds or more)
9. __ Fewer sleeping problems
10. __ Less anger toward spouse
11. __ Easier getting work done
12. __ More optimistic
13. __ Less worry
14. __ Better health
15. __ More energetic
16. __ Relief
17. __ More enjoyment in life
18. __ Better self-care
19. __ Other (What? _____)
20. __ None of the above

Q5. Compared with your previous spouse, how difficult was your recent divorce?
1. __ Much easier
2. __ Easier
3. __ Same
4. __ Harder
5. __ Much harder

Handling Emotions

Divorce slams into you like a tornado, leaving your home, relationships, and community uprooted and topsy-turvy. When it hits, depression, worry, and anger swirl around your head. Loneliness, guilt, and other feelings increase your upset even more. These emotions wreak havoc with your confidence and well-being. Luckily, there are many things you can do to reduce your emotional turmoil and move on to a happier spot.

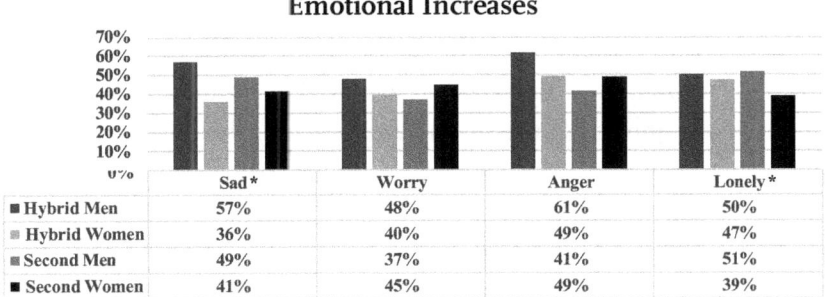

Figure 9-1: Men and women with an increase in four emotions. Note: Adults: 386, including hybrid first-timers 97 (women 53) and redivorcers 289 (women 170). * $p<.05$ gender difference.

Graph Takeaways:
1. Roughly half get sadder, more worried, angrier, and/or lonelier.
2. Men are more apt to become sadder and lonelier than women.
3. Hybrid first-time men tend to be the most upset.
4. Second-time men are the least apt to become angrier.

BANISHING THE BLUES

If you're the divorce seeker, you probably decided to call it quits after much soul searching and misery. After your decision, your sadness frequently lifts and your outlook improves. You're usually relieved and more optimistic than your spouse, unless of course the decision is mutual.

Conversely, when you don't want a divorce, your spouse's rejection throws you into a sea of disarray, grief, and tears. You feel like you're swimming in a turbulent ocean, gasping for breath and wonder if you will ever find your way out of the choppy waters and back to safety. You are sad, disoriented, and can't imagine being happy again. Throughout most of your journey, you are usually miserable, miss your former partner, resent your split, and are unhappy with the other losses in your life. You may cut corners on job assignments and neglect household tasks.

Unhappy, you are plagued with health and work issues. You have at least a fifty percent chance for sleep disturbances, trouble concentrating and finishing your work, and weight change. Increased smoking, drinking, and drug use are common and cause marked health declines for a third of you.

Men, especially hybrid first-time men, are more apt to become depressed than their ex-wives. Most of this is that you are often the rejected partner. There are several more reasons. You are usually not as tuned into the quality of your social relationships and, thus, the last one to deal with your marital end. You rarely have the deep friendships that women have, so you often lack the support system to help you get through the trauma.

If you become sadder after the divorce decision, you will land in one of two camps. Half the time, you start shedding your troubles by midway, relieved when your divorce is over, and are cheerful from then on. Most of the time, you can benefit from individual or group counseling, although you will probably lead a happy, successful life without this help.

The other half of the time, you are very upset long after midway and take longer to resolve the emotional pain and turmoil. For you, weekly sessions with a divorce therapist *and* a divorce support group are typically recommended. A divorce expert provides objectivity, calm, and effective advice sorely needed during a painful split. Joining a support group of other adults who are going through the same thing is reassuring, provides perspective, and adds to your recovery. Supportive friends and family are important, but they rarely provide essential clinical help.

About one in five men and one in eight women are so distraught that they do not care about themselves and are clinically depressed and overwhelmed. If this happens to you, promptly seek counseling. A good clinician will help you get through this stage as quickly as possible and onto a better future and a happy life. During this period, your medical doctor will probably want you not only to see a divorce therapist, but also to take an antidepressant.

If you are thinking about committing suicide or planning on hurting someone else, you need to *immediately* discuss these concerns with a psychologist, psychiatrist, or a physician at a local hospital emergency room.

You can almost always benefit from adopting my Blues Buster List. Start by taking good care of yourself. Maintain good grooming habits, dress well, exercise, eat a healthy diet, and get a good night's sleep. Improve your appearance. The more attractive you are, the easier it is to get what you want, like a new job or a new mate, and the better your self-esteem. Your home environment can have a major impact on your mood. A tidy space is calming.

Next, increase your social support system by spending more time with supportive others and if, possible, counseling. Good advice will help you weather the storm and make good choices.

Third, employ writing tricks. Write in your journal your thoughts, feelings, plans, and achievements. Praise yourself for every accomplishment, no matter how small. Develop a list of positive traits and put them on your refrigerator. Read this list every time you go to the refrigerator and when you are feeling negative about yourself.

Fourth, smile more. Recall happy memories. Look at selfies, a mirror or photos where you are smiling and smile back.[1] Go out of your way to have more fun.

Fifth, look for modest ways to help others in need. People who do are happier. The term for this is "Helper's High." [2]

Sixth, count your blessings daily just before you go to bed or some other designated time.

Being grateful is a well-established happiness booster.

Seventh, make your life more interesting by learning something new, trying a new activity, and/or traveling somewhere new.

> ### Exercise—Blue's Zapper
> Regular, daily exercise is the best blues buster. Get at least half an hour a day, more if you can. Alternate several activities or sports so you don't get bored.

> ### Blues Buster List
> 1. Take good care of yourself. Maintain good grooming habits. Dress well, eat a healthy diet, and get a good night's sleep.
> 2. Get daily exercise.
> 3. Increase social support by spending more time with others.
> 4. Join a divorce support group and/or get counseling.
> 5. Write in your journal your thoughts, feelings, plans, and achievements. Praise yourself for each achievement, even small ones.
> 6. Ask a friend to help you write up a list of your good points. Post it on the refrigerator and read part of the list every time you go to the fridge.
> 7. Replace negative self-thoughts with a positive one from your fridge list.
> 8. Have more fun.
> 9. Help someone else.
> 10. Learn a new skill, try a new activity, or travel to somewhere new.
> 11. Count your blessings. Once a day, record three things you are grateful for.

12. Keep your home and workspace clean and neat.
13. Smile and look at yourself smiling in selfies, mirrors, and photos
14. Recall a happy memory

DE-STRESSING

Stress patterns provide insight into you and your situation. When you are the most distraught is connected to your type of divorce, demographic factors, your personality, and who initiated the divorce. Your distress at any point in time is linked to your past, present, and future. This will be noted in more detail in the upcoming discussions.

When Is It the Hardest?

Stress varies and usually peaks in one stage, frequently the point at which you first think that your marriage is probably over. The sooner you do, the sooner you start your emotional uncoupling, the easier your breakup, and the better your early postdivorce adjustment.

Early Peak Angst

Your peak angst usually occurs in one of the first three stages: predecision, decision, or separation. If you want the divorce, you are probably 1) the wife and 2) slammed with high distress in the first or second stage. Your hardest stage depends primarily on your character and whether you have children from the union. Confident, divorce initiators are the most upset during the predecision phase, especially if they do not have children from the marriage. If you are a less confident divorce seeker, you are usually the most troubled during the second or decision phase, especially when you have young children. Most parents report that their decision was especially difficult because they were worried about their children's reactions and welfare.

If you are a deserted woman or a second-time man, your roughest time is customarily during the separation. First-time ditched men are different. You are the most upset later in the divorce, sometimes afterwards. One-third of you are the most distraught at the final decree or the first year after that.

During the breakup of a remarriage, your stress pattern has more to do with whether you are a man or a woman than whether this is your first or second split. Hybrid first-time men and women almost always copy the same stress path as second-time men and women, respectively. There are two exceptions. Deciding to divorce is harder for more hybrid-first women. Filing the divorce papers is harder for more hybrid-first men.

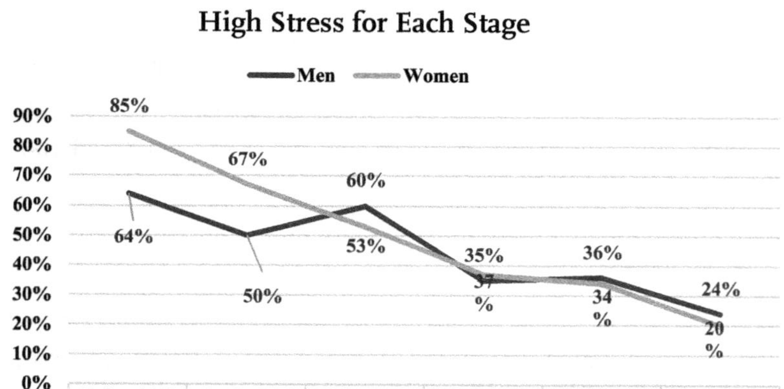

High Stress for Each Stage

	Before****	Decide***	Split	File	Decree	After
Men	64%	50%	60%	35%	36%	24%
Women	85%	67%	53%	37%	34%	20%

Figure 9-2: High stress during each stage for hybrid first-time and second-time men and women.

Note: Before is predecision stage. After is first year postdivorce. Adults: 500 include hybrid first-timers:135 (women 77) and redivorcers: 365 (women 218). ***p<.001; ****p<.000.

Graph Takeaways:
1. Most people have high stress near the beginning, but less and less stress as the split progresses.
2. Women are more likely to have high stress at the start than men.
3. After the divorce, almost everyone has low to moderate stress.

> **Get Organized to Increase Calm and Happiness**
> A clean, neat space promotes calm and smiles. Organize your work area and home one room at a time in small steps or sections until that room is done. Then, do the next room.

Stress Reducers

You are usually upset for a good part of your journey, especially at the start and during difficult negotiations. Reducing your worries is important not only for your well-being, but also so you can do your best at work, parent effectively, and make good divorce decisions. Luckily, there are many things you can do to reduce your irritability and strain. Start by adopting habits in the Blues Buster List, like a healthy lifestyle. Then add:

1. WORRY SESSION

One of the best de-stressors is the dedicated worry session designed by Borkovec.[3] Set aside a daily half hour to an hour early in the day to deal with your concerns. List these issues. Let go of those that you cannot control. For the others, tackle one at a time. For each, make a concrete plan to solve it. When your session is over, refuse to think about these worries until your next daily period. If you start fretting again at other times, like at night, remind yourself that you have a designated time to deal with these.

2. RESTFUL ACTIVITIES/ENVIRONMENTS

For many, a long hot bath, hiding from your laptop and cell phone, a massage, listening to music, and fun activities like gardening are calming activities. Organizing your home can also create a soothing environment.

3. DEEP BREATHING

Try deep breathing. In deep breathing, you increase the inflow and outflow of air and, at the same time, slow down your breathing rate. My favorite form is triangle breathing, which has 3 steps: inhale for 4, hold for 4, and exhale for 4. Repeat this cycle until you are calm.

4. PROGRESSIVE MUSCLE RELAXATION (PMR)

Jacobson originally designed Progressive Muscle Relaxation (PMR) in the 1920s. Since then, behavior therapists have used PMR to reduce anxiety and distress effectively. The procedure starts by siting or reclining in a comfortable position. Then one by one, you tense and then release each of the 7 muscle groups going from your head to your toes or vice versa. Emphasis is placed on the release of each muscle to maximize calm.[4]

1. **Face:** Tense muscles of your face, including squeezing your eyes shut for a count of 5 seconds, then slowly release for the next 10 seconds, focusing on your relaxation experience.
2. **Shoulders:** Tense the muscles in your shoulders for a count of 5 seconds, then slowly release for the next 10 seconds, focusing on your relaxation experience.
3. **Stomach and chest:** Tense the muscles in your stomach and

chest for a count of 5 seconds, then slowly release for the next 10 seconds, focusing on your relaxation experience.
4. **Hands:** Tense the muscles in your hands, making a fist for a count of 5 seconds, then slowly release for the next 10 seconds, focusing on your relaxation experience.
5. **Hips and buttocks:** Tense the muscles in your hips and buttocks for a count of 5 seconds, then slowly release for the next 10 seconds, focusing on your relaxation experience.
6. **Lower legs:** Tense the muscles in your lower leg for a count of 5 seconds, then slowly release for the next 10 seconds, focusing on your relaxation experience.
7. **Feet:** Tense the muscles in your feet for a count of 5 seconds, then slowly release for the next 10 seconds, focusing on your relaxation experience.

5. GUIDED IMAGERY

In guided imagery, you close your eyes and imagine a relaxing scene such as a day at the beach. Guided imagery is often added to PMR to increase calm.

6. EASTERN CALMING METHODS

Sign up for Meditation, Yoga, and/or Tai Chi. These are ancient methods from Asia. All three of these can calm your mind.

7. LOOK FOR THE SILVER LINING

Even in a bad situation, there is usually something positive—a silver lining. Look for the positive. How could this new development be turned into something good?

8. SELF-DISTANCING/THIRD-PERSON TALK

One of the fastest ways to calm down is to talk to yourself in the second person (you) or third person (she, he) instead of first person (I or me). When your heart starts racing or your mind swirls around in confusion, say to yourself: "(insert your name, like Jane) is upset. She should calm down." Or "You should calm down." Do *not* say I'm upset and I should calm down. This helps you be more objective about your situation and, thus, calmer.[5]

> **Bust Your Anger with Forgiveness**
> Tricks to reduce sadness and stress help reduce, but don't eliminate wrath. If you're angry, your ex may owe you an apology. Regardless as to whether you get one, you have two options: to forgive or stay mad and continue to suffer. Except for physical abuse, forgiving is better for your mental and physical health, eases co-parenting, and improves relationships. Consider a forgiveness meditation.

THE VOLCANO ERUPTS

During your split, you will be dealing with different levels of adult anger, both yours and your spouse's. Anger ranges from mild irritability to uncontrollable rage. It can be below the surface, ready to explode like a volcano, or more open, intense, and in-your-face. Regardless, for most, anger is normal at certain times, reasonable, and part of getting over and beyond the marriage.

As with other emotions, hybrid-first men tend to express the most anger for several reasons. First, you have the toughest men's divorce with the most difficulties, most trauma, and lowest relief. Second, you rarely initiate the break or see it coming.

Anger is routine when you and your partner try to work out a financial and/or parenting agreement. To keep wrath down, consider mediation or collaborative divorce methods reviewed in

Chapter 7 and use calming speech techniques with your partner discussed in Chapter 8. In these methods, you are respectful, develop listening skills, express concerns in a non-threatening business-like manner, and focus on creative problem solving, so together you and your spouse can meet the needs of everyone in the family.

In about one-third of failing remarriages in this study, physical abuse occurred. If your spouse has physically abused you, you need to protect yourself throughout your split, especially when you leave your partner. As explained earlier in Chapter 8, abusive adults often become particularly angry and violent when they feel that they cannot control and/or are left by their partner. To protect yourself and your children, you need to make emergency plans and leave quickly and quietly so s/he is not aware of your departure until you are in a safe spot.

Conversely, if you have a history of getting so angry that you physically abused your spouse, consider anger management counseling. Getting better control of your temper will help you journey thru your split and, if you have youngsters from the union, improve your co-parenting with your spouse.

Unlike depression, worry, and loneliness, persistent anger often occurs because you think your ex is untrustworthy. Usually, the issue is betrayal.

Some people make the mistake of jumping into a new relationship too soon to ease their loss. During the split, it's nice to have someone to help you through the process. Having an affair too early is understandable, but unwise. Finding a new partner, especially before the legal separation, causes complications and pain for others. Making this mistake will cause your spouse and children to mistrust you. Working collaboratively to finalize the divorce will be more difficult. Often, the divorce drags on and costs more in legal fees when this happens. If you have joint children, co-parenting will be tough during and after your divorce.

Co-parenting requires trust to work smoothly. An affair makes this process so much harder.

Substance abuse is another way to cause distrust and anger. If you engage in substance abuse, your spouse will probably think you're unreliable and be outraged by your behavior.

If you drink too much or take drugs, you have a lot of company. Many times, excessive drinking and marital problems feed on each other, with each increasing the other. It creates a negative cycle. Most of the time, it is hard to know whether marital troubles or drinking started the problem. Drugs can do the same.

Many counselors can assist you with substance abuse issues. The quicker you ditch these troubles, the more likely your ex-spouse is apt to rely on you again. Eliminating these problems and regaining your ex-spouse's trust will reduce your divorce trauma, accelerate your recovery, and improve other relations. When others think you are untrustworthy, or you drink excessively, most people start backing away.

If your ex had an affair, abused alcohol or drugs, or was abusive, you understand how these mistakes cause anger and trouble. Unless there was violence, work on forgiving your ex, and then determine when and under what circumstances you can trust your ex again. Forgiving doesn't mean forgetting, and it is important not to allow this behavior to happen again. In the final analysis, forgiveness for non-violent acts will benefit your whole family, especially your co-parenting.

Dr. Judith Rabinor, a psychologist, developed a friendship with her ex-husband so they could co-parent effectively. Befriending her former spouse mid-divorce made her divorce easier *and* cheaper. If you want the benefits of this approach, her 2012 book will show you how.

If, however, there was violence, do not forgive your spouse unless you are sure that you will not be physically abused again. Many battered women get into repetitive troubles because they forgive their spouse for hurting them, go back into the bad situation, only to be hurt over and over again. They cannot get out of this violent cycle, until and unless they are permanently angry with the perpetrator—so angry that they will never live with him again.

> **Anger-Busting List**
> 1. Forgive your ex for non-violent actions. Try a forgiveness meditation.
> 2. Forgive yourself.
> 3. Count to ten.
> 4. Write a letter stating all the reasons you are angry. Then write a response letter saying all the things you want to hear from the person who owes you an apology.
> 5. Write your negative feelings in your journal.
> 6. Talk out your anger with a therapist.
> 7. Daydreaming or fantasizing about getting revenge is not unusual and can get rid of some of your wrath, but take care that you do not do it lest you get yourself into legal trouble.
> 8. Scream where no one can hear you.
> 9. Forge a happy life.

The Blues and Stress Buster Suggestions include habits like exercise that will help reduce your wrath. My anger-busting list adds other ways to discharge anger safely and effectively—count to 10, scream where no one can hear you, talk to a therapist, write out your feelings in your journal, write a grudge letter, and fantasize revenge. In your grudge letter, explain why you are so upset.

After completing, write another letter stating all the things you want to hear from the person who owes you an apology.

Daydreaming about getting revenge is not unusual and can discharge some wrath, but be careful that you do not do this lest you find yourself in legal trouble. The best revenge and anger eliminator is to forge a happy life.

For most, anger subsides as the divorce progresses and practical issues get resolved. For a few, it continues unabated. For others, resentment subsides and then re-erupts later.

The first year afterwards, some men fall in love with another woman. As you do, you become antagonistic toward your ex as a way of ending your old relationship and cementing the new. For levelheaded men, anger is temporary and dissipates within a couple of years. If you're going through this, understand what is happening to you and tap down your wrath. Anger increases your risk for having a heart attack and other medical problems, and drives others away.

Loneliness

If you ask for a divorce, you have a one in three chance that you'll be less lonely after you separate. However, if your spouse initiated the divorce, you are more likely to be in the lonely camp initially, but rarely later. Most lonely adults are miserable, stressed, and miss their spouse.

If you are the husband, you are more apt to report loneliness than your wife. First, wives usually initiate the separation—leaving you to feel rejected and lonely. Second, in our society, you tend to have fewer friends than your wife, so you often have less emotional support during the crisis. Third, when couples separate, your children usually spend more time with their mothers than with you. These children stave off loneliness. For these reasons, you often rush into a new relationship with someone new because you just cannot stand being alone.

Loneliness is more of a problem if you have divorced parents, especially if you are a man (women 48%, men 61%). Why?

According to a 2019 study headed by Schaan[6], loneliness is often linked to low childhood parental care. During a split, many parents are so upset that they provide less support to their offspring. After the breakup, many parents, especially fathers, have less contact and a poorer relationship with their youngsters. If this happens, the children, especially sons, grow up to be prone to loneliness.[7]

When you are lonely and unhappy, you are commonly upset and slow to disengage. Compared to the depressed, but nonlonely, you are twice as likely to report weight changes, sleep disturbances, and increased smoking and drinking. Problems make your work and parenting harder.

Many men with divorced parents are in this double jeopardy set. As noted earlier, these husbands are at a high risk for depression and loneliness separately, so it is not surprising that they are at a high risk for this emotional duo.

To combat loneliness, you need to increase the time you spend with others. Life is better if you're outgoing and have close family and friends. If socially active, single status and freedom can be enjoyable. Good buddies encourage you throughout and help foster the next part of your life.

Reconnect with nearby friends. Expand your network by joining social, learning, or athletic clubs. Select an enjoyable activity or something you have always wanted to pursue, such as skiing, growing orchids, or joining a birding club. Another solution is to buy a dog, especially a cute, friendly one that will increase visibility and make it easier for others to talk to you. Dog owners gain companionship, get exercise, and meet people on their walks.

Reducing self-criticism and bad moods can improve your relationships and eliminate, in turn, loneliness. Most people do not like being around someone who is negative—self-critical, down, upset, or mad. Learning to control your emotions can be key to squashing your loneliness. This chapter should help you do this.

If childhood adversity or your recent relationship has left you with a fear of intimacy, rejection sensitivity, low resilience, distrust, or other emotional issues, consider counseling. Discard these problems, and you often eliminate the root cause of your loneliness.

> **Ghost Buster**
> Eliminate reminders of the past. If you are in the same place, change it in easy ways. Paint rooms a different color, add an accent wall, move your furniture, or add new art.

Me Time

For many, one of the most important steps toward self-care is learning to spend enjoyable time alone. It's a time to get reacquainted with your individuality and long-forgotten desires, and in doing so, redefine who you are and your goals in life. It can be quite exciting.

Pick a special period when you don't have any other responsibilities, like taking care of your children or work tasks. A midweek evening is often the perfect choice, but any carved out weekly set aside is fine. Start by making sure your special "self-date" can't be interrupted by cell phones, telephones, or other interruptions. Next, select an activity that lets you enjoy yourself uninterrupted and unbothered by others. Here is a list of ideas:

- Bicycle
- Go shopping.

- Take a long bubble bath.
- Take a walk through the woods, along the shore, or through your neighborhood.
- Get a massage or get your nails done.
- Book a spa day.
- Sit in a quiet, relaxing place like a park or your backyard.
- Go to the movies or read a book.
- Take yourself to lunch or dinner.
- Turn up the music and dance like no one's watching (They aren't.).
- Take a pottery or painting class.

Remorse and Failure Feelings

You often have regrets and/or feel like a failure. You have a one in three chance of feeling remorse and a one in two chance that you feel not only like a loser, but also sometimes like a two-time loser. If contrite, you probably initiated your breakup, are emotionally detached, and are in better shape than your ex-spouse. Failure-riddled individuals say the opposite. Often, you are the opposer, insecure, think you are worse off and more fragile than your ex-partner, and still feel emotionally married.

Frequently, normally considerate adults behave badly during their split by slinging insults or engaging in infidelity. Unfaithful spouses often have conflicted views of their behavior. Even if the affair helps you get out of your unhappy situation, it usually slams you with guilt. Saddled with guilt, you have more problems, especially child-related troubles. Sometimes, you feel awful because you think you have damaged or taken away their youngsters' relationship with the other parent. Self-reproach increases your distress further.

When your ex struggles with remorse, you usually struggle with failure, especially when you were left for someone else. Flooded with these thoughts, you feel rejected, lonely, and uncomfortable going solo. Failure feelings increase your depression, stress, and rumination. Self-esteem plummets. Slower recovery and a rougher second than first divorce will result unless these feelings are managed.

Women are more apt to have regrets and/or feelings of failure than their ex-husbands. When relationships become strained, you often shoulder more than your fair share of the blame for the breakdown and feel compelled to patch things up. Despite occupational advances and changing roles for men and women, you probably believe that you are more responsible for the social life and welfare of your family and friends than your brothers and ex-husband. Being a good wife, mother, and friend is often central to your identity. No matter how much you achieve occupationally, you, like other women, usually need to feel emotionally close to your family and friends to feel successful. In contrast, your brothers and husband probably define their success solely in terms of financial and occupational accomplishments, not close relationships.

So, how do you deal with these regrets and/or failure?

> **Method 1:** Forgive yourself. We all make mistakes and have regrets. You aren't your mistakes. Don't beat yourself up. Learn from your past, forgive, and move forward.
>
> **Method 2:** Swap your critical inner voice for a praising self-voice. Here are the steps:
> - Ask a friend to help you make up a list of your good qualities and put this list on your refrigerator.
> - When you start engaging in self-criticism, quickly replace these negative thoughts with positive self-compliments from your refrigerator list.[8]

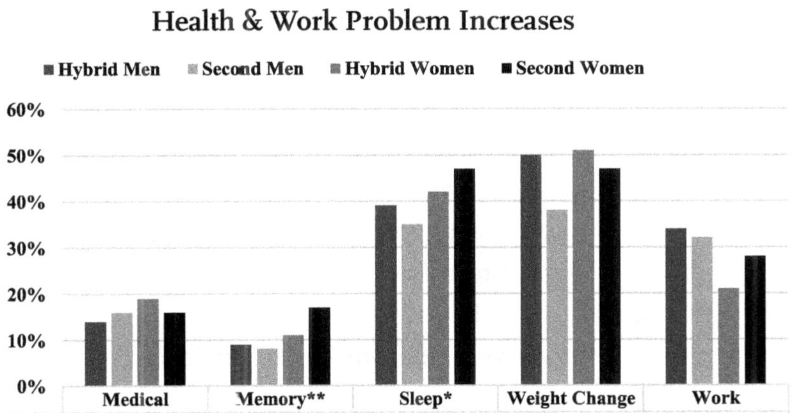

Health & Work Problem Increases

	Medical	Memory**	Sleep*	Weight Change	Work
Hybrid Men	14%	9%	39%	50%	34%
Second Men	16%	8%	35%	38%	32%
Hybrid Women	19%	11%	42%	51%	21%
Second Women	16%	17%	47%	47%	28%

Figure 9-3: Men and women with each health and work problem. Note: Adults: 386; hybrid first-timers: 97 (women 53) and redivorcers: 289 (women 170) * p< .05; **p<.01 for gender differences.

Graph Takeaways:
1. Sleep disturbances and weight changes are the most frequent.
2. Women are more likely to report memory and sleep issues.

Health and Work Issues

You almost always have some health and/or work problems, especially insomnia and weight changes. Health and work-related troubles are particularly acute if you don't want the divorce. Adopting a healthy lifestyle and tackling health troubles is one of your keys to successfully navigating your journey.

Insomnia

Sleep problems are common in a remarriage split, especially for women. Many divorce aspects like stress, sadness, anger, lifestyle changes, health declines, environmental issues, and financial strain can cause sleeplessness. Because insomnia is not only annoying, but also causes other troubles, make a special effort to get a good night's rest. Luckily, the most effective treatments for this problem are habits developed by sleep experts, especially behavioral psychologists, that you can easily learn and are summarized next.

The number one cause of insomnia is emotional upset, especially worry. If worry is your problem, try the suggestions for mind calming described earlier in this section, especially the worry session, regular exercise, and one or more of the calming methods like PMR.

A second key to a good night's sleep is the right environment. Scrutinize your bedroom. Is it clean, comfortable, and clutter-free? Is there anything that you might be allergic to that causes you to wake up from a sneeze? Maybe you're sensitive to certain plants, or your room is dusty. Do you need special pillows or sheets to control dust mites?

Next, check noise, light, and temperature conditions. Do you live in a noisy community? If so, and you cannot move, soundproof your bedroom with additional insulation. Alternatively, you can experiment with white noise generators or recordings of ocean waves and rain. If you have a noisy clock, move it outside your bedroom. Animals can be a problem, especially if they enter your bedroom and cause noise or allergies. Even if you love your pets, you may want to keep them out of your bedroom. At night, a dark environment promotes restful sleep. If there is too much light from the outside, invest in window shades and light-blocking curtains. When you get up in the morning, it is important to get sunlight through your windows or, better yet, take a walk outside. Light starts your wake cycle and helps develop your routine.

What is the temperature of your bedroom? Many rest better when the temperature is between 65 and 70 degrees Fahrenheit. If the bedroom is too cold, you will have a hard time going to sleep. If it is too hot, you will wake up more often, sleep lighter, and have less dreaming, restful naps. So set your thermostat to a slumber-inducing level.

If safety is an issue in your neighborhood, use standard measures. Place a phone near your bed and do a before-bed nightly check to make sure the doors and windows are locked. This way, safety concerns will not keep you awake.

Third, habits like smoking, drinking, meal regularity, what you do in your bedroom, and your pre-bed routine are other keys to your rest. Nicotine is a stimulant. Like all stimulants, it can disrupt sleep. Smokers take longer to go to sleep and have less sound, restful nights than non-smokers. Many not only smoke, but also increase their smoking during their breakups.

If you're a smoker, reduce this habit to improve your sleep as well as your health in general. When you reduce your nicotine consumption, do so slowly after consulting with your doctor, especially if you're a heavy user. Stimulants like nicotine are addictive. With an abrupt withdrawal, you may become restless, irritable, or have headaches.

Like nicotine, caffeine is a stimulant. Coffee is an obvious caffeine drink, but not the only one; colas, energy drinks, and teas, as well as chocolate, often contain the substance. If you consume more than two cups of caffeinated drinks, consider substituting caffeine-free beverages for at least some of your daily drinks, especially later in the day.

Increased drinking and drug use are common causes of sleeplessness. Even having a nightcap before bed is not a good idea. Alcohol induces slumber, but then causes you to wake up in the middle of the night and blocks REM, or high quality, deep rest. Without enough quality sleep, you will be sleep-deprived, have a hard time functioning during the day, and be irritable.

To reduce sleeplessness, stick to a healthy diet. If you're too upset to eat normal-size meals, consume a small portion at your regular eating times or drink a meal replacement shake. If you eat too often, substitute low-calorie options for some snacks and increase your daily exercise.

Sleeping well at night is partly good habits, habits that set your internal sleep clock and link going to bed with slumber. Getting up and going to bed at the same time every day is one of these routines. Eating regular meals at the same time, three to four times a day, is another. Eating breakfast at the same time every morning starts your day and your daily internal clock. At the end of the day, you should not go to bed too soon after a heavy meal, which may cause indigestion. Likewise, eating the right snack before you go to bed may induce sleep. The best choices contain L-tryptophan-rich foods such as milk, eggs, bananas, peanut butter, or ice cream. No wonder a warm glass of milk is a firmly established folk sleep remedy.

Make sure you use your bedroom for only sleeping and sex, so you associate your bedroom with only these behaviors. When you do other things in your sleeping quarters, like pay your bills, you start thinking about these wake-provoking habits instead of calm and sleep.

Develop a one-hour, pre-bed routine, incorporating not only the discussed sleep-promoting habits like a snack, but also stress-reducing activities like deep breathing and muscle relaxation.

As a final note, should you lie in bed unable to nap, get up and do something restful until you become drowsy, and then try to go to sleep again. Restful examples include deep breathing, progressive muscle relaxation, or reading a book.[9]

Good Night
- Dedicated daily worry session. Refuse to think about worries at other times.
- Mind calming techniques: progressive muscle relaxation, meditation, Yoga, Tai Chi, deep breathing.
- Keep your bedroom neat, clean, dark, quiet, and between 65 and 70 degrees.
- Only use your bedroom for sleep and sex.
- Limit your intake of caffeine, alcohol, and nicotine and avoid these after supper.
- Eat three to four regular meals at the same time every day.
- Get up and go to bed every day at the same time.
- Drink a warm glass of milk and/or do deep breathing exercises before retiring.
- If you can't get to sleep within half an hour of going to bed, get up and do something restful for half an hour to an hour, and then go back to bed again.

Get new clothes and a new haircut/hairstyle. Not only will your weight probably change, but also new clothes and a new haircut will help you kick start your new identity.

NEW WARDROBE

You will probably need to buy new clothes. Almost half the time, you either drop or gain weight.

Of the two, weight loss is the most common. When you lose pounds, you are having a grueling breakup with a long list of troubles, symptoms of high emotional distress, especially during the decision, separation, or total phases, and certain health or work problems such as sleep disturbances, increased smoking, and difficulty completing work assignments. Your difficult split usually includes increased loneliness, increased depression, and, for women, increased anger.

You often report high distress and weight loss when you are younger, the deserted partner, have an unfaithful spouse, a woman raised in a two-parent home, and/or a man with divorced parents. Fortunately, losing weight is often a blessing or silver lining.

If you're losing weight, don't be surprised if your ex is doing the opposite—gaining weight. One out of seven puts on pounds. Typically, if you are in the weight-gaining group, you have moderately high distress and aren't as upset as someone who is losing weight. You will probably get larger clothes if you are the plaintiff, middle-aged, a woman who grew up in a divorced parental home, or a man who grew up in a two-parent home. It is usually easier to be the initiator or to handle stress when you are middle-aged versus young, so these are predictable. But why do you often have an easier break and, thus, are more likely to gain pounds when you are a woman from a divorced parental home or a man from a two-parent home? Here is my hunch.

Compared to others, the woman from a divorced parental home is often less committed to her marriage.[10] In this study, she quickly launched the breakup. Initiating a quick exit from an uncommitted relationship, she usually had a relatively brief, high-stress departure.

On the other hand, the typical husband from a two-parent home has social, emotional, and financial advantages over the man who was raised in a divorced parental home. With more money in his pocket, greater stress tolerance, and better social skills, he is less apt to react with increased negative emotions such as impulsivity, loneliness, and depression; realistically more optimistic about his romantic future; can better ride out his breakup and; thus, more likely to gain than lose weight compared to the man with divorced parents.

SUBSTANCE ABUSE AND SMOKING

If you drink or smoke normally, you will probably increase these habits as your marital problems escalate. One-third upped one or both. Half the men and almost one in five women drink heavily or use drugs throughout the split. For these adults, reducing these habits is a step forward. If you drink heavily, take drugs, or drive under the influence, you need to seek treatment immediately.

If you drink more, you'll likely smoke more, have trouble concentrating and finishing tasks during the day, trouble sleeping at night, and experience other fitness hazards. If you add alcohol to your normal eating habits, you are adding calories. Many who drink, however, eat less because their appetite goes down as their mood goes down. For many, smoking increases and lowers appetite. The extra calories you're getting from alcohol usually balance out your reduction in food calories. Your body will not like the calorie swap or smoking and your health will suffer. If you want to hasten your healing, reduce your use of alcohol, drugs, and tobacco.

OTHER HEALTH CHANGES

Insomnia, weight changes, and increased smoking and drinking often lead to other complications like difficulty finishing tasks, forgetfulness, a general health decline, and, for women, a decline in their social life. Sometimes, you struggle to finish your work. Other times, you have fitness issues. Sleep-deprived and stressed, your occasional forgetfulness is not surprising. Nonetheless, you rarely report this trouble and probably underestimate it.

Well-being seldom affects how quickly you start dating again or find a new partner, if you are a man. Women are different. Your health determines whether you are socially active and re-partner. When you have a sleep disorder, difficulty concentrating at work, or health problems, you rarely date. When you are in good physical shape, you are usually actively dating or recoupled, especially if you are younger.

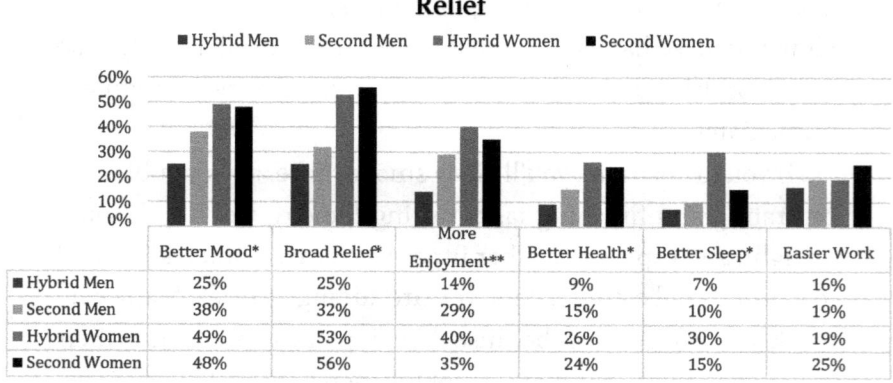

	Better Mood*	Broad Relief*	More Enjoyment**	Better Health*	Better Sleep*	Easier Work
Hybrid Men	25%	25%	14%	9%	7%	16%
Second Men	38%	32%	29%	15%	10%	19%
Hybrid Women	49%	53%	40%	26%	30%	19%
Second Women	48%	56%	35%	24%	15%	25%

Figure 9-4: Men and women with each relief reaction. Note: Adults: 386: hybrid first-timers: 97 (women 53) and redivorcers: 289 (women 170) * p< .05; ** p<.01 gender differences.

Graph Takeaways:
1. Many experience at least some relief during the divorce.
2. On average, women have more relief on five indexes: better mood, broad relief, more enjoyment, better health, and better sleep.
3. Hybrid-first women's relief was similar to second-time women's relief.
4. Hybrid-first men were less likely to have relief than second-time men.

Better Times

Chances are you'll start feeling better long before you are officially divorced. Most of the time, you are relieved midway through your divorce. Your relief is usually wide-ranging—an overall sense that things in general are on the upswing or that your stress has dropped. Anger tapers. Hope, lightheartedness, and reengagement with friends, a new lover, and activity replace your pessimism, sadness, loneliness, and lethargy. As sleep disturbances and worry disappear, your health and job performance improve. Your parenting is difficult, but easier. Your self-esteem rallies with these positives, and you start peeking around the corner toward better times.

If you have high relief, you typically started the divorce, had high predecision anxiety, recoupled prior to obtaining your divorce decree, and have satisfactory postdivorce adjustment. Immediately afterwards, you normally (most women, and to a lesser extent men), are indifferent toward your ex. If you don't have joint children, you often quickly forget the relationship.

Occasionally, you don't have any relief. You may report no upset during the breakup, so you have no problems to rid. You may have less stress, but it is still too high to feel relieved, or you are upset throughout the divorce and soon afterwards. You don't experience any let up.

WHO FEELS BETTER SOONER?

If you're a woman and your ex didn't have an affair, you'll probably feel relieved and in a better mood sooner than your husband. You are usually having more fun, in better health, and sleeping better, too. Your relief and improved attitude and health reflect many advantages. First, you probably started the divorce, so you're likely to end your journey earlier, too. Second, you are undoubtedly living a healthier lifestyle than your former partner.

Women, for instance, are less likely to drink or smoke heavily during a split. Habits like excess drinking have a dramatic effect on your health, mood, sleep, and overall recovery. Third, women often have more friends and social support. Fourth, you are typically better at asking for help than most men. Men tend to be too proud to ask for help, even when they are in terrible trouble. Fifth, women are more apt to seek advice from a counselor, friend, or books like this one.

Women like Bolta who divorced a once-married, second husband reported the most relief, while women like Beth, who left a twice-married, second husband, reported the least. Bolta, who came from a divorced parental home, had high relief because she swiftly left her husband and quickly put her marriage behind her. Beth was slow to emotionally divorce and worried about her future. In the long run, however, Beth probably has a better future than Bolta.

The reverse was true for men. Second-time men, like Nickolas, with second-time wives had the most relief, while once-married men, like Carter, who broke up with a remarried woman, had little relief until much later. Nicholas wanted the divorce, blamed their first-marriage children for the split—not himself or his wife, and felt little guilt or remorse over the split. Carter had little relief during the divorce because he was left, did not foresee the breakup, and a first-timer.

Actually, how quickly you recover is not directly dependent on whether you are a man or a woman or your divorce situation, but more on your approach to life and your habits. You are quicker to recover if you are sensible, sociable, and/or have a healthy lifestyle. Sensible people are faster to solve their problems, like divorce troubles, than others. Sociable individuals benefit from friends, family, or a new partner. Sensible and outgoing people often have a third advantage, a healthy lifestyle. A healthy lifestyle includes regular daily exercise, a healthy diet, and no addictions.

Case Studies

CASE STUDY: HOLLY

Holly, a 42-year-old bank loan officer, divorced Jake, an airline pilot. This was a second divorce for both. Like most with high relief, Holly's highest distress occurred at the start of her divorce. As she got angrier with Jake, her stress, resentment, and disillusionment escalated. To get up her nerve to leave, she took off her wedding ring for several days at a time to see if she could attract someone else. Once she discovered that she could, she asked Jake for a divorce. Her stress dropped dramatically.

Mid-divorce, she was more optimistic, healthier, and dating. She stopped picking up one cold or flu after another. Six months after her divorce, Holly was in high spirits; rarely thought about her past union; and had an active social life with friends, family, and a new partner. She felt indifferent toward her ex. Wiser than many, she attended individual and group counseling for a year and planned on continuing for another twelve months.

CASE STUDY: JOHN

John, a supermarket manager, was relieved. He started the divorce, had high distress initially, but had a quick recovery. Six months later, he was indifferent toward his ex-wife and rarely thought about his prior union. Several years later, he was married for the third time and satisfied with his new life. John was an exception, partly because he grew up in a close, intact parental home.

INSTANT OUT

Some predicaments are so outrageous that you immediately dash for the exit. Sometimes, the crisis spans several years with abuse, drug addiction, or criminal activity, but suddenly, you discover the truth or just can't stand it anymore. Hit by a mental lightning bolt, you have high relief as you scurry away.

An ambulance driver, Gigi, had an instant emotional exit from her second marriage. Three years after her first divorce, she met and married Harry, a bartender in his late thirties and four years her senior. Five years later, she discovered that he was molesting her daughter. They had a major quarrel and separated. At first, Gigi was livid, had insomnia, and lost weight quickly.

After the disclosure, Gigi entered counseling with her daughter and started to claw her way out of her emotional hole. She was soon relieved that her daughter would be okay, thanks to a talented therapist. Six months after their divorce, Gigi was upbeat, better off, but still angry with her ex. Three years later, she had a full, interesting life, but didn't want to remarry. She viewed her second divorce a relief, but still couldn't trust someone new.

THINGS TO REMEMBER ABOUT WEATHERING THE STORM:
- Half report an increase in sadness, stress, anger, loneliness, and failure feelings.
- Remorse bothers about one in three.
- Happiness and stress patterns differ for divorce initiators and non-initiators.
- Upset usually leads to work and health issues like insomnia, weight change, forgetfulness, and difficulty completing work.
- Two-thirds have some relief by mid-divorce.
- Traits such as age, gender, family of origin, and divorce type predict trauma and relief reactions.
- Chapter discusses many ways you can reduce stress and other unwanted emotions.

CHAPTER 10

First-year Postdivorce Transition

This quiz taps seven recovery indexes and personality traits. Items are similar but not identical to the ones in the original query. Questions 5 and 6 are part of a 41-item assessment, which measured trust, favorability, and other attributes in several of the sub-studies. As you read this section try to determine where you are in your journey, how your past, current life, and outlook are impacting your journey, and how you can improve your well-being and future.

Quiz #6: Transition

Q1. How stressful is your life now? Please use a scale of 0 (no stress at all) to 4 (very heavy stress) to answer this question. Circle your answer below.

   0 1 2 3 4

Q2. Compared with before the divorce, are you now?
1. ___ Much less happy
2. ___ Less happy
3. ___ About as happy
4. ___ Happier
5. ___ Much happier

Q3. What is your attitude toward your recent ex-spouse?
1. ___ Still in love
2. ___ Miss—but not in love
3. ___ Friendly—not miss
4. ___ Dislike
5. ___ Hate

Q4. How often do you go over what happened during your recent marriage?
1. ___ All the time
2. ___ Frequently
3. ___ Sometimes
4. ___ Rarely
5. ___ Never

Q5. Which of the following adjectives describe you?
1. ___ Attractive
2. ___ Cautious
3. ___ Considerate
4. ___ Confident
5. ___ Creative
6. ___ Cynical
7. ___ Dependable
8. ___ Dependent
9. ___ Fragile
10. ___ Friendly
11. ___ Honest
12. ___ Impulsive
13. ___ Intelligent
14. ___ Independent
15. ___ Loyal
16. ___ Reckless
17. ___ Reserved

18. ___ Selfish
19. ___ Sincere
20. ___ Stable

Q6. Which of the following adjectives describe your ex-spouse?
1. ___ Attractive
2. ___ Cautious
3. ___ Considerate
4. ___ Confident
5. ___ Creative
6. ___ Cynical
7. ___ Dependable
8. ___ Dependent
9. ___ Fragile
10. ___ Friendly
11. ___ Honest
12. ___ Impulsive
13. ___ Intelligent
14. ___ Independent
15. ___ Loyal
16. ___ Reckless
17. ___ Reserved
18. ___ Selfish
19. ___ Sincere
20. ___ Stable

Q7. Which of the following best describes your dating and/or partner relationship?
1. ___ Never date
2. ___ Date about once a month
3. ___ Date about 2 to 3 times per month
4. ___ Date weekly

5. __ Going steady
6. __ Cohabitating
7. __ Engaged
8. __ Remarried (date? _____)

Q8. Which love style best describes you? Please put a number between 0 (not at all like me) to 4 (very much like me) next to each statement below.[1] (modified RQ from Bartholomew & Horowitz, 1991)

__ A. It is easy for me to become emotionally close to a romantic partner. I am comfortable depending on others and having them depend on me. (Secure)

__ B. It is hard for me to get close to a romantic partner, because I am afraid of being hurt if I do. I am uncomfortable getting close to, trusting, or being dependent on him/her. (Fearful)

__ C. I have a hard time getting close to a romantic partner. I often want to be closer to him/her than s/he wants to be with me. I am insecure without a partner. (Preoccupied)

__ D. I am comfortable without a romantic partner. I want to be independent and self-sufficient. I don't want to depend on others or have them depend on me. (Dismissing/Dismissive)

Q9. Is your recent ex-spouse's Love Style closest to A, B, C, or D above? _____

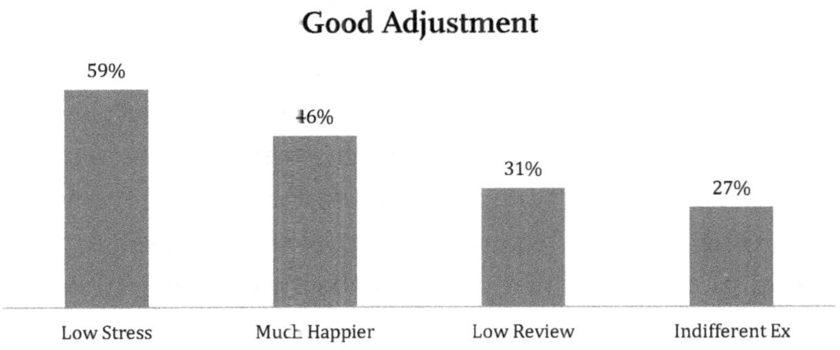

Good Adjustment

- Low Stress: 59%
- Much Happier: 46%
- Low Review: 31%
- Indifferent Ex: 27%

Figure 10-1: Good adjustment on four indexes during the first year postdivorce. Good adjustment is low stress, much happier, low marital review, and a neutral attitude toward their ex-spouse. Second-timers and hybrid first-timers: 386 (223 women).

Graph Takeaways:
1. Recovery is a process.
2. Most people start the transition before the divorce papers are issued, but still need more than a year to fully recover.

Recovery Chain Reaction

After the legal and financial arguing is over and the legal divorce is final, where will you be in your emotional journey? What is the recovery process like during the first transition year? Who are the quickest to get back on their feet? What accelerates or hinders your adjustment?

For most, the first year or so after your divorce is a transition phase from semi-turmoil and a quasi-married state to a relaxed, upbeat norm with a new social sphere. A healing period where you regain your sense of humor, develop a different routine, redefine yourself, and set your sights on new goals. After this period, you are usually in decent shape and almost recovered, but not quite there. Recovery is a process. It takes time.

At the start of the transition year, you are usually okay in some ways, but not in others. Typically, your first steps forward are a drop in stress and a feeling that you're happier now. These are *early-stage recovery signs*. Other signposts are your social activity, your attitude toward your ex, how often you think about your past, your self-esteem, and your trust level. The first three are normally *mid-stage healing tasks*. Marked improvement in these usually starts next. Self-esteem and trust, the remaining two, are *late-stage ones*. These take the longest to accomplish or stay undone even years afterwards.

Early Stage Rebound

DE-STRESSING KICK START—DOMINO EFFECT

Postdivorce strain reflects earlier aspects of your breakup as well as your progress. For half, you did not want the divorce and have either moderate or high tension. If you have made little to no advancement, you have high distress, are unhappy, recall a traumatic uncoupling, and deeply regret the breakup. You are frazzled and psychologically wed to your ex. You rarely see grounds for your divorce and adamantly deny communication troubles, marital unhappiness, or incompatibility.

When you have moderate strain, you are a bit further along and have started your emotional exit. You are quasi-wed/quasi-divorced. If asked why you got a divorce, you may admit that you had marital problems like long standing unresolved disagreements, but you rarely say that you and your ex were unhappy or incompatible. And you will not say you sought your divorce.

For just over half, you are even further ahead in your progress and have at most mild distress. You usually want the divorce and can easily list multiple credible reasons for the split including miscommunication, misery, and incompatibility. Commonly, you feel fine, have decent mental and physical health, and are relieved. Stress induced medical issues like insomnia and low immunity are rare. You recall an easier uncoupling than your ex, even if it was unpleasant and painful.

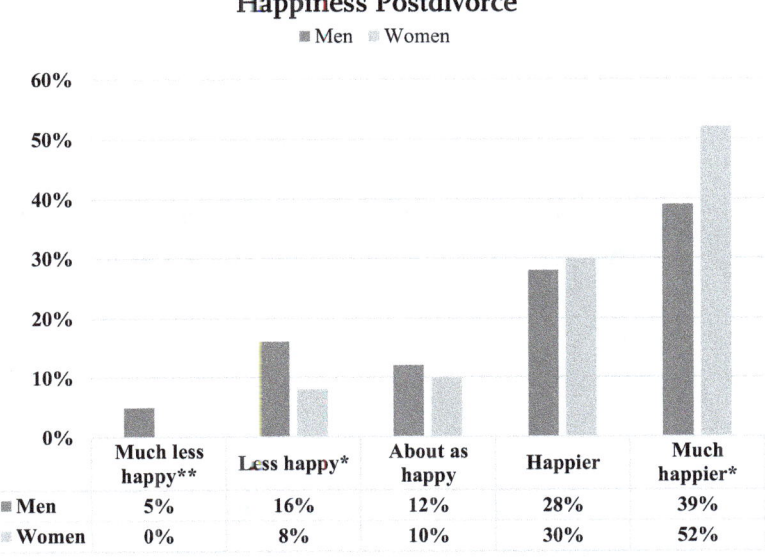

Figure 10-2: Men and women with each relative happiness level. Note: Redivorced and hybrid first-time adults: 384 (222 women). * p<.05; ** p< .01.

Graph Takeaways:
1. Most people are happier or much happier.
2. More women are happier or much happier than men (82% vs 67%).

If you are a woman, you are usually calmer than your former husband just after the divorce because you are more likely to want the change and started your emotional exit sooner. Your tension often goes down slowly during this year.

On the other hand, if you're a man, your stress is apt to drop rapidly over this period as you catch up, if not dash ahead of your ex. By yearend, you are usually less anxious than your ex-wife. Three out of four men, but only six out of ten women, are calm most of the time. *For both men and women, a stress decline sets off a domino effect—a recovery chain reaction.* Your next domino is a change in your disposition—you start to feel happier.

> ### *Stress Flip Flop*
> Just after the divorce, women are usually less stressed than their ex-husbands. By the end of the year, the reverse is true—men tend to be calmer than their ex-wives.

> ### *Smile*
> One of the quickest ways to boost your mood is to not only smile more, but also to see yourself smiling. Put a photo of yourself smiling in your home and look at it every day.[2]

Happiness Pop

Compared with before the divorce, how happy are you now? Are you less happy, about the same, or happier? If your mood has changed, is the change small or large?

A few adults are less happy after the divorce than before. Customarily, you did not want the divorce and had an excruciating breakup. You are still emotionally stuck in your past. During the first year after, you feel and act like Alfred. High-stressed, Alfred was miserable, constantly thinking about his recent marriage, and didn't date. He loved and missed his ex-wife. She was special, attractive, creative, and interesting. He wanted to get her back. Sometimes he even dreamed of remarrying her. To cite Alfred:

> I had a recurring dream that we had remarried. Some mornings, I would wake up half-hoping that Kara would be there next to me, but not finding her, I would cry.

Another small group is about as happy before and after the divorce. Your overall progress is slightly better than the worst-off crowd, but still low. Touchy and anxious, you carry a mini-flame for your ex-spouse, rarely socialize, frequently think about your past, and feel a little better, but not okay. Your divorce was tough. You still hurt.

Ronald missed his ex-wife and often thought about his recent failed marriage, especially when he wasn't working or busy with other activities. Perpetually downhearted, he resented her departure and wasn't dating. Ronald considered his parting excruciating, especially during the first few months of their separation. From then on, until the divorce decree, his stress was high with only a little relief near the end.

Until stress plummets, you are miserable and downhearted like Alfred and Ronald. Once it drops, your mood improves and you inch forward. Two out of three men and eight out of ten women are happier—either somewhat happier or much happier.

Sometimes during this first year, you are somewhat happier, calm, and have decent mending for this point in time. Commonly, you had a moderately difficult disengagement with your worst time either at the decision or separation phase. By the divorce decree, you were relieved. You started your emotional divorce long ago when you were still legally wed.

Roughly half the time, you are much happier during the first year and the farthest ahead in your emotional divorce process on this index. You are typically thankful to be out of a painful situation and mess. You probably started your breakup with high stress. Postdivorce, if you're much happier, you can now check this second milestone off your to do recovery list. Marylou was a classic younger, much happier woman. To cite Marylou:

> Before I considered leaving, I was consumed by stress, anger, and resentment. I drank and ate too much to reduce the pain. Many nights, I paced the floor, because I couldn't sleep. Once I decided to leave, my anxiety and troubles vanished. I stopped overeating and overdrinking. My health and outlook improved dramatically. I was relieved, optimistic again, and slept well at night, every night. After the divorce, I was my former, laidback self, happier, and had a lot of fun. Weekends, my new boyfriend, Lance, and I were out having a good time or visiting friends.

At the start of the transition year, you are usually happier or much happier. As the year continues, you have a small chance of becoming less enthusiastic. Bad as the marriage was, your first year or two afterwards can be challenging on many fronts. You may move down economically, lose friends, and have not found a new love yet. Reversing these losses takes time and persistence. You, however, have a better chance of becoming even happier. At the close of this year, you are almost always happy, especially if you are a woman (women 85%; men 75%)

To up your chance of being in and staying in the happier crowd, use the methods in the Blues Buster List in the prior chapter, especially exercise, increased socialization, and gratitude.

Getting to Know You
Get to know yourself better including your strengths and weaknesses, needs, and goals. When done, you will have redefined yourself, set your life path, and know who is right for you.

Drive Away Your Blues: Increase Your Social Activities.
Positive people spend a lot of time with others, especially friends and family. To up your social life, add a new activity like birding, ballroom dancing, or adventure travel. Which activity suits you best?

Increased Socialization is Key, but Different for Men and Women.
Usually with a career and an active social life, she is happy and heals quickly, even if she isn't dating. But he seldom recovers or is satisfied with his life without a new love.

Mid-stage Upturn

Once you are calm and happy again, you are set to start your mid-stage upturn. Your next change is often an enriched social life.

STARTING OVER

Increased socialization with your friends, family, and sometimes a new partner is a healing step. Dating per se is a survival move, readjustment technique, and in many instances, a healing barometer. For most, your dating lifts your spirits and indicates that you are moving on emotionally. Nonetheless, recoupling is an imperfect recovery measure.

Cautious men and women avoid intimacy during the first year after the marriage, even when they can and want to date. Often, on the advice of a counselor or other divorced friends, you give yourself a year or so to heal and become more confident and grounded. Or your second marriage was a rebound disaster. You do not want to make that mistake again. Regardless, you do not want to get involved with someone dysfunctional, form another bad match, or settle for an individual who blocks your healing in other ways.

Half actively date or have a new partner. Sometimes your intimacy is too high and leads to another marital mistake. *In my inquiry, those who rewed soon after their first failed union had the shortest remarriages.* You quickly popped in and out of your second marriage often discouraged by the double whammy. For others, however, your first different relationship is a superficial, short-term one. Your new lovers are not the same people you choose two or more years later when you are ready to make a good choice.

Over the first transition year, partnering often escalates. The number of partnered men goes from about one in three to half. The number of partnered women increases a bit less—from one in three to four in ten.

First-year Romantic Relationships

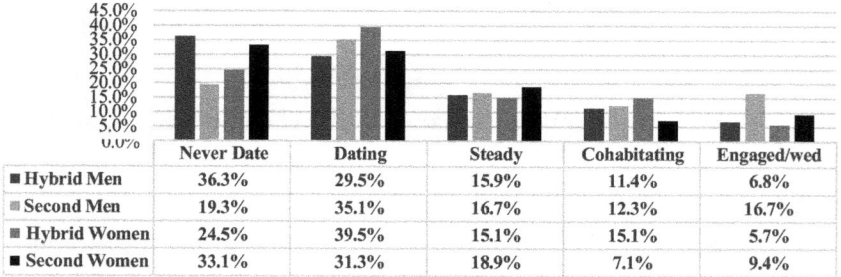

	Never Date	Dating	Steady	Cohabitating	Engaged/wed
Hybrid Men	36.3%	29.5%	15.9%	11.4%	6.8%
Second Men	19.3%	35.1%	16.7%	12.3%	16.7%
Hybrid Women	24.5%	39.5%	15.1%	15.1%	5.7%
Second Women	33.1%	31.3%	18.9%	7.1%	9.4%

Figure 10-3: First-year romantic relationships. Note: Redivorced and hybrid first-time adults: 491 (women 292). Men's total does not equal 100% due to data rounding.

Graph Takeaways:
1. Almost 30% are not dating.
2. Second-time men are more likely to have a new partner than other men and women (46% versus about 35%).
3. Hybrid first-time men and second-time women are the most apt to never date.

How quickly a woman recouples depends on whether she wanted the split as well as her age, personality, and education level/income. When you begin the divorce, you usually recouple quickly. Otherwise, you wait a year or two before venturing into the dating scene. If younger, you start dating sooner, especially if you are outgoing and confident. Regardless of your personality, you recouple slowly when you are middle-aged. For you, low stress, high self-esteem, and a positive outlook seldom predict active dating or finding a new love. This is especially true if you have close family, good friends, and are invested in your occupational life.

Many second-time women with second-time ex-husbands fall into this category. Peggy exemplified the over-forty woman who initiated her divorce. She encountered relatively low distress during and after her redivorce and enjoyed good recovery soon after her brief marriage. Among younger women, these factors would have predicted active dating, but because Peggy was in her forties and didn't cause the breakup with an affair, she rarely dated. She stayed active with friends, family, and new activities: ballroom dancing, birding, and tennis.

Overall, high school educated women are quicker to find a new love than their ex-husbands. Typically, you don't have the luxury, disposable time, or desire to stay single. You find a new partner to survive financially or emotionally.

On the other hand, college-educated women are usually

slower to choose a new love than their ex and the other women. Financially secure from your salary or alimony, you are almost always self-reliant, well informed, and assured. With this economic and pride edge, you tend to mend emotionally before actively dating. You prefer non-dating healing methods such as enrolling in a graduate or retraining program, starting a new career, traveling, taking up a new hobby, or counseling.

Unlike women, a man's happiness and self-esteem almost always mirrors his intimacy with a new love. Men like Carter, who rarely dated, had lower self-esteem and a dismal outlook. Six months after his marriage, he had marginal healing—he was miserable and riddled with self-doubts and worries. Tex's life demonstrated the opposite profile and life outcome. After his second divorce, he had a new girlfriend, good self-esteem, and a positive perspective. To cite Tex:

> Soon after my divorce, I was upbeat, confident, and in love again. I was successful. That year, I won the Top Employee of the Year Award.

Two characteristics predict a man's love life—divorce number and education (and higher income). The most active socially are second-time men. Roughly eighty percent have either found another partner (46%) or are trying to (35%). Just 19% are not dating at all. The hybrid-first-time men (and both groups of women) are more reticent. About one-third is recoupled, one-third is dating, and one-third is not dating at all.

The typical college-educated man quickly finds a new partner. The high school-educated man, however, is apt to be slower to date than other men and his ex-wife. With less income and education, it is harder for you to attract a new lover. Ironically, this may be good for you. Early on, you have more time to mend before you start a new serious relationship. With this extra healing, you are less likely to jump into a rebound commitment.

> **The First Year**
> Most take 12 to 18 months to recover from a major change like divorce. Don't remarry or make any other major decisions until you've been divorced for at least a year.

> ***Rewrite Your Past to Change Your Thinking***
> Rewrite your divorce story. In your new story, you're 1) an in charge, good person (not a victim or bad person), 2) grateful for your current situation, and 3) headed toward a bright, interesting future. Write your upbeat story in your journal now.[3]

I Love, I Love Not

Your next healing domino is almost always a shift in your attitude toward your ex. Especially for women, your healing improves in three steps as your feelings toward your ex-spouse become more and more dispassionate. The three steps are:

1. You have strong emotions (love, hate, or both reactions) toward your former spouse.
2. You miss, dislike, or have both reactions toward your ex-spouse.
3. You have a neutral stance toward your ex, best described as civil or indifferent, but you do not miss or spend time thinking about him or her.

During the transition, you are usually past step one. You do not hate, love, or feel ambivalent toward your ex. Instead, you dislike, miss, or, better yet, feel indifferent. At a minimum, you are beginning to wave goodbye to your past and starting to move on to a new social sphere. The door to your emotional marriage is closing or closed.

Typically, dispassionate adults emotionally divorce long before they physically separate or legally divorce. After your legal divorce, you are usually calm, upbeat, happier, and have a good social life.

You are the most likely to have a neutral stance toward your ex-spouse if you are a woman. This is expected. You, like other women, usually ask for the separation and divorce. You tend to start and end the emotional unlinking sooner. But there is a second reason discussed later—the impact of *the husband's re-partnering*.

During the transition year, women tend to become ever more indifferent toward their ex-spouse. Concurrently, some men go in the opposite direction—they become increasingly hostile. Men who dislike or hate their prior wife jump from one in three to half. As they pound the war drums, most of this upswing is a surge in hate—from near zero at the divorce decree to almost one in four a year later. Hybrid first-time men are especially likely to go on a war path.

A woman's dating and affection for someone new rarely impacts her feelings toward her ex-husband. Not true for him, especially if you are a second-timer. The more emotionally involved you become with a new partner, the faster you usually heal. You grow calmer, happier, more confident, and better adjusted. But as this happens, you often become more hostile toward your ex-wife. If cohabitating or remarried, you usually have an unfavorable view of your former spouse and either dislike or hate her by year end. Often this is temporary, especially if you are level-headed.

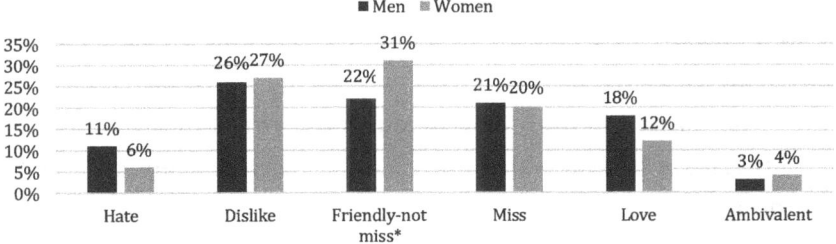

Figure 10-4: Men and women with each ex-spouse attitude. Note: Redivorced and hybrid first-time adults: 385 (women 222). * p< .05.

Graph Takeaways:
1. Women were more likely to have a neutral attitude toward their ex during the transition phase.
2. Most do not complete this emotional step during the transition year.

Don't Let Your Emotions Sabotage Your Relationships
Men often grow more negative toward their ex as they heal and fall in love with someone new. Don't let these emotions trick you into being hostile toward your ex and hurt your relationships.

Stuck in the Past, Focused on Present, or Going Forward?

As you continue to untie your marital bond and advance, your thoughts shift from thinking about your marriage and past to your current life. Oftentimes, your shift and your feelings toward your ex move in sync with each nudging the other and you emotionally forward.

You may obsessively review your former relationship during your divorce and early afterwards. Your marriage keeps swirling around in your head, blocking you from getting your work done or getting a good night's sleep. You continue to chew on your arguments and troubles. You keep trying to understand what went wrong, how you might have done things differently, and how you could have avoided your turmoil and woes. You usually love, hate, or feel ambivalent toward your ex, especially if you are the woman. Routinely, the deserted partner, you are upset, insecure, forlorn, and early in your journey.

Roger and Lisa ruminated on their prior unions. They didn't want the split, had their most difficult time after they separated, and were very upset for most of the dissolution and early post-divorce. Afterwards, they saw their ex as irreplaceable, did not date, and judged their recent divorce harder than their first. To cite Roger:

> It's been nine months since my divorce. I'm okay at work, but I don't socialize. I'm afraid that if I find someone new, she'll leave, too. I go over my second marriage all the time. I can't understand why she ran off with someone else. *What went wrong?* Until I can figure this out, I'm not risking another loss.

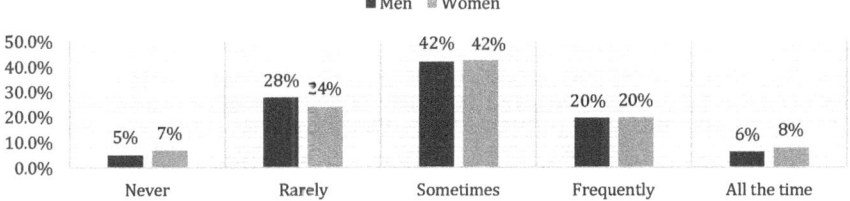

Figure 10-5: Men and women with each marital review level. Note: Redivorced and hybrid first-time adults: 386 (223 women). Gender sub-totals do not equal 100% due to data rounding.

Graph Takeaways:
1. Four out of ten think about their remarriage sometimes. The remaining seldom review their marriage or, conversely, do so often.
2. Marital review frequency is not related to whether you are a man or a woman.

As you heal further, you think even less about your past. Semi-recovered men and women think about their past occasionally. You are in better shape than those in the first set, but you have a way to go. Typically, your stress is moderate and you feel okay, but not great. Roughly forty percent of the time, this is how you feel.

About a third of the time, you can check this review problem off your recovery to-do list. You rarely or never think about your past. Your thoughts focus on the present and future. The leave-taking decision was yours or mutual. If this is your second divorce, it is often your easiest one. Calm, socially active, and satisfied with your life, you are in good shape. You are like Peggy. Peggy began her divorce and easily sailed through it. Her peak difficulties were at the start before she seriously considered leaving her husband. Problems centered in the marriage—not in the divorce. Postdivorce, she was fine. To quote Peggy:

> Most of my problems were marital, not separation troubles. By mid-divorce, I was happy and okay. I was relieved, no longer lonely, and healthier than at the start. Compared with my first, this one was a piece of cake—relatively easy.
>
> I divorced almost a year ago. I'm my former self, optimistic, and rarely think about the past. I'm making new friends and learning ballroom dancing. Charlie and I are dance partners and growing closer. We decided early on that we wouldn't date until we're both divorced for a year. We have a month to go.

You almost always spend the same amount of time thinking about your marriage throughout the first year. Dwelling on your past is not related to whether you are a man or woman or whether you are a hybrid-first or second-timer. It is, however, linked to and maintains other troubles like sadness and stress. So, getting rid of this issue can speed up your recovery.

As such, if you are spending a lot of time mulling over your divorce at the start of your transition year, you need to act quickly to reduce this problem, so you are not dealing with this and allied troubles next year, too. Try at least one of the following proven methods for reducing rumination: meditation[4], journaling[5], and the rubber band technique.

The root cause of marital review is often non-acceptance of your divorce. At some point, you need to stop caring about why you split and instead just accept that your partnership is over.

If you need a breakup cause for yourself or others, pick one of your marital problems as the major reason.

Proven Methods for Reducing Rumination
1. Meditation
2. Journaling
3. Rubber Band Technique
4. Counseling

Rubber Band Technique: Snap and Replace[6]
1. Develop a list of ideas to think about instead of your spouse.
2. Put a rubber band on your wrist.
3. Every time you think about your former spouse, snap the rubber band. Then, swap your spouse thoughts for something on your list.

Late/Final Stage Upswing

CONFIDENCE

Confidence is usually one of the last things you reclaim. If you feel insecure, you still have emotional work to do. Typically, you describe yourself as uncharacteristically shy, indecisive, or self-conscious. As you advance to midway, you become somewhat self-assured. Self-respect is acceptable and improving, but it is rarely as high as when you were still married, especially for women. When you are even further along and close to the end of your emotional trek, you are confident again. What are the secrets to regaining self-assurance?

Confidence Boosters
1. Up sociability.
2. Be supportive toward others and surround yourself with those who support you.

3. Up conscientiousness.
4. Be optimistic and persistent.
5. Always do the honorable thing.
6. Become kinder.
7. Learn or do something new. This keeps you and your life interesting, too.
8. Use positive self-talk—always say positive things about yourself.

Self-esteem Change During First Year Postdivorce
A woman's confidence seldom changes during this year, but a man's usually does. His often rises from midyear to year's end, especially if he's becoming closer to a new love.

Key one is sociability or extraversion. Extroverts have the confidence edge. Gregarious, you are open to chatting with or befriending almost anyone. The person on the bus or down the street may be 15, 45, or 85 years old. It does not matter. You want to talk to everyone. If you move, you keep your friends by calling, emailing, and visiting. At the same time, you make new acquaintances to do athletic, social, and other activities. When you lose friends, you make new ones. If something goes wrong, you have friends to buoy you up. You and other Extroverts are too outgoing to be lonely or without others for long. Smart Extroverts follow two important rules. You are supportive of loved ones, and you surround yourself with those who support you. Upbeat and surrounded by love and friendships, your confidence is solid, especially if you couple your sociability with the other keys like conscientiousness.

> **Be Conscientious—Reliable, Organized, & Timely**
> In this study, conscientious adults were not only adept at work, quick to solve their divorce problems, and confident, but also had happier, less upset, and less confused children.

Conscientiousness is the second key to confidence. Conscientious individuals are dependable, organized, and timely. Most are ambitious, hardworking, successful, and as a result, have mid to high socio-economic status.

Given your lifestyle, you face and solve your marital problems relatively quickly. Often, the split initiator, you almost always have a rough time early in the uncoupling, but you're usually calm and levelheaded near the end and later. Invariably confident, you seldom report feeling like a failure, guilt, or criticism. Compared with others, conscientious men (but not necessarily women) select a new partner once they are ready to move on.

In this study, conscientious adults were not only adept at work, quick to solve their divorce problems, and confident, but also had happier, less upset, and less confused children, too. Why?

Conscientious individuals have the makings to be better parents. Typically, you provide (1) more consistency to your children because you are reliable; (2) a calmer environment because you are usually organized and (3) more financial help because you typically have a good salary.

Predictability, a calm, environment, and better monetary support reduce stress for you and your children.

The third confidence booster in this study is optimism. Despite rough times, sooner or later, optimistic individuals are okay. You don't give up on yourself or on solving a problem. Fancy a better job? You persist until you find work that fits your needs. When your family wants to find a home in a better local, you keep on looking until you find one. If you want to remarry, you continue until you discover a new partner. Optimists have a growing list of accomplishments and resolved problems. Despite difficulties, you have a growing sense that you can control your own destiny.

> **Be Optimistic/ Persistent**
> Believing that you can have a good and better life will lead you there.

Secret four is love style. Two Love Styles, Fearful and Preoccupied, have lower self-esteem, but the remaining two, Dismissive and Secure, have solid self-esteem.

Normally, Fearful lovers are cautious, pessimistic introverts, and have the lowest self-respect of the four types. Often nervous, self-conscious, and timid, you tend to have fewer friends and accomplishments to sustain and augment your self-assurance. If you're cynical, you often do not date.

Preoccupied lovers are usually affectionate and outgoing, but overly sensitive, insecure, dependent, and a bit distrustful. Warm-hearted and sociable, you typically have many friends and a good social life. However, you may be anxious around others, because you tend to be distrustful. Sometimes, you're scared that your lover may desert you. You may be so cynical that you sneak a look at your partner's cell phone or email to see if your partner has another lover. You're likely to have a few, but not a lot of accomplishments to bolster your self-respect. So, you often have some confidence and the third best self-assurance.

Get Your Dream
1. Define your ideal life and make a plan to achieve your goals.
2. Work your plan and keep a record of your progress.
3. Reward yourself regularly with praise or treats for your progress.
4. Visualize your goal 10 minutes daily. This will keep you motivated.

Ordinarily, Dismissive individuals have good self-respect. Normally, you describe yourself as calm, levelheaded, occupationally successful, but less adept socially. Typically, your professional competency and self-reliance sustain your confidence, but your social relationships give you less or moderate assurance. Socially, you're like a turtle, cautious and hide under a tough exterior. Exceptionally self-sufficient, you're somewhat distrustful and shun close, interdependent relationships, especially love relationships. You usually weather a divorce and early aftermath well but need to learn to be more trustful to fully heal and find a new companion.

Outgoing, calm, agreeable, and capable, Secure lovers are like tall Redwood trees—solid despite surrounding turmoil. Your confidence usually stems from being good at work and love. Unlike others, you're likely to develop meaningful, interdependent relationships. Especially when you're a man, you tend to actively date or recouple by the second year afterwards. In sum, you're usually sociable, reliable, and relaxed—attributes in the first three secrets to self-respect. You are usually trusting—a trait for good social relations often missing with other love styles.

Remember too, that confidence is based on self-respect and respect from others. If you always do the right thing, are kind, and lead an interesting life, both you and others will admire you and your confidence will return.

THE GUTS TO TRUST AGAIN

Ask a redivorced or hybrid first-divorced individual for a self-description. In return, you will often hear a long list of positive adjectives—bright, attractive, sensible, generous, and so on. Then, ask the same person to describe his or her former spouse. In some ways, the second list will probably be upbeat. Half will say that the ex is attractive, friendly, or positive in some other manner. Nevertheless, on one trait—trust —the two lists will likely differ noticeably.

In this investigation, most redivorced and hybrid first-divorced people said that they were trustworthy, but their ex wasn't. Only about one in four men described their former wife as sincere, honest, or dependable. Even fewer women said the same thing about their ex-husband. Traditional first-time men and women were two to three times more likely to trust their ex-spouse than second-timers or hybrid first-timers (See Figures 3-2 and 10-6).

Sometimes you are wise enough to maintain your partner's trust and trust him or her when you divorce. If you do, you have avoided pitfalls like infidelity, financial mismanagement, or substance abuse. If prudent, you will postpone dating until after your formal split. After that, please continue to be cautious about your new love life and certainly don't flaunt it.

Distrusting your former spouse hurts your ability to deal effectively with him or her. How are you going to finalize your divorce or stick to an agreement if you can't rely on each other's word? You may need to co-parent. How are you going to do this if you mistrust each other? Like it or not, cheating, irresponsibility, and addictions precipitate partner rage and make your breakup and future dealings with your spouse harder.

The second trouble with distrusting your ex-spouse is that, if you are not careful, your mistrust of this one person spreads and hurts your new relationships.

You may distrust half the world. Men don't trust women. Women don't trust men. The problem is not only overgeneralization, but also you often question your own judgment as to whom to rely on, like, and love. So, you end up losing out on a lot of potentially wonderful friendships and another romantic tie.

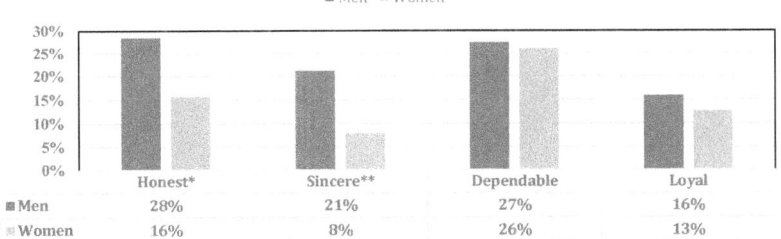

Figure 10-6: Men and women who described their ex-spouse as honest, sincere, dependable, and loyal. Redivorced and hybrid first-time adults: 222 (127 women). * p< .05; **p<.01.

Graph Takeaways:
1. Most redivorced and hybrid-first men and women distrust their ex-spouse.
2. Men are more trustful than women.

Your mistrust of your ex-spouse can destroy your future love life, if this means you don't trust your next companion either. When you trust your mate, you're programmed to make your relationship work. If a disagreement occurs, you look for ways to de-escalate the argument and to calm your partner. You have built-in rose-colored glasses when you look at your love. You may remember your partner as being more cooperative and adapting than s/he was. Trust replaces troublesome memories with nicer ones.[7] Over time, trust leads to greater trust and better, closer ties. If you're distrustful, you go in the other direction. You may end up with escalating partner conflict that is bad enough when it happens, but maybe even worse when you recall it.

> **Up Trust and Expectations**
> Be more predictable and reliable. Expect others to be trustworthy in at least some way. Within reason, you get what you give *and* expect. Give or expect nothing, you'll get nothing. Give *and* expect more, you'll get more.

Where Are You?

Now that you have read this section, which steps have you completed so far? Which ones do you still need to work on?

1. __ Calm
2. __ Happier
3. __ Active social life
4. __ Low marital review
5. __ Emotionally unattached to spouse
6. __ Confident
7. __ Trust your own decisions and most other people

> **Celebrate Your First Divorce Anniversary**
> You've forged through. Congratulate yourself and look forward to better times.

THINGS TO REMEMBER ABOUT THE TRANSITION YEAR:

- Most have satisfactory, but incomplete recovery and are still healing. They have mild to moderate stress, occasionally think about their recent marriage, feel happier, and are semi-detached from their ex.
- A drop in stress and greater happiness are the first dominoes in a series of healing steps. Often these start during the legal divorce process, especially for the divorce initiator, but may not occur until afterwards during the transition year. Mid-stage dominoes (greater social activity, reduced marital review, and less ex emotional attachment) are accomplished next. Late-stage ones (confidence and trust) are the last to be tackled and may be left undone long after the transition phase.
- Most increase their socializing/recoupling over the transition year.
- Compared to men, women have less stress initially, but higher stress by yearend.
- Compared to men, women tend to be happier and less emotionally attached to their ex-spouses.
- Marital review is about the same for men and women, and throughout the first year.
- Over the year, some men become calmer and happier, but more negative toward their ex-wives. Most of these men are becoming closer to a new love.
- On average, self-esteem is higher for extroverted, conscientious, optimistic, and Secure love style adults.
- Distrust is standard and much more common for redivorced and first hybrid-divorced men and women than traditional first-timers.
- At the end of the transition year, many have not fully recovered from their divorce.

CHAPTER 11

Second-Timers—Three Years Later

Quiz #7: Three-Year Follow-up

Q1. How happy are you now?
1. ___ Very unhappy
2. ___ Somewhat unhappy
3. ___ Neither happy nor unhappy
4. ___ Somewhat happy
5. ___ Very happy

Q2. How satisfied are you with your social and personal life?
1. ___ Very dissatisfied
2. ___ Somewhat dissatisfied
3. ___ Somewhat satisfied
4. ___ Very satisfied

Q3. How satisfied are you with your housing arrangement?
1. ___ Very dissatisfied
2. ___ Somewhat dissatisfied
3. ___ Somewhat satisfied
4. ___ Very satisfied

Q4. How satisfied are you with your job and financial situation?
1. ___ Very dissatisfied
2. ___ Somewhat dissatisfied
3. ___ Somewhat satisfied
4. ___ Very satisfied

Q5. How satisfied are you with your health?
1. ___ Very dissatisfied
2. ___ Somewhat dissatisfied
3. ___ Somewhat satisfied
4. ___ Very satisfied

Q6. Please describe yourself with any five words.

_____ _____ _____ _____ _____

Q7. How would you describe your dating and intimate relationships?
1. ___ Never date
2. ___ Date about once a month
3. ___ Date about 2 to 3 times per month
4. ___ Date weekly
5. ___ Going steady
6. ___ Cohabitating
7. ___ Engaged
8. ___ Remarried

Three Years Later

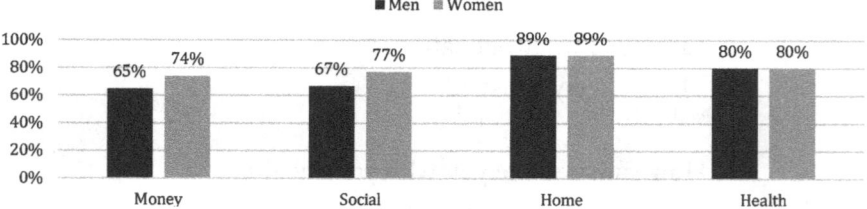

Figure 11-1. Men and women who are reasonably satisfied in each area of their lives. Note: Redivorced adults: 108 (62 women).

Graph Takeaway:
Most people are satisfied with their life.

What will your life be like three years after your second divorce? Will you be all smiles or down in the dumps? Will you be confident or insecure? Will you be satisfied with your finances, social life, health, and housing? What kind of relationship will you have with your former spouse? Will you be in love again? Will you remarry? These are the questions we will explore in this section.

FOR BETTER OR FOR WORSE?

As a general rule, the easier and simpler your breakup, the better your life during both the transition year and three years later. Nevertheless, this is not a firm, unbreakable rule.

Occasionally, especially if you're a woman, you did an outlook flip-flop. Sometimes, you were discouraged and distraught during your breakup and the transition year, but thrilled with your life a couple years afterwards. Maybe, you were so upset and tearful when you split that you thought long and hard about your marriage including how you might have contributed to your troubles or avoided your woes. Perhaps in counseling, you learned from the situation, worked through the hurt and loss, and emerged a year or two later strong and optimistic.

Women who went from a *negative to a positive* outlook—were usually those with twice-divorced ex-husbands. Lisa, for example, was in rough shape during her second divorce and for the first year afterwards. She was lonely, worried, chain-smoked, and because she was too upset to eat, lost weight. Nonetheless, three and a half years later, she had a new job and a new partner. Busy and outgoing, she was delighted with her life, especially her family.

On the other hand, sometimes you were happy and relieved just after your marriage, but landed back in trouble again, and were devastated by another loss. Women who go from a *positive to negative* outlook were usually women with husbands who had never been married before. Lolita fit this profile. She had high strain at the start of her uncoupling, but only mild upset during the rest of her breakup. Early afterwards, she was calm, upbeat, going steady, and rarely thought about her ex or past marriage. On the surface, she had all the attributes of a well-adjusted woman. Was she jumping from the frying pan into the fire with a rebound relationship? Probably. Had she figured out why her marriage failed and learned from her situation? Probably not. Three years later, she was unemployed and miserable. Bitter, she was not dating, because in her words, "Another man duped me again."

Pieces to the Life Satisfaction Puzzle

CASH IS KING

Money plays a major role in your recovery. As a general rule, your economic standing and life satisfaction are both roughly low

(30%), medium (45%), or high (25%). Three years down the road, you are probably at least somewhat satisfied, if not very satisfied, ,with your financial situation and, as a result, at least reasonably content in other ways. If, however, you are living from paycheck to paycheck, you are often in bad shape, especially in terms of your finances, social life, and health.

Better-off men are advantaged from the start—before marital issues surface, during the split, and long after that. You have simpler breakups with fewer economic and health woes. During the crisis, you are unlikely to be lonely, have insomnia, drink and/or smoke heavily, or have trouble concentrating on your work or paying your bills. Nonetheless, negotiating the property settlement can be a major hassle. After your divorce, your good fortune continues. By the third year postdivorce, if not sooner, you are normally happy, healthy, and have a new romantic partner. You are almost always blessed with high self-esteem and a strong sense that you can chart your own destiny, as well.

One-third of the men, however, are not only barely scraping by monetarily, but also miserable in other ways and for a long time. You tend to have more problems and troubles throughout the divorce and subsequently. Despite woes, you are usually okay with your living quarters, but seldom happy with your social or love life or health. More than half the time, you are not even dating. Only one in four of you is cohabiting or remarried. Limited social backing, loneliness, and elevated stress during the divorce are now cause medical problems for half of you.

Although women tend to have lower incomes than their ex-husbands, slightly more are pleased with their finances at the follow-up. As with the men, financially solid women have simpler divorces and better early and long-term adjustment. During the split, you have fewer budgetary worries; are less upset by social changes and losses; and are more likely to take the residential change in stride. In general, you are less upset and happier during the first-year transition. Three years out, you are usually fortunate across the board. You are almost always confident and pleased with your social life, health, and housing.

Again, like the men, low-income women tend to have a long list of complaints. Most of the time, you are disappointed with your finances as well as your love and social life. Thirty percent of you have inadequate housing, lower self-esteem, and health complaints, although you are about half as likely to have medical problems as your ex-husband.

MONEY IS NOT ENOUGH

Money is important, but not the only thing that matters. We are all social animals. Whether or not we are happy and confident usually hinges on whether we have loving social relationships including family, friends, or a new partner. How we heal often depends on whether we are a man or a woman.

For men, cohabiting or remarriage is pivotal. Men who do not have a new partner are almost always displeased with their lot in life, while re-partnered ones are content, if not upbeat. Why is this so?

Here is a clue. Next time you attend a social gathering, ask each attendee for the name of their best friend. Typically, in response, the women will give you the name of one of their girlfriends, but the men will point to their wives. So, when they split, men not only lose their spouse, but also their best friend. On top of that, women often organize the couples' social life. To regain companionship, most men must re-partner to find a close relationship, their next best friend, and a social director.

A man's love life is not just about being happy, it is also about self-esteem. Are you rewed or thinking about it? If so, you are normally very confident as well as very happy. If you are going steady or cohabitating but not ready to make another commitment, then you often have average confidence and are just happy, but not very happy. However, when you do not have someone special, you are usually insecure and down. This rule assumes that everything else in your life, like your finances, is reasonably okay.

As pointed out earlier, a single man's love life is determined in part by his wallet. Win the lottery or up your earnings in some other way, and your romantic luck will almost always skyrocket. You are now more attractive and better able to fund a comfortable life for you and your new romantic partner. Improve your income and love life, and everything else –your mood, lifestyle, and health –should take a turn for the better. Unfortunately, the opposite can happen. If you exit your split penniless, your love life, happiness, and self-esteem are often in the tank until you can get back on your financial feet.

For women, being surrounded by those you love in a secure environment is key to being happy and confident. Unlike a man, your mood and self-assurance are rarely based on your love life. And unlike a man, your mood and self-respect do not go in lock step together.

Some women are happy if they just get out of a bad marriage or find someone new, but that does not mean you are also confident. Physically abused women like Scarlett are almost always grateful to be out of their old home and into their new one. In general, you go through a rough and traumatic marriage and early divorce era before you give up on your marital tie, especially if this is your first. Commonly, you think about leaving for at least one year longer than other women— on average three years for remarrieds or six years for first-timers, instead of two. Once you leave, you are usually emotionally free and thankful for your new life with or without a new partner. But your self-esteem is almost always in bad shape.

Grace, and other unfaithful women are happier once they move in with their new love, but they are often insecure and riddled with guilt. A woman like Louise with a husband, who ran off to be with another woman, is usually both unhappy and insecure initially. She takes a long time to feel normal again. Typically, in a year or so, she is happy but saddled with feelings of failure and self-doubts.

Especially if you have children, you will usually consider a new partner nice, but not essential to your welfare. Close family and friends are often just as important to you, if not more important than a new partner, to your happiness and confidence. You may consider your first-marriage children a big social plus, especially if they are okay with the split. Normally upset by your second marriage, your first-marriage children may be relieved with the breakup. Importantly, many of your younger family members may assist and grow closer to you or your ex-. When Beth divorced Nickolas, her two children were central to her eventual recovery. A veterinarian, her financial success gave her monetary tools to solve practical issues and help her maintain and, then, rebuild her confidence.

After your divorce, you may like many women prioritize not only your relationships, but also work on your career, physical fitness, and talents. These achievements can boost your welfare.

In short, a woman's happiness and self-confidence are usually not based on her love life like her husband's, but rather based primarily on close non-romantic social relations and sometimes other achievements. Even if you are happier in a committed relationship, your new partnership may not necessarily up your self-assurance. Typically, you are happy *and* have decent self-respect as long as you have close family ties and friendships, even if you are not dating at all. Normally, if you are *very* confident, you are not only pleased with your social life, but also proud. You take pride in your job, talents, financial status, physical fitness, home, and/or younger family members like your children or grandchildren.

Avoiding Health Traps

College-educated men with good jobs are often adept problem solvers, who skirt health traps like smoking, increased drinking, or drugs. Typically, dating, if not recoupled, you are happy, calm, and have good social support at the three-year mark. These things—happiness, low stress, good social support, and a healthy lifestyle tend to protect you from illness. Your risk for medical problems is low, 10%.

High school-educated and lower to lower-middle class men with less money in their pockets tend to be beaten up and aged by their divorce. During the breakup, half of you smoke or drink heavily, are so depressed that you are sometimes suicidal, and have numerous health problems. Three years out, you are often frazzled, dislike your job and financial status, and have few close relationships. Half the time, you rarely date. High upset, low social support, dissatisfaction, and a harmful lifestyle increase your chances of health problems. Your risk for medical complaints is 50%.

Women are usually satisfied with their health, unless they have financial woes as well. Commonly, you follow the same lifestyle path as your former husband. Healthier women are in better stead money-wise and have healthy, financially solid ex-husbands, and vice versa. Why? Most couples have similar educational backgrounds and, thus, have roughly the same earning power, although women on average make somewhat less.

More often than not, better-educated women have solid incomes; make wise choices, including better health choices, and have social support from family, friends, and/or counseling. Your divorce may be painful, but you usually have low stress by the end of the first and third year postdivorce. At the follow-up, you often have the four keys to physical fitness—a healthy lifestyle, low stress, happiness or high life satisfaction, and good social support. Like the better-off men, you rarely have medical issues—only 10%.

In contrast, most unhealthy women have less education and income. Frequently, the high-school-educated woman chooses an unhealthy lifestyle, including sometimes smoking and excessive drinking (but less often than your ex-husband). You are often unhappy, especially with your finances and social relationships, and stressed. These disappointments coupled with your lifestyle cause you to be three times more likely to have medical problems than the more affluent man or woman. Your medical risk is about 30%.

Home Sweet Home

You almost always like your new home, unless you suffered a drastic drop in your standard of living. Men, who are the happiest with their new place, normally exit short second marriages, have first-union children who are untroubled, if not pleased and relieved with the breakup, and no second-marriage youngsters. In this setup, you rarely have remarriage alimony and child-support obligations that eat into your income and limit affordable housing choices. Unharmed money-wise by your recent past, you are not gun-shy about remarriage. You often find love with a new partner and plan to remarry within the next year or two.

As with the men, women who are the proudest of their dwelling, recall a relatively easy breakup with few complications and relief. Several years after the legal proceedings, you are content, calm, and pleased with your career and finances. Invariably, you're a college-educated woman with a redivorced husband and children from two unions. In this scenario, if you need it, you can secure financial help from your second husband due to your children with him as well as emotional support and assistance from your first-marriage children, extended family, and friends. Self-assured, you are almost always a Secure or Dismissive lover.

Unfortunately for your joint children, you rarely get along with your ex-husband.

On the other hand, a small group of lower-class and lower-middle-class men and women dislike their residences. Many were once financially secure but tumbled down the economic ladder during the divorce. Typically, you had longer marriages, second marriage-children, and a tough split.

Men were like Timothy, a commercial fisherman. When he separated from his wife, he had to make drastic cuts in his lifestyle. He moved from a comfortable, large colonial home in a nice section of town into a run-down, small apartment. Afterwards, he felt he had lost everything in his divorce—home, income, and family. He hated his new home and never wanted to remarry. Timothy was not going to take a chance on being hurt once more.

Women who were disappointed with their housing were not only unemployed or employed in low paying jobs, but also had little or no monetary help from their ex-spouse, so they could only afford minimal housing.

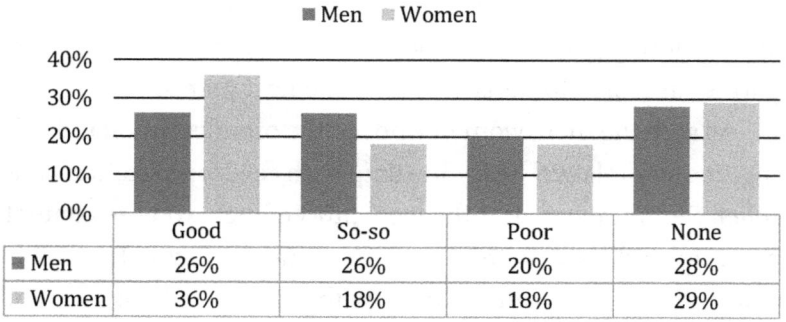

Figure 11-2: Men and women with good, so-so, poor, and no relationship with their second ex. Note: Redivorced adults: 108 (62 women).

Graph Takeaway: Half had a decent relationship with their ex-spouse.

> **Improve Communication and Parenting**
> If you are having a tough time co-parenting, get individual or group counseling. You will learn how to deal more effectively with your ex.

Relationships

THE GOOD, THE BAD, AND THE UGLY

Half the time, your relationship with your ex-spouse is at least passable if not good. You and your ex-spouse's personality and background as well as whether you have children in common, predict your post-marriage relationship.

Cheerful, sensible men usually end up with a civil relationship with their ex-wives by the third divorce anniversary, but rarely sooner. Sometimes, you argued viciously with your ex-wife throughout the breakup. During the first transition year afterwards, you may have grown even more bitter and hostile toward her. This was especially true if you were inching closer to a new love. Hopefully, down the road, when you are happier and more settled, you will quiet down.

In contrast, the typical, happier, even-tempered woman has a relatively neutral stance toward her ex-husband by the end of the first year postdivorce and from then on. You do not want to reconcile or even miss him. You are often emotionally able to establish a civil link with your ex early on, but he rarely is. Most of the time, you have to wait until your former spouse calms down to interact respectfully.

To emphasize, a levelheaded, upbeat woman calms down

sooner than a levelheaded, upbeat man. Typically, she is courteous toward him by the first divorce anniversary, while he is usually cordial toward her somewhat later—by the third divorce anniversary. Once this third year passes, they can often establish a pleasant, non-intimate rapport.

Among former couples, those of you with minors from the remarriage and no other children are likely to develop a civil relationship with your last partner. Characteristically, you try to be close to and involved with your youngsters. To achieve this, you allow the other parent to do the same, and strive to get along with him or her. You put the rough times behind you and move on to an unemotional, co-parenting liaison with your most recent ex.

Several years after the breakup, two groups of women in my study frequently had a poor relationship with their ex-husbands. The first type included women who were in rough shape early after the divorce like Cheyenne. Women with divorced parents such as Bolta were in the second set. Compared with other women, you were more likely to have an openly hostile or non-existent relationship with your ex. Only about 20% were on good terms with their recent ex-husbands and roughly 40% had no contact with them.

Cheyenne had an acrimonious relationship with her second ex-husband. Still bitter, she resented having to co-parent with him or deal with his new partner. Bolta, a real estate appraiser with divorced parents, avoided her ex. As you will recall, Bolta left her artist, financially strapped, second husband, Carter, in their old apartment. Why? According to her, she had a better credit rating and could easily secure a new place, but he could not. She also had a second and more important motive. They did not have joint children, so she saw no reason to see Carter again, by choice or by accident. When she left, she moved to a new neighborhood and established a new home and a new routine—a routine that prevented her from accidentally seeing Carter again on the street, in a grocery store, or some other neighborhood spot. By doing so, she quickly moved on physically and emotionally and ducked his wrath and loan requests, too.

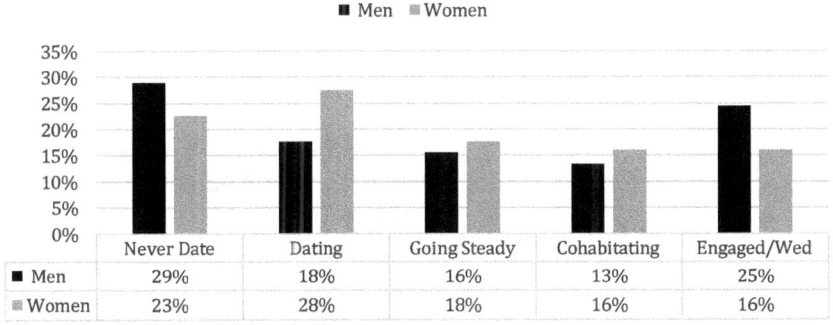

Figure 11-3: Third-year romantic relationships for second-time men and women. Note: totals do not equal 100% due to data rounding. Adults: 107 (62 women).

Graph Takeaways:
1. Half have not found someone new. About 25% are not dating at all and about 25% are dating.
2. About half have a new partner.
3. More people cohabitate or go steady than remarry.
4. Men are somewhat more likely to have a new partner.

Searching for Mr. / Mrs. Right

After your first marriage ended, you usually calmed down, moved forward socially, and swiftly found another romantic partner. Three years later, you were almost always rewed.

Typically, after your second divorce, you are more cautious, reticent to commit, and slower to hitch up once more. Initially, about a third of you are not even looking for someone. Although you may quickly find a different love partner, often these links are short-term, transitional ties soon discarded or swapped out. You are rarely remarried.

A couple of years later, you have usually inched forward, but not by much. Twenty-five percent of the time, you are not looking for someone new. Seventy-five percent of the time, you are dating, going steady, or maybe cohabitating, but you are probably not wearing an engagement or wedding ring. You are rewed only 20% of the time. Who is game for a third try?

If you're a woman, you are probably more willing to tie the knot than your ex-husband. Three out of four women, but only six out of ten men are either wed or want to walk down the aisle again. Regardless of your gender, if you are open to a third marital union, you are usually confident, seeing someone special, and do not have any second marriage children.

Can You Get Back in the Saddle?

If you're part of the "never again crowd," you have a lot of company, but you have not recovered from your divorce. Three years after your second divorce, you have a one-in-three shot that you have sworn off marriage for good.

Men from divorced parental homes, like Pluto, and those who experienced a drastic drop in their lifestyle, like commercial fisherman, Timothy, avoid marriage like the plague. Pluto was mad that he had lost not only his second wife, but also so much more including even the couple's wedding gifts and dog, Barker. He was living with a new love, Marylou, but had sworn off a third marriage. When part-time secretary, Rosemary, divorced Timothy, he felt he had lost everything—his family, home, and money. He felt burned and never wanted to marry again.

Characteristically, marriage-avoidant women feel betrayed, bitter, shamed, or discouraged. At times, you feel like an outcast—socially guillotined by your last husband. Many times, you are burned and humiliated by the ending of your relationship, especially if you were left for another woman. Pessimistic, you may feel too defective to be happily married.

Sometimes you rarely date or stop dating completely—you give up on finding a new partner. Instead, you find friends, activities, and a more enriched life as a single person. Deserted women like Cheyenne often follow this path. Cheyenne spent weekends with her daughter Lilac on sports and church activities. Her local Methodist Church became her church family. Other times, you are like Bolta and cohabitate or actively date, but run from a partner who presses for greater commitment.

Because of the financial and emotional burden of the legal process you may be cynical about the institution of marriage itself. Years after the split, you may question your ability to stay happily wed. Thus, after two failed attempts, you may not believe that a marriage is a lasting obligation or best for you.

Routinely, the wedding-adverse voice cynicism. "I don't trust myself to choose a safe, compatible partner." Or, "I don't trust men (women)." If you are in the "never again crowd," you will try to avoid matrimony for the rest of your life and are comfortable with this decision. Naturally, you may seriously reconsider marriage later, if like Pepper, you heal further, learn to trust again, and discover the right person.

Happily Married for the Third Time Example: Pepper

An only child, Pepper had a passion for traveling and writing. Her father was a salesperson, while her mother worked part-time as a registered nurse. After college, Pepper joined a New York firm to begin her writing career. At 24, she had a nine-month marriage to an accountant. At 27, she met a local executive, Barnaby, in New York City. When the relationship became too serious for her, she broke up with him and ran away by taking a temporary assignment investigating a story in the Midwest. Still in love, however, she dated Barnaby again after she returned to the city. Six months later, they wed. Soon thereafter, Barnaby complained about her frequent out-of-town assignments. The couple divorced two years later.

Pepper decided that she could not be professionally successful and remain happily married. Given the choice, she chose to concentrate on her career. Over the next twelve years, Pepper had an interesting writing career and dated, but avoided another marriage.

In her early forties, she dated another writer, Howard. A warm-hearted, mid-forties, recent widower, he had a twelve-year-old son and a ten-year-old daughter. When Howard first asked her to marry him, Pepper panicked, became angry, and refused. From the start, she made it clear she was not interested in marriage. However, he didn't share her fear of marriage and pursued her until she finally agreed to marry him. Five months into the marriage, Pepper's parents died in a car accident. Howard and her stepchildren were compassionate, shared her grief, and were now her only family. Happily married for the first time, she no longer had one foot out the door. From then on, they were a close couple until Howard's death twenty years later.

Reverse Cynicism
If you don't want to remarry or even date, enter counseling to eliminate your fears and distrust. Once you open your heart and become more trusting, most of your relationships will improve, including your romantic ones.

Things to Remember about Second-timers—Three Years Later:

- Twice-divorced men and women are usually happy and reasonably satisfied with their financial situation, social life, housing, health, and themselves.
- Adequate finances and a good social life are key to other aspects of life satisfaction, like self-esteem and health.
- Self-esteem and happiness are rooted in social relationships. For a man, self-confidence and happiness are both based on his love life and go in lock step together. For a woman, happiness and confidence are more about her social life with family and friends, not her love life. Her joy and self-esteem are related, but they do not necessarily move in lock step.
- Socializing and recoupling increase slowly over the first couple of years.
- Recoupling, especially remarrying, is much slower and less likely than after the first divorce.
- Few have remarried, and one-third have sworn off a third try.
- Often, redivorced women with twice-married ex-husbands have poorer early recovery, but better long-term recovery than redivorced women with once-married ex-husbands and vice versa.
- Half of the ex-couples have a civil relationship.

CHAPTER 12

Mono-Redivorce: What to Expect When Only *He* Is Redivorcing

Janet's Story

Janet opened the door to Fairhaven High School and followed the colorful signs leading to her tenth reunion. On the way, she passed a long line of glass-encased trophies. She stopped, smiled, and looked at the awards from her class, almost hidden among the many others. She smiled too as she looked at her own reflection in the glass case. With a recent haircut, she looked stunning, sophisticated, but cautious in her new navy suit. Having divorced last year, she was starting to venture forth to reestablish old friendships and find some new ones. Behind her, she heard a familiar voice. "Janet, is that you?"

Janet turned and burst out, "Mari, I was hoping you would be here. Want to sit together so we can catch up? It's been almost three years."

"All right."

"How are your husband and the kids?" Janet inquired.

"Fine. How are yours?"

"Guess you didn't hear. Stanley and I got divorced last year," Janet told her.

"Sorry to hear that. Are you okay now?"

"Yes. But I feel so strange doing things by myself. My sister pushed me into coming today. She said I needed to get out and get in touch with my old friends."

"Guess we're lucky you came to our tenth."

"I'm here. But I'm not going to stay for the whole thing."

"Wow, Janet. You look so thin and fit."

"I've lost weight. It was about the only good thing that happened in the last couple of years. I've been through the meat grinder."

"What happened?"

"Stanley cared more about taking care of his first wife and son than us. Any extra money or time went to them. Our daughter Lilly and I got shortchanged. We were his current family, why shouldn't we get more than less?"

"What do you mean?"

"We didn't have enough money to pay child support, his son's special requests, and all our bills. Stanley spent more leisure time with his son than he did with our daughter. His son disrespected me and did whatever he wanted. Stanley ignored it. If I complained, Stanley would defend him and get mad at me. But if our daughter was rude or did something wrong, he would punish her immediately. I got tired of watching Stanley favor his boy over our daughter and me. Why should we play second fiddle?

"It's been a while since we both got married. I remember thinking at the time that your parents weren't happy like mine. Yours looked so glum during the ceremony."

"Mom and Dad felt he was a bad bet. They wanted me to marry a single guy who hadn't been married before like your husband. No problems with an ex-wife and kid from another marriage. They were right. Stanley didn't like my parents, either. He says they ruined our marriage. Can you imagine that?"

"How long did you think about getting a divorce before you decided?" "Two years."

"Why so long, Janet?"

"I worried about our daughter, so the decision was tough. But one day I looked up. I felt unloved and miserable. I couldn't take the indecision or arguing anymore. I had to get out. So, I called my parents. Within a week, they found me a lawyer."

"How did you and your daughter handle the divorce?"

"We were initially unhappy and upset. Then, we got counseling, hired a tutor so Lilly could catch up at school, and got more exercise. I started running with a friend. Lilly took up swimming. Counseling, tutoring, and exercise all helped. We're both okay now."

"Did you like your lawyer?"

"Yes. He gave me great advice that got me through it. He prevented Stanley from intimidating me. Stanley is older than us, so he tends to run rough shod over me, especially when he's mad. My child support isn't great, but okay."

"What's your lawyer's name, Janet?"

"Murray Morrison. Why?"

"I may be getting a divorce, too," admitted Mari.

At every annual high school and college reunion in the United States, classmates catch up on each other's lives. Updates, of course, include classmate divorces. When adults like Janet and Stanley explain their breakups, they usually fault financial strain, social problems with children and in-laws, or infidelity. Invariable, friends look for details about these separations. They also wonder. Was the divorce harder for her or him? How does this split compare to other divorces? How did this marriage and divorce differ from his first ones?

Scenario Snapshot

In mono-remarriage, he's the sole remarried partner. When the marriage unravels, she's a young adult, like Janet, but he is older and middle-aged, like Stanley. Unless she had an affair, most assume that he is primarily responsible for the breakup. Why? Like Janet, she's young, much younger than her husband, and once wed. Family, friends, and professionals are often sensitive to her needs and lack of knowledge about the legal process. On the other hand, most presume that he already knows how to get a divorce and can handle the situation without their aid. After all, he is older and has been divorced previously. Not surprisingly, his family and others are more critical of his role in the marital demise and rarely give him much help or sympathy.

Falling Through the Cracks

Typically, the ex-husband blames his divorce on conflict with his in-laws, infidelity, and disrespect. Other men are less apt to mention these. She usually faults the split primarily on financial difficulties or infidelity and secondarily on other issues like his emotional problems or his substance abuse. Unlike the second-time wife, you rarely complain about your children/stepchildren. In contrast, almost one-half of the redivorcées blame their children for their marital problems. You, like most, assume that if someone has an emotional problem, it must be him, not you, because he is the only one who is remarried.

> *Decision Therapy*
> Most once-married women benefit from talking to a divorce counselor to determine if they can patch up their marriage or should leave.

Divorce Process

HER DIVORCE—SITTING ON THE FENCE BEFORE THE PLUNGE

Like two-thirds of the women, you usually ask for the divorce, but before you do, you usually sit for a long time on an emotional fence, struggling to decide whether to leave. As a result of your drawn-out dilemma, you are more likely to have high decision distress than other men and women. Not surprising. This is your first divorce.

If you have an affair, you are quicker to leave. Janet, who was faithful, mulled over her decision for several years, but Grace darted off as soon as she found a new love. Before you separate, you are almost always miserable. Like eight out of ten women, you are in purgatory when you suggest the separation.

Typically, your husband moves to a new residence, while you and your children remain in your current dwelling. About a year later, you usually relocate to another, more affordable place as well. Downsizing to cover the cost of maintaining two places is your primary reason for the shift. Sometimes, you consider the move disturbing and time-consuming. Despite aggravations, the change often leaves your unhappy reminders behind and kicks starts your recovery with new friendships and activities.

If you began the divorce, you start healing as soon as you split. Your divorce may be grueling, but the worst is now over. From then on, you are sensitive and adjusting to your new routine, but less likely to be downhearted or irritable. Your stress continues to drop as you proceed.

If you didn't want the divorce, you go from bad to worse when your husband leaves. Your separation is painful. You almost always lose weight and pace the floor at night because you can't sleep. Typically, you are angered by your husband's affair or rejection, lonely, sad, and worried. Your difficulties may pile up. Half the time, you can't stand being alone. About a third of the time, you feel embarrassed and ridiculed. Discussions with your ex-husband are strained.

Commonly, your finances are a major stumbling block. Your household income drops from two paychecks to one. Sometimes, you quickly solve your monetary challenges. Other times, you have a harder time. Despite cutbacks, your increased expenses are a major hurdle. A third of the time, you bitterly fight over your financial settlement. The real conflict is rarely money per se. Because of your pain and conflict, you and your ex seldom think cooperatively and flexibly about how to make the settlement a win-win solution.

Child-related questions are a central issue for mothers like Janet. You struggle with these questions. "How do we calm our children? How do we make sure our youngsters aren't harmed by our divorce? How do we work out a parenting plan that works for everyone?" Single or part-time parenting, unpleasant visitations, or suspicion that your spouse is undermining your personal relationships may add to your stress.

Especially if you left your husband, your distress declines as you work out your practical problems. After the papers are filed, your life is better and you are relieved and more relieved than your husband. On average, three aspects of your life and health improve. You are probably more lighthearted, sleep thru the night, and calmer. Yet, when the divorce papers are finalized, you and other plaintiffs like Janet are temporarily frazzled or distraught knowing that this marks the legal end of your love relationship. In the same situation, twice-divorced women rarely cry or express upset.

Your recovery depends on whether you wanted the divorce. If you left him or the decision was mutual, you are self-confident, cheerful, and calm. You rarely think about your past. If you left to be with another man like Grace, you are living with him, but are often haunted by guilt. When you didn't like Janet, you slowly started to date again.

If deserted, you are like Louise. You have low or modest recovery for the first year afterwards. Typically, you are emotionally semi-wed to your ex, angry, and miserable. You often feel abandoned and like a failure. Your marriage keeps popping into your thoughts. You continue to obsessively think about your past wondering how you got into your mess, miss him, rarely date, and are bitter. However, you often brush off your misery by the end of your first transition year and begin dating again, ready to find someone new.

Starting over socially can be daunting. Like Janet and one out of three women, you are initially uncomfortable being single again. You need a nudge from your family and friends to attend social events like your reunion. Nevertheless, you seldom fear social rejection. Family, friends, and others are usually quite empathetic with your situation and uncritical. Unlike your husband, you can often count on social support from your family and friends regardless as to whether you left him or he left you. If either of you had an affair, you rarely get along and have a tough time co-parenting your minors in the immediate aftermath.

> *Four Traumatic Reactions*
> You usually report four traumatic reactions such as anger, depression, and loneliness or health issues such as insomnia, weight loss, and substance abuse.

> *Men Ask for Help*
> Men should ask for emotional support and help. Family and friends will assume that he does not need it, unless he asks. Savvy men join a support group.

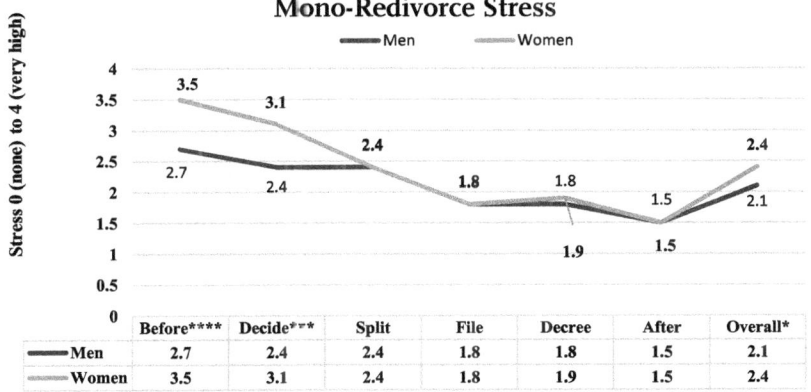

Figure 12-1: Mean stress for each stage and overall for mono-redivorced men (twice wed) and women (once wed). Note: Before is predecision. After is the first year postdivorce. Adults: 151 (77 women). * p< .05; *** p = .001; **** p = .000.

Graph Takeaways:
1. Women usually have high and higher stress than men at the start.
2. Men often have moderately high stress at the start.
3. Most men and women have moderate stress from the separation until the end of the split.
4. After the divorce, men and women usually have low stress.

HE GOES DOWN THE STAIRCASE

Your journey depends on whether you wanted to end your marriage, or your wife thrust it upon you. Most of the time, she leaves you. In about a third of the cases, however, you desert her or the decision is mutual. When you want out of the marriage, you are usually quicker to come to your decision—you take half as long as she or about a year.

For the most part, you have staircase stress—stress that drops multiple times as you uncouple. Often, you start drinking and smoking more, your eating habits change, and you gain or lose weight early in the process. When you engage in an unhealthy lifestyle, your health declines, which in turn, slows your recovery.

If you want the divorce, your most difficult time is at the start. For half, your misery plummets as soon as you decide to leave. Otherwise, you are miserable until you depart. Like John, your distress drops when you walk out of your home for good and slam the door on your marriage.

If your wife began the legal proceedings like Janet, you are bound to be like her husband Stanley. Like six out of ten men, Stanley quickly faced his marital demise and, thus, had moderately high early distress during the first two stages. When he separated, his angst continued until he developed a new routine and found someone new.

Jealousy, social strain, and loss are standard early to midway in your breakup. In most divorces, one or both of you have an affair. If she does, you usually feel betrayed, bitter, rejected, and flooded with self-doubts and worries. Other times, you have an affair, and she often feels the same anguish. Sometimes, you miss her even when the separation is your idea. Damage to other familial relationships compounds your troubles and riles almost everyone in your extended family. Most of these glitches are temporary if the two of you behave in a respectful manner and reach out to form new friendships.

Characteristically, you have more complications with your minor children when you want the divorce, but she does not. If you precipitate your breakup with an affair, you invariably have difficult child visitations and upset children.

Economic challenges of one sort or another are standard. You are often distressed and angered by your financial settlement talks. During your first divorce years ago, you rarely felt disadvantaged during your negotiations. But this time, you may be convinced that your higher income puts you in a poor bargaining position and resent it.

During the decision and separation phases, you are often very upset. As the divorce progresses, however, calm, cheerfulness, and improved concentration replace your tension, rage, sullenness, and distractibility. Slowly, more and more positives crop up. As troubles vanish one by one, your health improves, your work becomes easier, your relationships improve, and your optimism returns. When the divorce papers are filed and the divorce decree is issued, you are usually okay, calm, but still recovering. If you initiated the split like John, the supermarket manager, you are relieved, upbeat when you receive your divorce papers, and in better shape than if you hadn't wanted it.

At the end of the transition year, if you sought the divorce, you are almost always fine. However, if you didn't want it, you usually have ongoing troubles. Sometimes, you are touchy, down in the dumps, and frequently think about your ex-wife. Other times, you are a bit luckier. You are semi-recovered and better off than predivorce. You reflect on your divorce off and on, miss your wife, and date sporadically.

If you want social support or affection during or after your split, you usually turn to a new love. Unlike your ex-wife, you rarely have social support or help from your family and friends. Dating or better yet, recoupling improves your outlook and well-being immensely.

Three years out, a mono-redivorced man's chance of being reasonably happy is split down the middle. About thirty-five percent of the time, you are engaged or rewed. You are often happy and confident. Twenty percent of the time, you are cohabitating. Typically, you are somewhat satisfied and the next most likely to be grinning and confident. However, half the time, you are unattached, dissatisfied, especially with your financial and social lot, and insecure.

> **Easier for her?**
> Just under half (44%) of the women think they had an easier divorce than their husbands. About a third said their divorce was harder (34%). The remaining 22% said the two splits were about the same.

> **Take the High Road**
> Ideally adults should not start a new relationship until they have separated. An extra-marital affair renders your divorce longer and harder for your family.

IS THE DIVORCE EASIER FOR HER OR HIM?

For most, the breakup is in some ways harder for her, but in other ways harder for him. Most once-married women face higher distress and angst than their twice-married husbands before they separate (pre-decision and decision phases). Why? She is normally younger, usually starts the split, and this is her first union, but his second. Mid-course, typical couples like Janet and Stanley report equivalent distress and difficulties. Emotional trauma reactions, such as increased sadness, and complications, such as financial difficulties, are about the same for both. If, however, she has an excruciating divorce start, which Janet, Grace, and most women do, she usually has high and higher relief later than her ex-husband. She almost always has the social advantage. Relatives and friends often give her more backing and general assistance than her ex. Many shun him thinking he is at fault and a two-time loser.

Afterwards, when she compares her experience with that of her ex-husband, what does she conclude? If she sought the divorce, she tends to view her divorce as easier than his. If she opposed the split, she often saw her breakup as harder. Occasionally, she concluded that it was equally thorny for both.

To come to one of these conclusions, she typically recalls whether she wanted the divorce, her stress and relief, but also her major advantage—her high social support and help getting through the ordeal and moving forward. Janet, for example, had assistance from her family and friends so although she was almost as distrustful as her ex and hesitant to find someone new, she eventually started looking for someone. Her ex was socially and financially beat up, cynical, and afraid of another marriage. He felt like a two-time loser and ostracized. His pocket had been picked twice. He was not up for a third drubbing.

Thus, if you are a first-time woman, you customarily think you had an easier divorce than your redivorcing ex-spouse, although you often reported more stress. The same thing happened in Chapter 3 when I compared a different group of first-timers, *traditional first-timers,* versus second-timers in general, except the effect was even stronger. The hardest parts of a second divorce are often not the mechanics of exiting the relationship or stress during and after the split, but rather being tagged a two-time loser and the discouragement and self-doubts that often come with making the same mistake twice.

> **Women's Hindsight**
> Whether a woman thinks she had the easier divorce depends on two things: 1) whether her parents are married to each other and 2) who initiated the divorce.

Case Examples

FINANCIAL PROBLEMS AND HER PARENTS: JANET AND STANLEY

Janet and Stanley's marriage was undercut by money troubles and conflict with her parents. When they wed, she was a mid-twenties dental hygienist, while he was an early-thirties plumber. They had two children, Bobby from his first marriage and Lilly from theirs. Janet said:

> The most difficult part of my breakup was deciding to get a divorce. I was trapped for several years, unable to decide whether to stay with Stanley, my first love, or exit the marriage and my misery. I felt unloved, shortchanged, and resentful. Eventually, I left. I couldn't correct the situation, stand the stress, or tolerate the indecision.
>
> As I wavered back and forth, I was frazzled, lost weight, and had insomnia off and on. Once I decided to leave, my angst dropped noticeably and continued to drop during the divorce. Three difficulties stand out—negotiating the settlement, my daughter's distress, and the loss of my everyday relationship with Stanley. He should have given me more child support—at least as much as he was paying his first wife. Again, I was second best to his first wife. I had a hard time explaining the divorce to our daughter and calming her. Lilly kept on asking. "Where's Daddy? When is Daddy coming home?" Like her, I missed him.
>
> During the breakup, I was lucky. Almost everyone was sympathetic and supportive. My parents found and paid for my lawyer, were there for me emotionally, and paid the bills Stanley wouldn't and I couldn't. They took care of Lilly after school and several evenings per week, so I could continue working full time and go out with my friends.
>
> Near the end, I was relieved and could sleep all night without waking up thinking of our problems.

At the end, I knew I wanted the divorce. Yet, I was sad and stressed the week I got my divorce. Afterwards, I was all right, happier, and rarely thought about my past. I waited a year before I started dating again. Three years later, I married a nice guy, who loves both Lilly and me.

As Stanley explained, his experience was quite different.

Like Janet, I was the most upset during the last year we lived together. When she asked for a separation, I didn't want to get a divorce, but I understood that things were not working for us and moved to a new apartment. Janet was unrealistic about what I could do financially. Settling the property division was a long, fiery dispute. My daughter Lilly was upset. I had a hard time explaining to her why we broke up and why I had left. She kept asking me to make up with her mom and to come home. I had to keep telling her that I would always love her. Showing her my new apartment helped to reduce her anxiety.

Unlike my first divorce, no one offered to help. After I got into my new place, I was lonely, but I started to calm down. Weekdays for a long time, I missed Janet and Lilly. Without them, the apartment seemed empty. My teenage son was delighted and companionship on weekends. It was fun, but hectic to have both kids visit at the same time. We had a hard time coming up with things all three of us wanted to do together. I was more upbeat and less lonely as soon as I found a new honey, right before the divorce decree.

Overall, my troubles were on par with Janet's. Yet, she had somewhat more distress early on or during the first half and I had somewhat more anguish and less relief during the second half. Afterwards, I was okay, especially after I found a new love. As I got closer to her, I felt better and better, but also more hostile toward Janet.

HER INFIDELITY EXAMPLE: WILLIAM AND GRACE

When the couple wed three years after William's first divorce, he was an early-thirties salesman, and Grace was an early-twenties hairdresser. Each of his two marriages lasted between six and seven years. In this, his second union, the couple shared three children: his son, Lane, from his first family and their two children, Mark and Steve. Grace recalled her divorce experience.

> My affair helped me get out of a bad situation, but it also made me feel guilty and like a failure. Four months after the divorce, things were better. My new love, Doug, and I were closer and happier, yet my past still haunted me. I kept wondering why my previous relationship ended so badly. William is still mad. When the children go to his house or back to mine, I try to do it as quickly as possible or get Doug to do it for me. I try to avoid William and his nasty comments.

In a different interview, William gave his side of the story.

> When Grace left me, I was numb. It came as a total surprise. At first, I was lonely, depressed, and angry with her. The stress was excruciating at the start of the split—but not later—not after I started dating.

Midway through, I felt relieved and less down. Our divorce was harder than my first split eight years ago. The breakup was harder on me than on Grace. By the time we got our divorce papers, I was dating and okay, but continuing to recover and hated Grace. She's unstable, untrustworthy, and selfish. We've had a hostile relationship ever since. Co-parenting is tough. If we meet, I have a hard time being civil and so does she.

His Infidelity and Family: John and Louise

John's affair precipitated his divorce from Louise. A florist, she met John when she was in her twenties. John was a supermarket manager with a teenager, Cody. According to John, he had the easier divorce, but his affair backfired and made their financial settlement talks harder. John said:

> Most of my troubles were before Louise's discovery and volcanic outrage. Her blow-up got me out of my tight spot and slammed the door on our marriage. Louise was upset for the longest time. It took her over a year to calm down enough, so we could work out a financial settlement. With a new woman, I was happy during most of the split and afterwards. My son and parents were thrilled.

In a separate interview, Louise described her divorce differently.

> Once I confronted him about his affair, John went from an affectionate husband to a cold, hostile stranger. He acted like he was the victim not me—complaining that I had put him through hell and

hurt his relationships with his family. I was in a state of disbelief and bewilderment. For the first few months, I cried every day. I lost weight. At work, I tried to hide my grief, but my friends couldn't be fooled and came to my aid. Like Sherpa, they led me to an attorney and a support group, covered for me at the store, and helped me find my way through the rough terrain. Throughout, I was ambivalent about John, loving him one minute, hating him the next. At the end, the pain was still there, but less intense. I was better and spent weekends with my friends. Still, I cried the day I got my divorce.

The first year afterwards, I didn't like John or want him back. I was happier and relieved to be out of the awful situation. Hallelujah!! But I kept going over our relationship. I tried to figure out what I did wrong, and how I got into such a pickle. After this year, I was tired of being upset. I had been miserable for too long. I stopped thinking about our past.

THINGS TO REMEMBER ABOUT MONO-REDIVORCE:
- Women are usually the first ones to leave the marriage and initiate the divorce.
- On average, women suffer from a relatively long, early stress period compared to other men and women.
- More of these women have high or very high decision distress than others in this survey.
- Stress is about the same for women and men from the split onward.
- Most women think that their divorce was either easier (44%) or about the same (22%) as their husband's.
- These second-time men often have a harder time recovering than bi-redivorced men.

CHAPTER 13

Uni-redivorce: What to Expect When Only *She* Is Redivorcing

PUG TELLS HIS DRINKING BUDDIES ABOUT SAVANNAH AND PARIS

A mid-thirties architect, Pug had a whirlwind romance, a short first marriage, and a difficult divorce from Savannah. Savannah was a mid-thirties bank teller with an eleven-year-old daughter from her first marriage. Three months after the divorce, Pug had a brief affair with Paris. Through it all, every Thursday after work, he went to George's Tavern to see his drinking buddies before going home to his Boston apartment. Until today, he had not revealed much about his love life.

Pug had broken up with his recent love, Paris, over lunch earlier that day and wasn't in a good mood. But today was Thursday and Pug, a man of habit, headed as usual to George's. When he arrived, he spotted Sam, Larry, and several other regulars, sat down next to them, and ordered a pitcher of draft beer. Sam nodded and asked:

"You look down, Pug. Something wrong?"

"I just broke up with Paris. I was just getting over Savannah and now I'm back in the soup again."

"You've come to the right place," chuckled Larry. "You need a beer and a new woman."

"I ordered a pitcher. Now, how do I order the right woman? I don't want to go through this again. It's tough going through two splits back-to-back like this."

"How'd you meet Savannah?" Sam asked.

"I was on vacation at Moon Lake. Bumped into Savannah on the beach the first day there. We hit it off instantly. A month later, I moved in with her and her daughter."

Across the table, Larry chimed in. "Too soon to move in, Pug. Did you get along with her daughter?"

"No."

"You knucklehead, you have to win over the children before you move in. Otherwise, you don't get along."

"Really?"

"Really. Did you get married or just live together?" Larry asked.

"When we first met, Savannah was separated and waiting for her divorce decree. Three weeks after it came through, we got married."

"Sounds like she married you on the rebound. You got married too quickly. Your marriage didn't have a chance from the start," Larry said.

"What do you think went wrong, Pug?" Sam asked, ignoring Larry's comments.

"A lot. We're different. Savannah and I are used to doing things in a certain way, but in a different way."

"What do you mean?" Larry asked.

"I wanted to eat a formal dinner every night at 8 pm, so I could see you guys or watch the news. She liked to eat earlier in the kitchen so she could do something afterwards. We argued about everything, even how to put the toilet paper on."

"Toilet paper?"

"I'm used to the hotel method with the end at the top like my mom does. She puts it on the other way with the end of the paper on the bottom."

"Couldn't you work this out?"

"Whenever I explained to her that my method was the right one, she would just snap back that I was wrong, controlling, or domineering."

"You divorced over toilet paper, Pug?"

"Not just that, Sam. We disagreed on everything. She is a Democrat and I'm a Republican. She thinks religion is stupid, but I'm a devout Lutheran. The worst was that I felt excluded. Savannah and her daughter, Princess, were close and closer than I was to either of them. I felt like an outsider in my own home and disrespected by my stepdaughter."

"I told you, you have to win over the kids before you move in with the woman. Otherwise, they consider you an intruder, and you don't get along," Larry said.

"Okay, I got it," Pug quipped.

"Did you leave her or did she leave you?" Sam asked.

"I left. We were both unhappy and drifting apart. Didn't feel close to Savannah. Once I realized that things were never going to work out, I left and filed for divorce. Savannah is emotionally unstable and impossible."

"Left my second wife a couple of years ago. She was cute, but wacky, too. Was your hardest time in the beginning before you separated, like mine?" asked Larry.

"Yup. The worst was early on, before I decided to get a divorce, and we separated. We were constantly arguing. I dreaded going home. I was angry, miserable, and stressed out. I lost weight, kept on picking up one cold or flu after another, and couldn't get to sleep many nights. Once I walked out, I was better, but still upset. I know Savannah is not my type of woman, but who is? Well, that and Savannah are in the past. Now I have to get over another one, Paris."

"Does anyone want another beer?" Larry said.

"Why not. Let's all drink to my next gal," Pug said as he eyed a bunch of women just coming into George's.

> **Telepsychology—Zoom**
> If you find it difficult to talk with a therapist face-to-face, consider talking with with a counselor on the phone or on the internet instead.

The Basics

In a uni-remarriage or stepfather family, the husband is in his first marriage, like Pug, but the wife is in her second, like Savannah. Usually wed in their late twenties to mid-thirties, the husband regularly has an instant family with not only a wife, but also one or two children from her six-year or shorter earlier marriage. Her children often resent the new husband.

Sometimes, you fail to form a close marriage because one or both of you are unwilling to commit to the marriage. Other times, you have a hard time bridging different religious and political beliefs, or you come from different socio-economic backgrounds. And maybe, you give up on the relationship too quickly, falsely thinking you are incompatible. You don't understand that it normally takes a stepfamily several years before everyone in the family is close. Invariably, the husband feels excluded and disrespected, like Pug.

When these families separate, you tend to blame a combination of substance abuse and infidelity, or sexual problems, intimacy, and/or emotional problems. Often, you and/or your spouse could benefit from therapy for substance abuse, trust, self-esteem loss, sexual dysfunction, or lack of intimacy. Counseling to combat social rejection sensitivity and up resilience can be effective tools to reduce these five common troubles.

Who Initiates the Divorce?

Typically, as the wife, you are the first to withdraw emotionally, suggest the separation, and file for the divorce. If you file, you spend on average two years thinking about it before you decide.

One of the unique features of this group is that you are quite variable in your decision time – much more so than other couples. Almost one-third of the time, you make your decision in only a few months, or conversely, in about one in five instances, you take five or more years to do so. You are particularly quick if you were raised in a divorced parental home.

Likewise, if your husband asks you for a divorce, he may come to his decision slowly or quickly, but usually faster than you. Pug and other men who file for divorce take on average a year to mull over the decision, but one third take only a few months, and another one third spend at least two years.

Occasionally, you start thinking about ending your marriage and then your husband starts thinking about it, too. Then, you come to a joint decision. This is usually the best scenario for everyone.

> **Men Have the Social Edge**
> Most people blame the wife for the divorce and are more likely to help him.

What Makes These Divorces Challenging?

Financial matters are your most common snags—they challenge nearly 75%. Compared with other men (but not women), this challenge is frequent. Your monetary troubles include intra-family obligations such as the property settlement, child support, and alimony; income changes, higher expenses, residential moves, and difficulty getting a better job to cover increased costs.

Typically, you argue about the property division. If you had financial troubles before the breakup, property division means splitting up bills, especially credit card debt, as well as a few other things. When you have a modest income, you divide up furniture, wedding gifts, pets such as the family dog, and maybe one or two cars. You may have a longer list including a house, bank accounts, retirement funds, and occasionally things like a sports vehicle, a country club membership, and a vacation timeshare.

If you are the wife, you usually stay in the couple's place with most of the furniture. You almost always want some help paying your bills, because your income is rarely enough to cover your expenses in your original home, and your husband usually has a higher, more secure salary. Often, you worry first and foremost about paying basic bills like utility, food, and rent, and just surviving financially. Compared to others, you and other women in your situation are the most likely to fall down the economic ladder and end up in serious financial trouble.

Once in a while, you, but more often your husband, are better off money-wise and the first to move out, like Bolta, who divorced Carter. To improve her situation, Bolta found an affordable place in a different neighborhood, but still in her son's school system. However, the change was expensive, time-consuming, and socially unnerving.

Backlash from youngsters, in-laws, ex-spouse, and friends is common. Bolta's son Max was upset and missed his stepdad. Carter's parents and sister were hostile toward her. Some of their friends stuck by him, didn't feel they could continue their relationship with her as well, and dropped her socially. Most of all, Bolta resented having to tell her boss and so many other people about her split, even though they were usually sympathetic. She was embarrassed and chastised enough without opening herself to more criticism.

Your husband normally has the social edge. Many think that if you're divorced once, you have minor emotional issues, but if you're redivorced, you must have major ones that caused your second split. So, most blame and criticize you and are reluctant to help you. Instead, they side with your husband. As a first-timer, he can count on social support and aid from his family and friends, including help finding someone new. However, no one asked Carter how he was coping with the loss of his stepson, since they falsely thought it was unimportant.

Especially if left, your husband tends to be devastated and suffers a blow to his self-esteem. Unfortunately, he seldom receives professional guidance and support. In the few cases where he does, he is normally a confident father with children from the marriage, who left you for another woman. Once he decides to leave, he is rarely upset unless he is concerned about his youngsters. His chief therapy goal is often retaining his relationship with his children and making sure they are okay. After, he is happier if he is close to them and his new love.

Commonly, you, like many wives, receive some help from others, but not as much as the first time you divorced. Occasionally, you are slammed with criticism. Sometimes, even your family lights into you and tries to push you back into your marriage, if you are the one who wants the breakup and do not have a very good reason for leaving him.

Although you are more likely to receive professional advice than your ex-husband, you rarely do unless you have children from the marriage, have a substance abuse problem, and/or he left you for someone else. If you do, you worry about how your problems and the divorce will affect your children, or losing custody. Many times, riddled with guilt and low self-esteem, you are envious of your ex-husband and his new love and depressed.

His Divorce is Often Harder than Hers
Just over half the men (54%), said their divorce was harder than their wives'. The other men claimed to have an easier (23%) or equally difficult (23%) split. This is the opposite of what hybrid-first-time women said.

Divorce Coach and Support Group
Most, especially the men, benefit from a divorce coach or therapist and a support group.

Stress, Trauma, and Relief Patterns

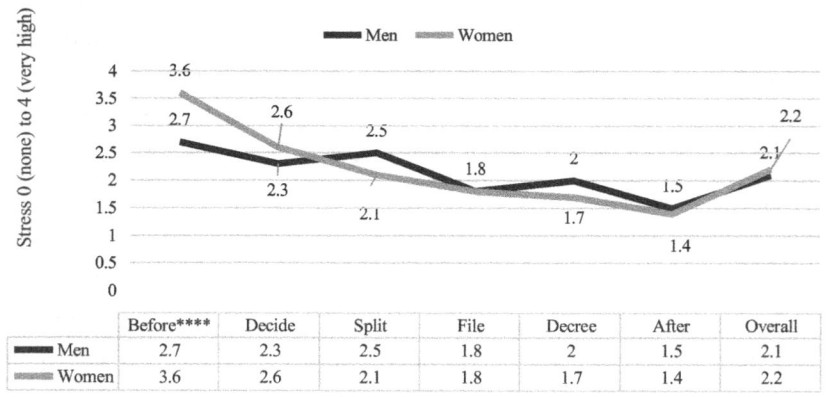

Figure 13-1: Mean stress for each stage and overall for uni-redivorced men (once wed) and women (twice wed). Note: Before is predecision. After is first year postdivorce. Adults:150 (men 58; women 92). ****p=.000.

Graph Takeaways:
1. Most women have "alpine stress." Initially, they have intense stress that dissipates quickly.
2. Typically, the man has less stress than his wife at the start, but as much if not more distress than her from the separation until the divorce decree.

WOMEN HAVE ALPINE STRESS

Unlike other research women, you normally have "alpine stress." Like a skier who starts at the top of a lofty mountain and descends quickly, your stress starts high, but falls rapidly. Overall, your journey is a relatively low stress breakup, even though you usually list more aggravations than your ex-husband. Half the time, you fume during the first half of the breakup, but defuse long before the divorce decree. Characteristically, you have extensive relief near the end—better health and more energy, fun, and confidence. Unlike others, you are rarely lonely.

There were exceptions. If you were left for another woman, have emotional or substance abuse problems, or have severe financial strain, you may experience a tough time, even afterwards.

> **Toughest Time for Men**
> Most men in this group have their roughest time either before or after the separation. Other men and women rarely go through this.

MEN TOUGHING IT OUT

You do not swoosh down the stress slope as gracefully or quickly as your wife. Instead, you are in unending "deep powder" convinced that you will not get off the stress slope in one piece. Commonly, you erupt with high outrage and hostility—rail endlessly about the hard-hitting situation and your impossible wife. Worried and lonely, you regularly enter and get stuck in a deep funk. Throughout, you are twice as likely to be depressed, lonely, or drink too much than your wife. Roughly half the time, you are very upset at every point during the divorce, gain or lose weight, and think that you had a rougher divorce than your wife. Other times, you decide that your experience was easier (23%) or about the same (23%).

You are often more upset than the second-time men—in part because this is only your first and in part because you rarely initiate the split or see it coming. In many ways, you typically have the toughest men's divorce with the most difficulties, the most trauma, the lowest relief during the breakup, and the lowest self-esteem early after the divorce. However, you walk away from the experience without your wife's second divorce tag.

Your separation is seldom the most difficult stage. Your greatest anguish usually occurs before you separate, if you initiate the divorce like Pug or the decision was mutual; or near the end of the divorce, when you do not. Unlike your wife, you rarely have any relief.

More fortunate couples agree that the marriage is not working and decide to divorce simultaneously. When this happens, your breakup is much easier on everyone. You work cooperatively to expedite the split; both of you have moderate and the lowest stress and few difficulties throughout; and best of all, you often end up friends. Normally, at first, you retain a relationship with your stepchildren, but you may fade from the picture as you move on.

First Year Postdivorce/ Transition Year: Easier for Her Than Him

When the wife initiates the split (which you usually do), you are usually in relatively good shape afterwards. You feel upbeat, indifferent toward your ex-husband, and better off than he. Half the time, you are actively dating or recoupled. Your husband routinely emerges from the divorce still upset, usually more upset than the typical redivorced man. Characteristically, he misses you, ruminates on your past marriage, and is not dating. Over the next year, he often starts going out socially and becomes happier, less irritable, and more self-confident.

On the other hand, if your husband initiates the divorce, the reverse happens. You are the most upset, while he feels relieved, has little stress, and is dating or recoupled long before the two of you get divorced.

Over the transition year, both of you inch forward socially, solve your practical problems, and heal further. Oftentimes, the person who started out in the worst shape, usually the husband, catches up. By year's end, almost everyone is reasonably okay, despite ongoing self-doubts. Still, you may need more time to feel all right.

The Tables Turn

By the third divorce anniversary, some wives are still happy, but others have done a flip-flop adjustment. When you split, you were almost always all smiles, relieved, and at least on the surface doing much better than not only your husband but also most other women. Half of you continue to be happy. But half are frowning. You are dissatisfied with your financial situation, social life, and health. Commonly, you are so distrustful of both yourself and others that you have slammed the door on another romantic relationship. If you have a new love, your relationship is defined as going steady. You are rarely living with him, with or without a wedding ring. Regularly, you have not figured out how to get back on your financial feet or how to make an interesting, happy life.

Half the ex-couples are like Savannah and Pug. They have a civil relationship. Bolta and Carter were like the other half: they never saw each other. Bolta avoided him from the separation on.

After the transition year, Carter did not want to see Bolta either, although he still cared about his stepson and made a point of calling him on his birthday every September.

Case Examples:

CASE EXAMPLE: SCARLETT DIVORCED ELVIS

Scarlett recalled her divorce:

> Before we split, I wept easily, chain-smoked, and ate a lot of junk food. I gained weight. My mind spun wildly trying to figure out why I was in this bind again. Once we separated, my crying and worry decreased, but didn't stop. I was less lonely and felt mildly relieved. Yet, it was tough being a single mom. Money was tight. Elvis was unable to help me with the bills. He had his own ones. I went on welfare. Luckily, Mom helped watch the kids, so I could date. A year after the divorce, life was better. My marriage was a bad memory, but it rarely crossed my mind. Elvis meant nothing to me. I hoped that he would find a new honey, so he would leave me alone. Two years later, the kids and I are okay. I date occasionally, nothing too serious.

Elvis was upset from the separation through the first-year transition. During the split, he was depressed, agitated, lonely, and angry with Scarlett for deserting him. He drank heavily on the weekends. Immediately afterwards, he was gloomy and bitter, but less irritable, drank less and less often, dated frequently, and was no longer lonely. A couple of years later, Elvis was fine. He remarried and moved to Georgia. From then on, he carried a photo of Elle in his wallet, but only saw her when she visited him in July and then again when he came North to see her and his parents for Christmas. In between, they texted, phoned, or used email to keep in touch.

Case Example: Bolta divorced Carter

In earlier chapters, Carter recounted part of his marriage story. Here, I start with Bolta's recollection of her marital history, including her first and second, and then add to Carter's earlier version.

As in so many uni-redivorces where the wife's parents are divorced, Bolta bolted from her marriage, and had an easier divorce and better early recovery than her prior husband, Carter. Afterwards, she was optimistic and dating. Bolta said:

> I have been married twice. In the first, I had my son Max. A couple years later, my first husband became depressed and stopped talking to me. He wouldn't get any help. So, I left. His second wife told me he did the same thing to her. After she left, he committed suicide. I feel awful that this happened, but there was not much either of us could have done. He was the problem not us.
>
> At 28, I married Carter. This was his first. We were too quick to marry. My parents disliked him and his parents disliked me. We both resented their attitudes. Yet, we didn't know how to handle it or fix it. Unlike my first, Carter added fun and was initially upbeat.
>
> That's part of the reason I married him. He drew bright, happy scenes for our home. In the living room, he hung an ocean scene depicting the three of us walking on a pink-sanded beach at the edge of a turquoise sea. In the kitchen, he added a

sketch of Max with a gigantic basket of citrus fruit and bananas in his arms. Evenings, he played his guitar to soothe away our daily troubles. This was the good part. The bad part was that I was the only one with a full-time job. Carter worked part-time and rarely sold a painting. I was angry he didn't get a better job. Upset too, he said that I wasn't committed to our marriage and his artistic goals.

I suggested that we separate and filed for the divorce. I went through hell at the start before I decided to leave. Carter was miserable, too, but less so. As I have good credit, but he doesn't, I had to find a new apartment. He stayed in our old place. Max and I took our personal items like clothing and our computers. Carter kept everything else. Higher expenses—attorney fees, replacement furniture, and higher rent—all ate into my income. Single parenting was a new issue. I had to find a carpool, so Max could go to his basketball practice and games. When we settled into our new place, life got better, but Carter's life got worse and his problems spilled over on to us. He didn't show up on time for art shows, lost weight, and squeaked by financially. When we met to settle things, he was angry and needed money. I bought his sketch of my son carrying a fruit basket and paid his first two months' rent. After the divorce, I was okay. Max was upset for months—he missed having a stepdad. Carter was depressed, bitter, and in a financial mess for the first year after. I avoided Carter whenever I could. We're doing fine now. Max is doing well in school and is in the Big Brothers Program. I like my job and new steady.

Carter's story below details how he had a harder divorce than his wife during and early afterwards, but not three years later.

> I was okay until Bolta left with Max. I painted bright, colorful Haitian scenes depicting parrots, orange sunsets, and exuberant dancers. Afterwards, my paintings became dark. I listened to the blues and hummed sad songs. I was in a mental fog, lonely, and felt like a failure. My thoughts kept spinning around as I struggled to understand the breakup and what was happening. Early after, I was still miserable, thought about my marriage nonstop, missed Bolta and Max, and didn't date. A couple of years later, I found Madeline. Since then, things have been great, but I still think about Max and wonder how he is doing.

THINGS TO REMEMBER ABOUT UNI-REDIVORCE:
- Normally, women are the divorce seekers and reach their decision in about 18 to 24 months. Men, who initiate the divorce, often finalize their decision quicker or in about a year. Both are much more variable in their decision-making speed than others.
- She usually has a relatively easy breakup and good early adjustment compared with him and other women. He tends to have a traumatic split and lower early adjustment compared with his wife and other men.
- Sometimes, at the three-year mark, she has done a recovery flip-flop and instead of doing better than most men and women, she is not doing as well.
- Half the ex-couples have a civil, non-intimate relationship three years afterwards.

CHAPTER 14

Bi-redivorce: What to Expect When *Both* Are Redivorcing

CHEYENNE AND HOLLY COMPARE NOTES

Holly emerged from the parking lot, took a right turn, and walked briskly toward Bob's Grill. She was eager to meet her high school friend, Cheyenne, for lunch and to catch up. When they last met two years ago, they had just celebrated their thirty-seventh birthdays and were remarried to twice-married men. Since then, both had divorced.

From Christmas cards, they knew about each other's divorces, and that Holly wanted hers, but Cheyenne had not. Neither, however, knew the other's full story. Lunch would fill in the details. Holly reached the restaurant first and had her eye out for her friend. Ten minutes later, she spotted her and called out,

"Cheyenne, I'm over here."

"Hi, thanks for getting here early. It's starting to get packed."

"I've ordered Dell's Lemonade for us. I know how you like it."

"Thanks. It may be only June tenth, but it's sure hot today." Cheyenne said.

"So, what's happening with you?"

"Remember how you had a harder first divorce than me? Well, this time, I bet I had the worst one," declared Cheyenne.

"Maybe. My first was his decision, but this time, I was the one who wanted out and I was prepared," Holly said.

"You prepared?"

"I figured out the practical stuff...how to make it financially on my own; where I wanted to live; and other things. Then, I started looking around to see if I could find someone else."

"How'd you check who was out there?"

"Whenever I went on a business trip or some other place by myself, I slipped off my wedding ring, just to see what would happen," Holly revealed.

"And?"

"From time to time, guys would approach me. They'd sit next to me on the commuter train or in the cafeteria, and strike up a conversation. I didn't go out but my confidence grew. I decided I could find someone else nicer. I contacted my lawyer and asked for a divorce. Then, I took off my wedding ring for good."

"How'd your children react?" Cheyenne asked.

"My two are from my first and didn't like Jake or his kid, so they're fine. The three kids caused a lot of our arguments and marital troubles, but they weren't the whole story. We clashed on a lot of things," Holly quipped.

"Sounds familiar. I didn't have the best relationship with my step, either. Comes with the turf. Do you have someone new, Holly?"

"Kind of. I've got a steady, but we have an understanding. We're not going to live together until we are serious and we can all get along. I'm still cautious. I don't want to rush into another mistake. It's a work in progress. Now what's with you, Cheyenne?"

"Ralph suddenly left me for the next-door neighbor."

"Whoa! Next door neighbor?"

"Yup. I was shocked, didn't see it coming. The two of them just moved out one day to a rental twenty minutes away."

"Tough break."

"I was a basket case for months. I felt abandoned, humiliated, and jealous of Ralph and his new girlfriend. My self-esteem tanked. I cried a lot. Couldn't sleep at night. Lost weight. By the divorce last year, I was better, but still struggling and miserable."

"Sounds like you're still upset."

"Guess so. I have bad days. I feel like a two-time loser and resent what happened and my situation. Until a couple of weeks ago, we both taught in the same building. I just transferred to another school, so I don't have to work with him anymore. What a relief!"

"Have you found someone new, Cheyenne?"

"No, for now I'm not interested. I'm scared the next guy will leave me, too. I don't trust men any more...financially, emotionally, or otherwise. I don't think I will ever find the right one or be happily married."

"I wonder if I can be happily married, too. We have good jobs. We're friends and survivors, so we'll be okay," Holly remarked to break the tension.

"Let's drink to us," Cheyenne offered, raising her glass.

"To us!" They clicked glasses. "Let's order lunch, I'm starved."

> **Exit Preparation**
> Considerate second-timers try to make the divorce decision a joint one, are open about their feelings, and don't have an affair before they separate.

Landmines

The largest group of divorced couples in this study includes two remarried spouses—they make up half. Compared with others, they are usually older and have left longer first unions. Typically, when they marry, they are middle-aged, like Holly and Jake with adolescents from both prior marriages. Unlike the other remarriages, they enter these new relationships on equal footing, both knowledgeable about marriage and split-ups. Each brings with them potential complications in the form of first-marriage children, ex-spouses, resentments, and emotional scars.

Comparatively, they have a high risk for child-allied challenges and external interference. Major subtypes include the younger couple like Desirée and Saul with two or three sets of children or the older, more typical middle-aged couple like Holly and Jake or Beth and Nickolas with two sets of adolescents from their earlier marriages.

Who Initiates the Divorce?

In unhappy marriages, most women are usually the first to recognize their marital troubles, first to consider leaving, and as a result experience high early angst. Half are like Holly and initiate the split. Some unhappy wives, however, are hesitant to separate and don't start the divorce. Eventually, as the relationship deteriorates, their husbands begin thinking about ending their union, too. Although men are often the last spouse to contemplate divorce, once they begin considering it, they are usually quicker to decide than their wives. On average, male plaintiffs like Nickolas or Cheyenne's husband, Ralph, think about breaking up for about nine months, while female plaintiffs like Holly contemplate leaving for about fifteen months. Although women in other couples tend to initiate the divorce, in these couples, just as many men as women kick off these divorces.

Generally, the woman starts the official proceedings if she is under forty or has a new intimate relationship. Typically, when the man begins the legal action, he is over forty, financially secure, and has a new lover. Personal characteristics determine the dissolution speed. Younger, outgoing women move at a moderate to quick pace to begin the separation and end the marriage. Likewise, over 40, confident husbands move at least at a moderate pace to dissolve their marital ties, unless, of course, their wives act first. Other men and women are slower to exit.

> **Be Kind**
> After all you did love that person at one time.

> **What To Do with Fluffy?**
> If you both want to keep your pet, consider
> 1. Giving the pet to the one who is most upset and lonely. She or he needs Fluffy's companionship and calming influence. OR
> 2. Breed Fluffy. You can have the original pet and your ex can have an offspring.

HE HAS FEWER PROBLEMS THAN OTHER MEN AND WOMEN

The typical husband has an easier divorce than most of the other men and women in this study. Especially if middle-aged, he rarely has second marriage children, so he seldom worries about children's complications, including financial issues such as child support or social issues such as criticism. On the flip side, his wife almost always has a longer list of tasks or challenges to resolve than everyone else in this research report. These, of course, are just the averages. Men like Holly's husband, Jake, have a tough time because they don't want a divorce, while women like Holly want the divorce and have an easier exit.

Nonetheless, economic concerns are common and a top issue. Half the men and three out of four women face new monetary troubles and turmoil. About half the couples argue over how to divide their joint property. Usually, they are discussing the equity in their home, vehicles, furniture, and bank balances.

Sometimes, they must include other items such as credit card debt, antiques, retirement benefits, a small business, or a family pet. For most women, fiscal troubles are more troublesome and severe than for their husbands.

While men rarely complain about a drop in their incomes, half the women do. Some women are scared they can't make ends meet. Normally, she downsizes her home and lifestyle. Income is no longer joint income and drops. He seldom chips in as much toward her household and other costs, so her expenses go in the other direction—up. Beth could no longer afford to live in the same house, let alone the same section in town. Instead, she chose a smaller place in a new neighborhood and reduced the family's discretionary spending. That way, she could shoulder the costs of running her new residence without any help from Nickolas.

In contrast, many of these men continue to have solid, stable salaries; higher incomes than their second wives; and despite higher costs, don't have to drastically downsize their lifestyle. Sometimes, men like Nickolas can afford to stay in their current marital home and assume the mortgage or rent payments and do. Alternatively, other men move to a new residence to get a fresh start or have already left as part of the separation process. Like most couples, the loss of Beth's income had less of an impact on Nickolas than the loss of his income on her.

Couples with second-marriage preschool or school-aged youngsters like Cheyenne and Ralph or Desirée and Saul, face multiple child-related issues such as worrying about their children's welfare and concern about their distress.

Middle-aged couples with only first-marriage children seldom worry about their youths, quite the contrary. Children in these homes usually help their parents through the split with empathy, chip in more with the housework, and may even get a part-time job to help financially. Pleased with their split-up, Beth's Sarah and Nickolas's teens assisted their parents in multiple ways. While many parents are relieved, if not enthusiastic, about becoming single again, some of course are not. Middle-aged, stay-at-home mothers who don't initiate the split often feel rejected and resent their new single status. Introverted men and women, divorce opposers, and those with substance use complications have more challenges and are slower to adjust to the dissolution both during and after the formal divorce decree.

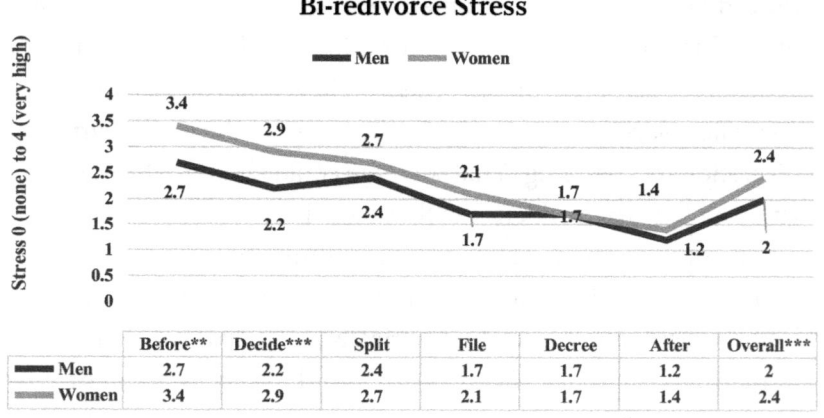

	Before**	Decide***	Split	File	Decree	After	Overall***
Men	2.7	2.2	2.4	1.7	1.7	1.2	2
Women	3.4	2.9	2.7	2.1	1.7	1.4	2.4

Figure 14-1: Mean stress for each stage and overall for bi-redivorced men and women. Note: Before is the predecision stage. After is the first year postdivorce. Adults: 199 (women 126). * $p < .05$; ** $p < .01$; *** $p = .001$.

Graph Takeaways:
1. Most women have very high or high stress during the first two stages and then moderate stress for the remainder of the split. Afterwards, she usually has mild distress.
2. Most men have moderate stress throughout the split and then low stress afterwards.
3. His divorce is usually much easier than hers.

At first, most are miserable. If they initiated or wanted the divorce, like Holly or Cheyenne's husband Ralph, they are the most upset at the start, either during the predecision or decision stage, but begin to heal and feel better as soon as they separate. As the divorce continues, they ordinarily feel better and better.

However, those who don't want the divorce are just beginning their misery upturn. They often have upside-down U-shaped distress. After the divorce decision, their unhappiness escalates, especially after they separate. From then on, divorce-opposing women are like Cheyenne. Midway, Cheyenne was livid, downhearted, and lonely. She lost weight and had insomnia. Near the end of her divorce, her misery declined gradually until she was okay at the end of the transition year, but still dragging emotionally. She felt like a two-time loser and thought finding a future, solid marriage was hopeless.

Between five and six men out of ten have high strain during the first half of the breakup. That rate drops in half by the filing and divorce decree phases, and then plunges again to one in five thru the first year post-decree.

Stress for women descends like a staircase, with high strain common at the start. Out of every ten women, high stress impairs eight in the pre-decision, seven during the decision, six at the separation, four at the filing, three at the divorce decree, but only two thru the first year afterwards. The typical woman is like Holly. Holly's stress plummeted from high at the start, moderate midway, and low at the close.

Although at least some grief continues until the end of the marriage, divorce plaintiffs, as well as half of their spouses, replace despair with hope and relief by midway. Most report some relief. As relief, optimism, and calm replace anger, pessimism, and stress, work becomes easier and health improves. Month by month, as they edge toward the conclusion, more and more join the forward-looking, happier camp. Yet, just below the surface, self-doubts usually hover and bubble up from time to time.

> **Visualize Better Times**
> Visualize that you and your children are okay for about 15 minutes every day. If you have joint children, imagine that you are cooperatively co-parenting them.

WHAT IS IT LIKE AFTERWARDS?

During the first-year transition, most feel reasonably okay. Typically, they are calm, happier than before, and occasionally think about their recent past. Nonetheless, they seldom trust either their ex-spouse or a new partner. Only one in five is indifferent toward their ex. Translation: only one in five is almost over their divorce and unscarred by it.

At the bottom of the recovery spectrum, Cheyenne and about half the deserted partners sweat through poor adjustment in the early postdivorce era. Stuck in their old marriage and downhearted, one in five still wears a wedding band both physically and emotionally. They love or hate their ex-spouses, frequently think about their past, and don't date. They are heartbroken and wish that they could erase their dissolution or cause their ex-spouse to love them again and prompt reconciliation. Rarely do they get their wish.

Over the first year afterwards, men are like Holly's husband, Jake. Jake grew progressively more negative toward Holly as he became closer to a new partner and mended. Women, on the other hand, don't do this. Holly stayed indifferent toward Jake, even as she inched closer to a new lover.

Men have a distinct advantage in the dating arena. About half the women (or twice as many women as men) never or rarely date.

Cheyenne did not date. At the other end, close to half the men or 50% more men than women have a new partner—they are going steady, cohabitating, engaged, or remarried. Cheyenne's second ex, Ralph, was cohabitating. Few, however, rewed within four years.

Recoupling predicts these men's well-being. Un-partnered, ex-husbands such as Samuel are downhearted, anxious, and emotionally stuck in their previous marriage. Conversely, men such as Cheyenne's ex Ralph, who love a new partner, are upbeat, calm, and emotionally detached from their ex.

Three years after, half are in a serious relationship—going steady, partnered, engaged, or remarried. Many of these partnered individuals, especially among the women, instigated their re-split because they had found a different partner.

Remarriage rates, nevertheless, are still low with less than 20% rewed. To emphasize the point, almost everyone married their second spouse within three years after their first divorce, like most other once-divorced men and women. Moreover, at least at this point, many are adamant that they never want to marry again. This wedding ban is rooted in cynicism. Too often, they don't trust other potential lovers. Or, they doubt their own judgment as to whom they can safely love again.

Nonetheless, long term most are in good spirits and satisfied, particularly if they have a solid income and social life. During the three years, many couples have done an adjustment flip-flop. Instead of the man being happier than his wife, now it is the opposite. Most women are better off and more satisfied with their lives than their ex-husbands. Why?

The change was mostly due to certain women catching up with, if not speeding by, their ex-husbands. Many were like Beth. They not only wanted to get back on their feet, but also had the financial and social wear with all to do so—not via a new lover like their husband—but rather through deep social connections with friends and family and an interesting life. Some benefited from counseling. Others figured it out on their own. They used the last couple of years to claw their way back to a happy spot.

Half, including Beth and Nickolas, have a civil, non-intimate relationship with their former mate. The other half, however, have either a hostile or no relationship with their second ex-spouse like Cheyenne and Ralph.

> ***Don't Flaunt a New Love***
> If you're the first to find someone new, don't flaunt your new relationship.

> ***Be a Gentleman***
> Commonly, men feel increasingly negative toward their wives as they grow closer to someone new. Be a gentleman, stay respectful, and don't act on your emotions.

Case Studies

DESIRÉE DIVORCED SAUL: HIS, HERS, AND OUR CHILDREN

In their early thirties, Desirée was a teacher's aide, while Saul was a construction worker. Both were splitting after a brief second marriage. They had a teenage son from his first marriage, a grade school daughter from her earlier marriage, and a preschooler from their relationship. Desirée divorced Saul, because she felt unloved, abused, and that he cared more about his son than her or the other two children. Saul, in turn, felt Desirée discriminated against his teenager. Desirée described her divorce:

> I was on a stress rollercoaster. Stress was high when we first had marital problems, later when

we initially separated, and again at the divorce decree. In the roughest times, I had insomnia at least twice a week, hated Saul, and lost weight. Between these bad times, things were better, but not great. I slept well at night, felt relaxed, and was healthier. Yet, I still got upset when I talked about the breakup. Afterwards, I was relieved. My first and second divorces were equally tough.

Like other substance abusers, Desirée's husband, Saul, dealt with high stress late in the uncoupling and was very unhappy for a long time afterwards. Even a year after the marriage ended, Saul whined about his plight; with gnashing teeth and tears in his eyes, he railed on endlessly about his traitorous wife to his family, friends, co-workers, and even strangers. Three years later, both Saul and Desirée were happier, satisfied with their lives, and cohabiting with others, but neither wanted to marry again.

Ralph Divorced Cheyenne: His and Our Children

As the initiator of her first divorce, Cheyenne had a hectic, but comparatively easy breakup. At 23, she divorced Watson, secured a scholarship, and went back to college. By 26, she received her teacher's accreditation and a high school history position. On the job, she met her second husband, Ralph, a recently divorced mathematics teacher her age. They had two children—Lilac from this marriage and Rose from Ralph's first family. Five years into the marriage, Ralph left to live with their neighbor, Sabrina. Cheyenne had no idea that Ralph had been having an affair and was about to leave her. Stunned, Cheyenne was initially confused, then hurt and upset. She had upside-down, u-shaped distress; her stress climaxed when Ralph departed to live with his new girlfriend, and then after about six months, dropped thereafter. To quote Cheyenne,

I was miserable, especially just after Ralph left. A month later, I had to move to a cheaper rent to make ends meet. I carried a bottle of gin with me, even when I drove. When I became anxious, I took a sip of gin to settle my nerves. I lost weight and thought non-stop about my marriage. Many nights I couldn't sleep as our problems kept rolling around my head or I had nightmares. I had this recurring bad dream about Ralph and Sabrina. Over time, my anxiety seeped away like water draining from a tub. When the divorce came thru, I was relieved and stopped drinking during the day. I changed jobs to get away from him. I started dating a couple of years afterwards, but nothing too serious.

Lilac and I spend our leisure time on church activities or sports like biking. The Methodist Church is always doing something—chicken potpie dinners, Bingo, and Sunday socials. Last summer, we helped our church build a Habitat for Humanity House. Lilac still sees her dad and stepsister Rose every other weekend and a couple of weeks in July. Lilac and Rose like doing things together.

Ralph was miserable until he started his affair and decided to leave. When he ran off with Sabrina, his stress dropped sharply, but returned from time to time as he dealt with practical issues like the settlement and wrath from hurt people—Cheyenne, Sabrina's ex-husband, and extended family. Ralph mistakenly thought leaving with a girlfriend would make it easy. Sometimes, it was, but often it wasn't. Sabrina's husband got so angry that he punched Ralph in the nose the first time he saw him after the split. Eventually, everyone calmed down, but it took a solid two years to get there.

Beth and Nickolas: His and Her Adolescents

Beth, a veterinarian, and Nickolas, an accountant, married about three years after they had both divorced their first spouses. Beth had two children from her first union, Sarah, twelve, and Ann, seven, while Nickolas had two teens, Bret, fourteen, and Carol, thirteen. Their three oldest children were upset by their parents' remarriage and did not like their new stepparents and stepsiblings. Ann, the youngest, like other younger children, accepted the remarriage and liked her new stepfather. Beth recounted her past marriage to Nickolas:

> We knew our older children did not like our dating, but we thought they would calm down once we wed. Instead, things got worse. My daughter, Sarah, was the most upset. She stopped speaking to me, got into trouble at school, and argued with everyone—Nickolas, his kids, and me.
>
> When his two visited on the weekends, they spent most of their time with Nickolas. If they were with my kids or me, they would start a scuffle. After three years of nonstop arguments, Nickolas and I threw in the towel. He verbalized the decision, but I knew the marriage wasn't working.
>
> At first, I missed his friendship, our conversations, and snuggling. I stopped going to church so I wouldn't see him with his new girlfriend. Ann liked her stepdad and was sad like me. My expenses went up with legal and counseling fees, higher rent, and higher utility costs to cover. Thankfully, I had a good job and could support my children and myself with cutbacks. The children didn't like the cuts. It was hard to find a new, affordable place we all liked in their current school district. We cut

food costs, bought clothes on sale, carpooled, and took a cheaper summer vacation.

We had a prenuptial contract. So, we didn't fight over money issues. Most of my divorced friends had a tougher time getting through it because they did not have a prenuptial agreement or a professional salary.

Several months after we settled into a new routine, my anxiety dropped. I felt better. Sarah was happier, dropped her negative behaviors, and helped out more at home. Both girls were sympathetic. By the divorce, Ann was okay and her former self. After, the kids and I were happier. Nickolas and I are still friends. We have found other people, but three years later neither of us has remarried.

THINGS TO REMEMBER ABOUT BI-REDIVORCE:
- Men and women are as likely to initiate the split.
- Typically, men have the easiest divorces in this study, while their wives have the hardest.
- Stress, wrath, depression, weight changes, and loneliness are common reactions during the first half. Relief is normal near the end of the breakup, particularly for those who initiated the divorce.
- Half the men and three out of four women struggle with economic challenges.
- Most have satisfactory, but incomplete adjustment during the first and third years after. Distrust is common and prevents many from a full recovery.
- Typically, men are happier than their ex-wives at the one-year mark, but many wives catch up and shoot ahead of their ex-husbands, such that they are happier at the three-year point.
- Few rewed by the third divorce anniversary.
- Three years later, roughly half the couples have a civil relationship.

CHAPTER 15

How Will My Children React? How Can I Help Them?

Quiz # 8: Children's Reactions

Q1. How old are your minor and adult sons, daughters, and stepchildren?
1. Ages of daughters? _____
2. Ages of sons? _____
3. Ages of stepdaughters? _____
4. Ages of stepsons? _____

Q2. Please go back to the prior question and circle the children and stepchildren from your recent marriage.

Q3. Select your child with the most recent birthday. What is this child's age, gender, and birth marriage/partnership?
1. Age: _____
2. Gender (Circle): Boy   Girl
3. From which marriage/relationship? (Circle)
   First Marriage   Second Marriage
   Another Relationship

Q4. Did this child want the remarriage? (Check all applicable)
1. __ No
2. __ Indifferent
3. __ Yes
4. __ Asked you to remarry
5. __ Unsure
6. __ Not applicable

Q5. How upset was this child during your recent divorce process?
1. __ Not at all upset
2. __ A little upset
3. __ Upset
4. __ Very upset

Q6. Please describe this child today with any five words or adjectives.
1. _____
2. _____
3. _____
4. _____
5. _____

Q7. Does/did this child have a negative emotional reaction to your recent separation or divorce? (Check all applicable)
1. __ Abandoned (felt)
2. __ Angry
3. __ Anxious
4. __ Confused
5. __ Felt deprived
6. __ Embarrassed

7. ___ Lonely
8. ___ Sad
9. ___ Scared
10. ___ Self-blamed
11. ___ Self-esteem lowered
12. ___ Worried
13. ___ Other (What? _____)
14. ___ None

Q8. Does/did this child have any negative behavioral reactions to your recent separation/ divorce? (Check all applicable)
1. ___ Behavior problems in school
2. ___ Delinquent
3. ___ Demanding
4. ___ Disobedient
5. ___ Drugs/alcohol
6. ___ Immaturity
7. ___ Lower grades
8. ___ Poorer health
9. ___ Self-control lower
10. ___ Suicidal
11. ___ Acted too grown up
12. ___ Other (What? _____)
13. ___ None of the above

Q9. Does/ did this child have any positive or indifferent reactions to your recent separation/ divorce? (Check all applicable)
1. ___ Calmer
2. ___ Delighted
3. ___ Happier
4. ___ Incifferent

5. ___ Relief
6. ___ Other (What?
7. ___ None of the above

Q10. Which of the following parent-related reactions does/did this child have to your recent separation/divorce? (Check all applicable)
1. ___ Blamed one parent
2. ___ Became closer to father
3. ___ Became closer to mother
4. ___ Disappointed in parents
5. ___ Feared loss of a parent
6. ___ Feared parent would stop loving him/her
7. ___ Reconciliation (wanted)
8. ___ Supported father emotionally
9. ___ Supported mother emotionally
10. ___ Withdrew from father emotionally
11. ___ Withdrew from mother emotionally

Q11. How would you characterize your current relationship with this child?
1. ___ Very poor
2. ___ Poor
3. ___ Ok
4. ___ Good
5. ___ Excellent

Children

Your children's reactions depend on you, your former spouse, and your child. If you take the high road, do whatever you can to put the best interests of your children first, and take good care of yourself; you are likely to reduce the short- and long-term difficulties for everyone. Most children mirror and react to their parents' outlooks and emotions. The sooner you and your ex-spouse recover, the sooner your children are likely to recover, too.

Parenting suggestions are listed below for making the process easier on your children. My advice is primarily for youngsters born or adopted during your latest marriage, but children from a prior marriage often benefit from these proposals, too.

After discussing these guidelines, I will consider how birth family, age, and gender affected children's reactions in this study. Then, I will discuss how to tackle your children's two most likely troubles—emotional and academic. My fourteen favorite rules will help your youngsters.

GUIDELINES:
1. **Tell your children that you love them every day.** Doing so will promote your children's happiness, confidence, and mental and physical health.
2. **Protect your relationship with your minor children.** If the two of you have decided you will move out, leaving your spouse and children in your home, work out a written parenting plan with your spouse before you leave.
3. **Don't leave just before or during a special event, unless you must to protect yourself or your children.** You don't want your children to link your divorce to their birthday or a holiday. Doing so could ruin that occasion for them in the future.
4. **Shield your child from nasty arguments.** Parental conflict can damage his or her emotional security and self-control. Many adult children from high-conflict homes have poor relationships, especially love relationships.
5. **Do your best to stay calm in front of your youngsters. Make the best of your situation. Work at remembering and sharing the good times.** Children mirror their parents' emotions and

outlook. If you and your ex-spouse are levelheaded and try to adapt to the new household routines, your children will probably do the same. If you are the primary custodian parent, it is important that you stay positive. In this study, upset parents tended to have upset children, but calm parents tended to have calm children.

One of the best tricks to being happy is to appreciate the good things in your life. Tell your children that from now on ,you will tell them three things you are grateful for every day, and that they are to do the same. Pick a gratitude time, like at bedtime. With practice, they will start looking for positives and be more upbeat.

6. **As tempting as it may be, don't say insulting things about your ex-spouse in front of your children.** If you do, your children may withdraw from you either when they are young or after they grow up and realize you prevented them from having a positive relationship with their other parent. If you can't afford to do something, say so, but don't go on to blame your ex for it.

7. **Discourage your youngsters from saying negative things about your (ex-) spouse or his or her new partner.** Children benefit from having a positive view of other people. Tapping down spousal criticism promotes the welfare of your children, including first-marriage ones, and makes both your and their interactions with your ex-spouse and next partner easier now and in the future.

8. **Maintain consistency and predictability in your children's lives.** Keep as much of your youngsters' lives the same before and after you separate. If possible, keep your children in the same school system and close to their best friends. Peers will help get your children through your breakup. When you set up a new residence, show your children your new household, including their new bedroom. This will help them have a

better understanding of where you and they live and add to their sense of belonging.
9. **Comply fully with your parenting schedule and financial arrangements.** Make your support payments on time. Make sure your children are ready to leave on time and/or pick up and return them promptly. If you can't avoid being late, call ahead to let your former spouse know about your delay.

    Commonly, divorcing couples don't trust each other. If you have joint children, one of your tasks is to establish a civil, trusting co-parenting team with your ex-spouse. Your children's welfare depends on this. Being prompt and sticking to your word helps reduce distrust and relieves stress on your youngsters.

    If this is difficult, remind yourself that compliance with your agreement is an investment in your children's long-term sense of emotional and financial security.

10. **Do whatever you can to keep the two of you in your joint-children's lives.** To do so, make school administrators aware of your divorce, any updated contact information for both parents, and put in a formal request that all school communications (including progress reports, teacher messages, announcements) be sent to both parents. Maintain open communication with your ex about your children's schoolwork and activities, and attend as many of their special academic and extra-curricular events. Encourage your children to email, phone, or Zoom you and their other parent. There is no reason why they can't talk to each of you at least a couple of times a week, if not daily.

11. **If your ex-spouse doesn't show up for set visitations or doesn't stay in touch with your joint children, there are things you can do to reduce their pain.** First, reassure your children that you love them. Second, explain that the absence has nothing to do with them or their self-worth. Third, have backup

plans, so they have other things to do if visits are canceled. Fourth, if you can, explain to your ex that it is important for the well-being of your children that they spend time with each of you. If this doesn't work, drop the issue. Fifth, try to foster relationships and outings with other relatives, including your in-laws, so your children have a sense of being part of a larger clan. Children benefit from having loving, extended kin, even if they are close to their siblings and parents.

12. **Be flexible and considerate.** Job obligations, sickness, flat tires, and other unpredictable events may mess up your routine. If you can graciously accommodate your ex's unexpected need to modify the schedule, you run a better chance that when you have similar troubles, your spouse will adapt as well and help you later.

13. **Postpone dating at least until you separate, and preferably not until after you divorce.** Early dating will make your divorce more contentious and harder for your youngsters. Even after the divorce, be cautious about introducing your children or ex to your dates until you establish a committed, stable relationship. Then introduce your children slowly with a brief initial interaction, and then have them spend progressively more and more time with the two of you. This will give your children time to adjust to your new partner. When you are certain, make sure they hear about it from you directly not from someone else.

14. **Lastly, please remember you are doing these things for your children, despite your ex-spouse's reactions.** Some people calm down and recover quicker than others. If your ex has a hard time being courteous, you will need to continue being polite for the sake of your children. Don't give up.

In my research, many men (and some women) grew more hostile toward their ex during the first year or two after the divorce. This was primarily true of men who were forming a serious, love relationship. A secondary cause was envy. Some were jealous of their former spouse's new relationship. After that, levelheaded individuals defused and could have a civil relationship with their former spouse.

The Child's Birth Family: First or Second?

How Do First-Marriage Children React?

First-marriage youngsters almost always navigate their parents' second divorce better than the first. Most are happier, indifferent, or at least ambivalent and find some positives to their new situation (Figure 15-1). The child's age and the length of your remarriage influence their relationship to their stepparent and their reactions to the divorce.

With brief remarriages, children are rarely upset by the second split and usually support their parents' decision. Commonly, children are temporarily confused, indifferent, happier, or relieved. They often think that you and they are just as well off now before the split, especially if you feel that way, too. If you are the mom, your school-aged and adult children usually chip in more around the house if you ask for it, are empathetic when you are distressed, and grow closer to you. Many dads can count on the same caring and increased closeness with their children, but this happens less often.

In longer second unions, you are in a different situation, especially when your children still live with you. Ask yourself these questions. "Is my child close to his or her stepparent? Am I unusually upset?" If your answer is no to both, your children usually handle your divorce well. Your minor and adult children mostly behave like children in short remarriages—indifferent, pleased, or assume things are okay for everyone after your divorce.

However, if you answer yes to one or both above questions, research indicates that your child's reaction depends on his or her age. Your minor child is likely to be ambivalent or have a negative reaction. Some youngsters are mirroring your distress. Others dislike losing a stepparent.

Your young son often resents losing his stepfather if he sees him as his emotional dad. His upset is especially high when this is the only father he recalls and he sees your split as a repetition of the loss of his biological dad. Repeat hurt is a double whammy and can be emotionally harder for him than the first time. If your daughter has a close relationship with a stepparent, the same is true. These children are especially distraught (angry, worried, and/or sad) if they are school-aged. Those who feel trapped in a loyalty conflict are normally angry and worried.

When school-aged children are upset, problems at school are common. They often get into scuffles or have lower academic performance and success. These can impact their self-esteem. Once this happens, your child is at risk for getting into all sorts of difficulties with school personnel or law enforcement. Fights, substance abuse, and depression are common. If you see these behaviors surface, you need to respond quickly. It is important that they talk out their feelings instead of acting them out.

If need be, help your child retain a relationship with his stepparent. Even spending one afternoon a month and having regular phone or email contact with your ex could reduce your child's distress. In some states, certain judges support co-parenting plans between a stepparent and parent when it is in the best interest of the youngster. The stepparent needs to request a co-parenting role after the divorce.[1] This is a new but increasing trend as more and more children are spending the bulk of their childhood with an alternative or supplemental mother or father.

Unless the divorce initiates a loyalty conflict between you and a beloved stepparent, adult children are rarely upset or concerned about the impact it will have on them. Typically, they check to see how the divorce is affecting you and their siblings. If you and they are okay, they calmly accept the situation. Conversely, if your family is distressed, expect them to be empathetic, emotionally supportive, but unhappy about your dissolution. Respect and don't interfere with your adult children's connection with your ex. They are adults and have a right to choose their personal relationships.

Seriously consider making your over-25-year-olds from your first union *part* of your support group. When needed and asked, these children almost always emotionally support their moms. Sometimes, they back their dads' too, but less frequently. This is due in part because fathers are less likely to ask for help.

Case Example: April

Seventeen and a high school senior, April was thrilled and relieved when her mother and stepfather divorced after a difficult nine-year relationship. Gone were the endless arguments and abuse. According to Lynn, April's mother, the breakup was due to her husband's infidelity, alcohol abuse, and long-standing marital unhappiness. This included emotional and physical abuse, and arguments about April. Despite their miserable marriage, April's mom was upset for several years. Her finances were tight. Her mother's darkest days were during the pre-decision and filing stages.

April helped by making dinner as soon as she got home after school and cleaned up afterwards. Once a week, she did her laundry and helped clean the house. As they spent more time together, they became closer. Six months after the divorce, her mother remained a bit anxious, but was calmer and started to take over household chores again. Although her mother wouldn't admit it until much later, she was better off without him.

Case Example: Bolta's Son and Carter's Stepson: Max

At 14, Max was upset and struggling with academic problems initially because of his parents' conflict and later because he missed his stepdad, Carter. From early on, Max couldn't concentrate on his schoolwork. As a result, he didn't complete his assignments on time, barely passed tests, and watched his previous B+ grade-point average drop to a C. After the separation, he was angry, depressed, and worried. He missed hanging out and doing things with Carter. He was unhappy that he rarely saw him and might never again have a live-in father. Until the split, he was emotionally close to his stepdad, his only father figure. Max hadn't seen his biological father since his parents divorced when he was a preschooler.

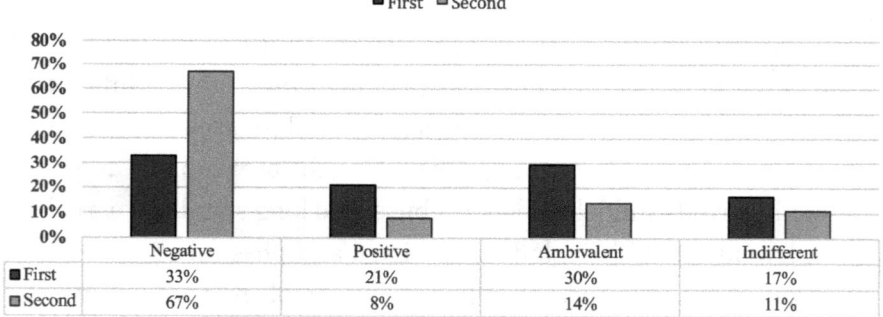

Figure 15-1: First and second marriage children with negative, positive, ambivalent, and indifferent reactions to a redivorce. Note: Children 182 (sons 91).

Graph Takeaways:
1. Second-marriage children have the most negative reaction.
2. First-marriage youth reactions fall into three equal groups: a) negative, b) ambivalent, or c) positive/indifferent.

> **Be Sensitive**
> Most second-marriage children, even adult children, are unsettled by their parents' divorce. Be sensitive when you tell them about your divorce.

Case Example: Maxine

Maxine, 17, blamed her stepfather's affair for her mother's second divorce. In a rage, she withdrew from her stepfather and stopped speaking to him. Worried and sometimes confused by her mother and stepfather's behavior, she acted out at school and got into trouble. Her work was either incomplete or late. She was now working part-time after school to help her mother pay for everyday expenses and earn some spending money. This further limited her study time.

Maxine had mixed feelings about her job. She enjoyed having her own money and increased independence, but resented that she had to work and share her earnings.

How Do Second-Marriage Children React?

If you have two children, one from a first marriage and one from a second marriage, expect them to react differently to your second divorce. Chances are, your older child is okay with the split, but your younger one is distressed. Unless you have severe problems in your remarriage, like physical or substance abuse, most children from this marriage are going to be upset, especially if they are school-aged. Many are confused, insecure, and want their parents to reconcile. Some are angry, worried, and have academic problems.

For certain children, the risk for problems is high. Among teenage boys, for example, scholastic and self-esteem difficulties are standard, but reversible with counseling and tutoring. On the bright side, your second-marriage child will probably have at least one positive emotional reaction, such as relief, and become closer to one, if not both of you. One in five is indifferent or unruffled by the divorce process.

First- and second-marriage children differ. Your first-marriage youngster is watching a parent and a stepparent separate, but your second-marriage child is watching two parents separate. Psychologically, the breakup of two parents is harder. A remarriage child has two distressed parents, who are less emotionally available to and supportive of him or her. In contrast, your first-marriage child sometimes has your first-marriage spouse. Uninvolved in your divorce, this adult can provide an oasis—stability, calm, and assistance with daily needs such as help with homework, personal troubles, and transportation. Just knowing that he or she has an unconflicted haven can make all the difference to your child, whether he or she chooses to take advantage of this.

Keep it Simple and Visual
1. Children benefit from a simple explanation of why you are divorcing and how their lives will change.
2. Make sure they know who will take care of them and when. A calendar can help a younger child "see" the new routine with mom days marked in one color and dad days highlighted differently.
3. Show your child your next home as soon as possible. This helps him grasp the new situation. Make sure he has his own room or spot in your place. This tells your child that he is loved and an important part of your life.

Another difference is age. Most second-family children are preschoolers or school-aged and younger than those from first marriages, who are often teenagers, if not adults. Your younger, remarriage children are still dependent on you, but your firsts usually are less so. So, most second-marriage youths are more upset by your split (See Figure 15-1).

The Child's Age During the Turmoil

As children mature, they typically become more socially insightful and independent from their parents. As a result, their reactions to a parental divorce change, too. For purposes of this discussion, children are divided into five age groups: those under five, elementary school children, adolescents, young adults, and mature adults.

THE YOUNGEST

This group almost always comes from the most recent marriage. Although affectionate and fun to be around, these youngsters have a limited understanding of personal relationships.

Infants are just starting to form an attachment to their mother and father. If they receive good physical care, feel loved, and are protected from conflict, they usually thrive.

Toddlers and preschoolers have egocentric thinking, don't understand cause and effect, easily misunderstand social situations, and don't understand time concepts like the future. They assume that everyone thinks and sees what they do. They're rarely empathetic because they don't understand your or another person's point of view or experience unless it is just like theirs. They may falsely think they are causing things like your divorce. Thus, you need to make sure they don't feel guilty about your divorce when they had nothing to do with your breakup. They live in the present and have a hard time grasping the future, including when future events will occur.

They do understand simple concepts like Mom and Dad are or are not getting along. Divorce is too abstract a concept for these young ones to grasp. They need a simple reason for the changes that are occurring and how it affects their schedule. Most importantly, they want to know who will take care of them. If possible, they benefit from as much consistency with their prior lives as possible, such as continuing the same daily routine.

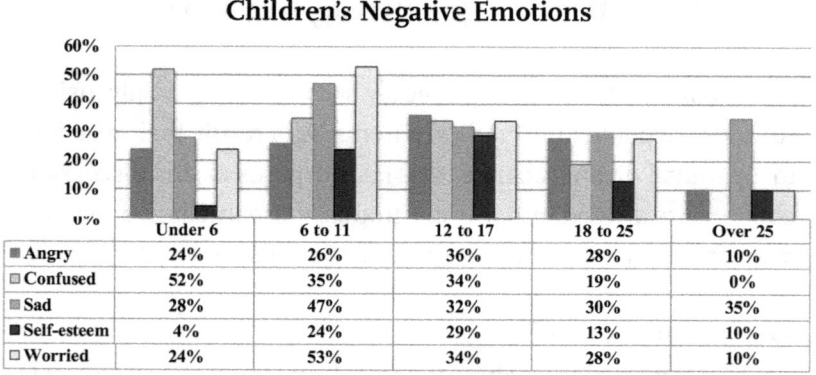

Children's Negative Emotions

	Under 6	6 to 11	12 to 17	18 to 25	Over 25
■ Angry	24%	26%	36%	28%	10%
□ Confused	52%	35%	34%	19%	0%
■ Sad	28%	47%	32%	30%	35%
■ Self-esteem	4%	24%	29%	13%	10%
□ Worried	24%	53%	34%	28%	10%

Figure 15-2: Children in each age group with each negative emotional reaction. Note: Children 182 (sons 91).

Graph Takeaway: School-aged children have the most negative reactions.

Two-thirds are angry, anxious, and/or sad. Most of them are also confused—too young and upset to understand what is happening. In many instances, they are mirroring your distress, so you can help them by taking better care of yourself and investing in your own recovery. As you calm down and adjust, so should they. Good parenting skills usually reduce child distress further. As they become calmer and recover, you will be less distressed, too. Child and parent adjustment is a two-way street with both affecting the other.

One-third are either indifferent or pleased. Children who seem indifferent are almost always under two, are first-marriage children, or have well-adjusted mothers and fathers.

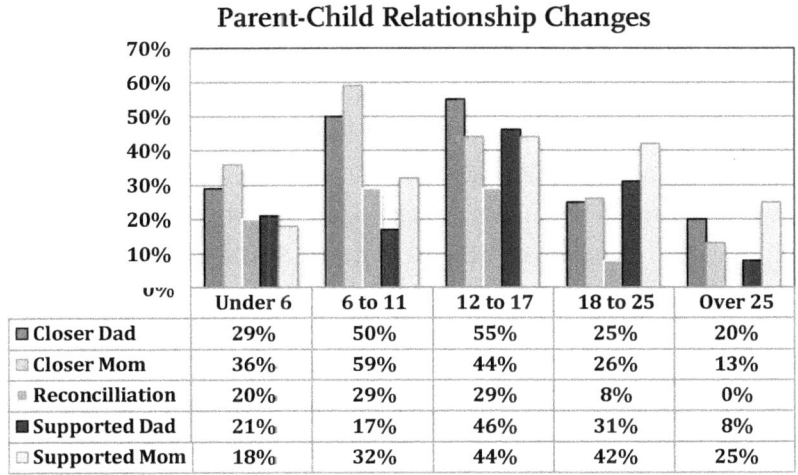

	Under 6	6 to 11	12 to 17	18 to 25	Over 25
Closer Dad	29%	50%	55%	25%	20%
Closer Mom	36%	59%	44%	26%	13%
Reconcilliation	20%	29%	29%	8%	0%
Supported Dad	21%	17%	46%	31%	8%
Supported Mom	18%	32%	44%	42%	25%

Figure 15-3: Children in each age group with each parent-child relationship change. Note: Children: 182 (sons 91).

Graph Takeaway: Many school-aged minors grow closer to and support a parent.

In this study, minor children's reactions in general were related to their parents' adjustment and reactions, especially their mother's if she had primary custody. Typically, upset mothers and fathers reported that their children were angry, anxious, or otherwise upset, while calm and happy parents reported well-adjusted children.

Most toddlers and preschoolers become closer to you and/or their other parent. Others withdraw if they blame you for the divorce or think that you are abandoning them. Yet, some want the two of you to reconcile.

> **Parent and Child Reactions Often Similar**
> In this study, minor children's reactions usually reflected their parents' reactions, especially their mother's if she had primary custody.

Toddler Case Example: Elvis and Scarlett's Daughter Elle

Elle was a second-marriage child, two and a half years old at the beginning of her parents' marital breakdown and almost five when the divorce was finalized. In their thirties, her father Elvis was a bus driver and her mom, Scarlett, was a stay-at-home mother during the marriage, but went on welfare after the divorce. It was his first divorce and her second one. Before the separation, Elle was a happy child who loved playing with her dolls, classmates, and neighborhood children.

For the first year after the separation, Elle was confused and anxious about the changes. Initially, she repeatedly asked: "Where is Daddy? When is Daddy coming home?" Much of the time, she clung to her mother. Saturdays, she was happy during her visit with her dad, but disappointed when he dropped her back home. As her parents calmed down from the dissolution, Elle became more cheerful, less clingy, and more outgoing. Living with her mother and half-sister, Elle became closer to both, but withdrew somewhat from her father during the two-year divorce process. From time to time, however, she asked her parents to get back together and she continued to enjoy her Saturdays with her dad.

Preschool Case Example: Desirée and Saul's Son Tucker

After seven years of marriage, Tucker's parents separated. In their mid-thirties, his mom, Desirée, was a teacher's aide, while his dad, Saul, was a construction worker. Tucker was their only child from the relationship. Desiree had a grade-school daughter from her earlier marriage and Saul had a junior high son from his first union.

Initially, five-year-old Tucker reacted to the turmoil with confusion, anger, fear, and sadness. After the separation, he often balked at going to preschool and got into trouble when he was there. He had temper tantrums, kicked or pushed other children off their tricycles, or threw classmates' things on the floor.

Despite his anger, Tucker always looked forward to visiting with his dad. Sundays after breakfast, he would sit by the front door with his dog "Happy" waiting for his father. In public, he would clutch his father's hand, while Happy ran along on his other side. After the divorce was finalized, he was calmer and his misbehavior subsided as his mother and father's arguments became less vicious and frequent, but he kept on asking his dad to come back home.

ELEMENTARY SCHOOL CHILDREN

Elementary school children (aged 6–11) are more varied in their reactions to their parents' second divorce than the youngest cluster for two reasons. First, unlike the younger ones, who are usually from the second union, these children are from both first and second marriages.

Second, they are typically less self-centered, more socially aware, and better able to reason and grasp time concepts. From age seven years they understand that you often see things differently than they do and, thus, can be empathetic with your situation. With a better grasp of the world, including a better understanding of how their life is changing and their parents' perspective and feelings, they are less apt to be confused. Nevertheless, they are literal thinkers, dependent on their parents, and don't comprehend all the ramifications of the divorce.

Often, these youngsters react negatively or ambivalently to their parent's disunion. Initially, they may be sad or worried, but later they typically adapt and become used to the situation. Ambivalent children, of whom there are many, are calmer, happier, and/or relieved despite their other negative reactions and the difficult situation. Expect your child to be relieved or cheerier, when the conflict stops, an abusive person departs, or you and your ex-spouse calm down and recover.

If you are caring and see them often, they are bound to grow closer to you. Because of this closeness, they often give you social backing and want the two of you to reconcile so you can stop the suffering.

Like the youngest, they want and benefit from a simple explanation of what divorce means, why their parents are splitting, and how their everyday life will change. In most homes, especially high-conflict ones, a simple explanation for a child is this.

> Mom and Dad don't get along because we disagree about some basic things. Mom and Dad are going to live separately so we will be happier. Mom will take care of you for the first half of the week and Dad will take care of you for the second half of the week. Let's mark Mom time with a blue crayon and Dad time with a red crayon on your calendar now so you can see your new schedule. Do you have any questions?

First and foremost, children want to know who is going to take care of them and that they will be well taken care of and loved. Children are almost always eager to see a parent's new home and, if possible, their new room or place where they can store things. This, in turn, helps children better comprehend the new situation, adapt, and feel loved and a part of your new life.

> **Who Will Take Care of Me?**
> Children want to know who is going to take care of them and that they are loved.

Case Study: Janet's and Stanley's Daughter Lilly

Like most elementary school girls during divorce proceedings, seven-year-old Lilly acted out initially. With counseling and the use of several tips (playing sports, daily gratitude sessions, and tutoring), Lilly's acting-out behavior disappeared, and she was much happier. The daughter of a remarriage (her mom Janet's first, her dad Stanley's second), Lilly had an older half-brother from her father's first marriage named Bobby, who was in high school. Unlike Lilly and most second-marriage children her age, her brother was pleased with the split.

At the start of the academic year, just four months after the couple separated, Lilly's teacher described her behavior in this report:

> **Marking Period #1:** Lilly is not keeping up with her studies. She is frequently sad, anxious, or in a mental fog. Often, she sits in class staring out the window, unaware of what is going on around her. When she is particularly unhappy, she sits by herself during lunch and recess, looking down at either her uneaten food or the ground.

At the end of the school year, just after the divorce decree, she noted Lilly's improved attitude.

> **Marking Period: Final:** Lilly is doing better in school. She is attentive, participates in class, and easily learns the day's assignments. She hangs out with her classmates at lunch and joins in with the other children during recess and gym.

Lilly's mother reported that her daughter's home behavior was similar during the breakup.

At the start of our divorce, Lilly usually went to the family room to watch TV, but didn't pay any attention to what was going on. She was miserable. She missed her dad when she was with me and missed me when she was with him.

On the advice of her pediatrician, her dad and I made some changes. We all started counseling. To get Lilly back on track, she got tutoring, took up swimming, and began a daily gratitude session before dinner. Within six months, she perked up, dropped her irritability and aloofness, and became more sociable and upbeat.

With the divorce behind us, we're both calmer and happier. Lilly enjoys being with the neighborhood kids, looks forward to her swimming sessions and team events, and is doing well in school. We're emotionally closer. We've come a long way.

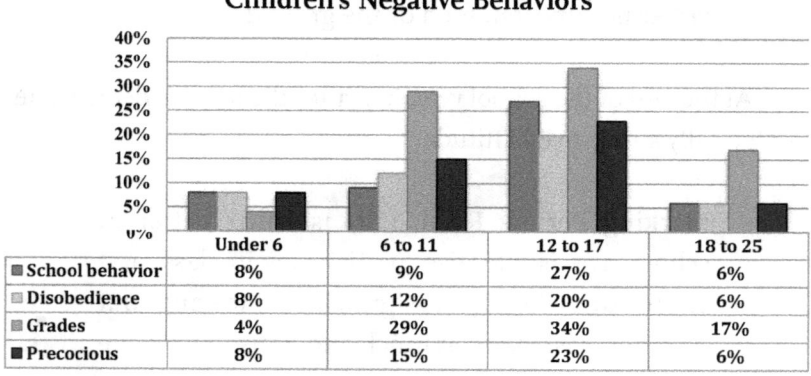

Children's Negative Behaviors

	Under 6	6 to 11	12 to 17	18 to 25
School behavior	8%	9%	27%	6%
Disobedience	8%	12%	20%	6%
Grades	4%	29%	34%	17%
Precocious	8%	15%	23%	6%

Figure 15-4: Children with each behavior problem in each age group. Note: Children 182 (sons 91).

Graph Takeaways:
1. Teens are the most likely to have behavior problems.
2. A drop in school grades is the biggest issue for teens.

TEENAGERS

With good abstract reasoning and a better understanding of human relationships than their younger siblings, teenagers almost always react intensely to your split. Close to half grow closer to and emotionally support you and/or your ex-spouse (Figure 15-3).

First-marriage teens who don't like their stepparents are usually pleased with the breakup. If this is true with your child, then their grades, behavior, and mood will usually improve, sometimes quite dramatically. If your relationship has been strained because they didn't like their prior situation, they are likely to befriend you and thank you for leaving their disliked stepparent or stepsiblings.

Second-marriage youths often respond in the opposite fashion. Some are angry with you, nervous, or have school problems such as lower grades, especially if they are boys. Many children slide into academic troubles and suffer lower self-esteem; they are twice as likely to have these problems as your first-marriage ones.

Teenage Example: Sarah

When Sarah was nine and her younger sister Ann was four, her parents divorced. Three years later, Sarah's mom, Beth, married Nickolas, an accountant with two teenagers, Bret and Carol. Like most young children, Ann quickly adjusted to the remarriage and liked her stepfather. However, Sarah was older and, like many teenagers, she was upset by her mother's remarriage, disliked her stepfather, and became rebellious. This is Sarah's story in her own words:

> When I was twelve, Mom married Nickolas, a know-it-all accountant with two teenagers: Bret and Carol. He was super neat and did everything just so. Before my stepfather moved in, my sister and I had few, if any, rules. Afterwards, Mom let him take charge with a whole set of new laws. My life was ruined. I had Mr. Perfect constantly telling me what to do and what to say. I hated Mom for putting me in this situation. I stopped talking to her and avoided my stepfather. In classes I didn't like, I did as little as possible. I found new friends who were mad at their moms for marrying a jerk. When we got together on weekends, we would share horror stories as we drank beer.
>
> When they visited, my stepsiblings caused all kinds of trouble. My stepbrother liked to tease me about something that I had done in school within earshot of Mom or Stepdad. Then, he would walk away and wait for them to scold me. My stepsister loved to hog the bathroom. If I showered after her, I would miss breakfast. My steps thought they could boss my sister and me around like Stepdad, because they were bigger and older than us.
>
> I found ways to get even. Mornings, I would use my stepbrother's towel. He would start yelling that I was a bitch and demand a clean one from Mom. To stop the mix-up, Mom went out and bought new towels in a different color for each of us. Mine was green. Bret's was blue. But I kept on using his. Then my stepfather put up hooks in our

bedrooms. So, I found something else to pretend to use—his toothbrush. I would run it under the water just before he used the bathroom. When he noticed and complained, I shrugged my shoulders and told him he was being silly. To stop this, Mom bought each of us a bathroom caddy. From then on, he kept his stuff where I couldn't get at it.

The nightmare lasted three years. When I was 15, Mom and Stepfather split up. My sister Ann liked Stepdad, so she was unhappy for a while. But God was I happy. My stepsiblings were thrilled too. I emailed my friends and celebrated for a full week. Then, I stopped messing with Mom and helped at home. Mom and I started talking again. Most of the time, I did my homework and I stopped drinking. I didn't really like my new friends or beer, anyway. But I missed fighting with my steps.

> **Adolescents React Strongly**
> Typically, adolescents have a strong reaction to a second split with first-marriage teens thrilled or relieved and second-marriage teens upset. Be prepared for these reactions.

Teenage Example: Katie

Katie's parents, Melissa and Donald, ended a 16-year relationship. After several years of marital unhappiness, Melissa precipitated the breakup by revealing her relationship with another man. For Donald, a firefighter in his early forties, this was a second divorce, while Melissa a librarian in her late thirties, was experiencing her first. They had three joint children: Katie and her two younger sisters.

During the divorce, Katie was so upset that her grade point average dropped from an A to a C. She felt emotionally torn between her two parents, angry, and put upon. Throughout, she comforted her younger siblings and her parents as if they were all children in the family and she was the mother. To quote Katie:

> After my parents separated, everyone was unhappy, and the house became chaotic. Dirty clothes piled up in the laundry. Many nights, Mom was too upset to cook. After about a week, I couldn't stand the clutter and turmoil. I took over many of Mom's old jobs, like cooking or helping my sisters with their homework. If someone looked unhappy, I would try to help.

After the divorce, Katie was relieved, because she had less work to do and felt less frazzled by the loyalty conflict. After, both parents said that they were now closer to Katie than before, because of her help during the split.

Teenage Example: Mathew

Mathew, 14, was the older of two children from his parents' remarriage. His father, Jonathan, was in his forties and leaving his second wife, Nancy, due to his affair. This was Nancy's first marriage. Jonathan was a financial analyst, while Nancy was an elementary school teacher.

Emotionally torn between his parents, Mathew was upset and had trouble paying attention in class and concentrating on his studies. His grades plummeted and, as a result, he became less confident academically and socially. He missed his father and wanted his parents to reconcile. He spent more and more time with his friends. They provided Mathew with a sense of independence as well as a time-out from the chaos at home.

Children's Positive Emotions

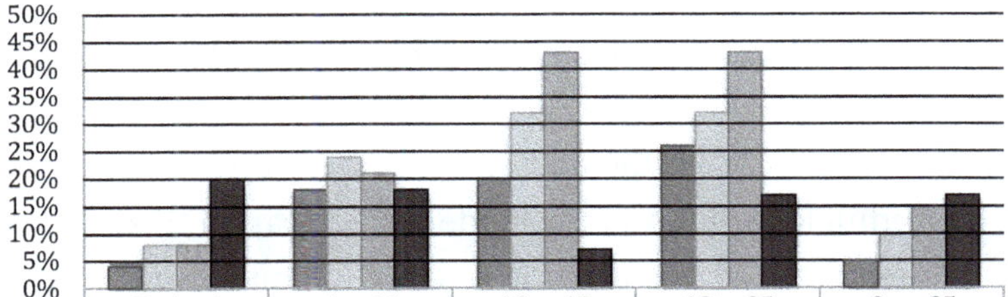

	Under 6	6 to 11	12 to 17	18 to 25	Over 25
■ Calmer	4%	18%	20%	26%	5%
■ Happier	8%	24%	32%	32%	10%
■ Relief	8%	21%	43%	43%	15%
■ Indifferent	20%	18%	7%	17%	17%

Figure 15-5: Children with each positive or indifferent emotional reaction in each age group. Note: Children 182 (sons 91).

Graph Takeaway: Twelve- to twenty-five-year-olds are the most apt to be positive.

Young Adult Children Are Not Immune!
In response to a second divorce, young adult children (18-25) are usually less upset than teens, but more upset than your children who are over 25. You will need to be sensitive to their emotional needs and distress.

YOUNGER ADULT CHILDREN: STILL SENSITIVE

Adult children fall into two age categories: the 18-to-25-year-olds and the over-25-year-olds. Although technically adults, the younger ones are often still in school, unemployed, living with you, and still somewhat dependent on you. If you have such a child, he usually has a stronger reaction than an over-25-year-old, but a milder reaction than one of your teens.

Younger adults are just as likely to react positively, negatively, or ambivalently with both positive and negative reactions. Like adolescents, they are usually relieved. Unlike their younger siblings, however, they almost always withdraw. At this stage, they are separating from their parents as part of their search for their own adult identity and independence. So, part of this withdrawal is age-based and has nothing to do with you or your divorce. If you are fortunate, some will help you.

Case Example: Linda

Even though this was a second marriage for Linda's mother and father, they both considered this their only real marriage. Years ago, Carol and Carl exited short, childless first marriages to other people. This remarriage lasted twenty years and produced two children: 20-year-old Linda and her younger brother. Linda was a college junior when the divorce was finalized. During her freshman and sophomore years when her parents were getting a divorce, she was upset, angry at her father, and caught in a loyalty conflict. This is Linda's story:

> When I went off to college, I had a new sense of freedom where I left my parents' constant bickering behind. They fought all the time, but I never thought they would separate. They loved each other.
>
> Halfway into my first semester, a policeman called and said my dad had reported that Mom was missing. His hunch was that Mom had simply left Dad. Before he agreed to investigate the case, he wanted to know from me if my mom might be in

trouble. I thought this was odd and asked him to find her. Two days later, Mom called and said she was at a conference. She hadn't told Dad because she was afraid he wouldn't let her go if she had. I accepted this explanation. I didn't understand what was happening.

Right after Christmas vacation, I got another call from Dad. Mom was gone again. This time, she had filed for a divorce. He asked me to talk her into coming back home. This was the beginning of one call after another from both Mom and Dad, trying to convince me to take their side against the other. I was unhappy, torn, angry, and couldn't do my homework. History courses reminded me of Dad, so I couldn't study that without getting upset. Theater and art reminded me of Mom, so I didn't want to do those either. Second semester, I got Ds on half my mid-term exams.

My friends were a great help. They told me that I should stay out of their problems. They helped me find things to do during breaks, so I rarely went home. My advisor gave me great advice—take courses like anthropology that didn't remind me of either parent. So, I did. My grades shot up. When they got divorced, I was relieved. I continued to avoid Dad but kept in touch with Mom.

Over-25 Children

Parents with older children seldom need to worry about their reactions, unless they are from the most recent marriage or losing a beloved stepparent. Most are indifferent. Some are sad that the marriage ended for your sake, not theirs. Some help you get through your breakup, so the two of you grow closer. Unlike younger adults, older ones rarely withdraw from their parents. They are too involved in their own personal lives and occupational pursuits to be upset by your personal situation. Besides, with few exceptions, they are from a first union. Unlike your younger ones, they have the objectivity and maturity to be members of your support team if they aren't from this marriage. Make sure, however, they are only a small part and not your whole support system.

> ***Ten Signs Your Child is Upset***
> - Lower grades
> - Trouble sleeping at night
> - Inappropriate anger—getting into fights at school, breaking things, etc.
> - Withdrawing from family or friend, overly quiet and silent
> - Depressed: no longer interested in former favorite activities, crying, or sad.
> - Anxious: worried and/or having physical problems like dizziness and stomach aches
> - Lower self-esteem
> - Substance use
> - Change in appetite and eating
> - Self-Injurious behaviors (such as Cutting)

Case Example: Valerie

In their late twenties, Valerie and her younger sister, Lola, were concerned about their mother Mary's well-being during and for the first couple of years after her second divorce. In her mid-fifties, Mary was a twice-married factory worker. Her second marriage was 17 years long and about twice as long as her first. Although Mary suggested the separation and filed for the divorce, she was really the abandoned party. Her husband, Barney, had precipitated their divorce by revealing his relationship with another woman. Throughout the divorce, she was frazzled, lonely, and unhappy.

Through the split, Valerie and Lola emotionally supported and kept close tabs on their mother. At their request after the divorce, Mary entered counseling with her pastor, became more involved in church activities, and joined several social organizations. By her first divorce anniversary, she felt lucky to be out of her abusive second marriage. Three years later, Mary was cheerful and reasonably satisfied with her life. In turn, Valerie and Lola were relieved to see their mother happier and socially active again.

Sons versus Daughters

BOYS WILL BE BOYS

Compared to daughters, sons are more likely to respond with anger, academic and self-esteem problems, and side with their father or stepfather. These differences are most pronounced with second-marriage children.

Often angered and/or worried by parental divorce, school-aged sons are frequently too upset to concentrate on and complete their schoolwork, and as a result, have academic problems. Because learning problems cause self-esteem loss, boys have a higher risk for both issues.

Unlike daughters, sons are apt to worry about losing a parent, especially their father. Many boys view their stepdads as their true fathers, and seeing this as a rerun of their original father loss, they are typically angry and distraught.

Helper's High

A daughter is more likely to act too grown up, become more demanding, and feel embarrassed by your split than her brother. Often, she grows closer to her mother and withdraws from her father.

Unlike her teenage brother, an adolescent daughter may take on the role of caretaker and mother figure toward her younger siblings and, sometimes, even her mother. As side benefits, her stress sometimes declines, and she inches closer to her mom. As her parent, you need to be careful that your daughter helps some, but not too much. When you help someone else, you can become happier if it isn't extensive and overwhelming. This is known as "helper's high."[2] However, if she starts doing a lot of work, she may become exhausted, resentful, and/or depressed. It is also not good for your daughter to do a lot of parenting, especially for you. She is still a child and needs your parenting, not vice versa.

Alternatively, some daughters feel deprived and become demanding. If they do, they are usually angry, anxious, and rebellious, and will withdraw from you. Typically, these daughters land into trouble for their behavior, sometimes for the use of drugs or alcohol, or they run away. If your daughter is starting to have this type of reaction, you should get her into counseling quickly. Enter counseling, too. Your therapist can speed up your adjustment. As you recover, you should calm down and find it easier to take care of your obligations—job, home, and children. In response to your progress and improved parenting, your daughter is likely to become happier, more levelheaded, and drop her upset and rebelliousness, too.

> **Don't Let Your Daughter Become the New Mom**
> Be careful that your minor daughter doesn't act like a new parent in your home. She needs you to continue parenting both her and your other children.

Solutions for Emotional or Academic Issues

Although your children may not need your help with emotional or academic problems, here are some solutions and ways to protect them if they do.

GETTING BACK ON TRACK

Counseling is your first line of defense. School counselors routinely provide individual and group sessions for children struggling with parental separation and divorce. Your pediatrician or school can provide you with recommendations for clinical psychologists.

Second, make sure your child is doing well in school. When students go through parental divorce, academic troubles are common. Doing poorly in school compounds emotional distress and causes self-esteem loss (See Grades Back Up below for methods to do this).

Third, try to be as conscientious (organized, timely, hard-working, and reliable) as possible and teach your child to do the same. Conscientious parents are usually calmer and more predictable, which in turn, makes your child's life the same—calm and predictable. *In this study, children with conscientious parents were in better emotional shape—happier, calmer, and less apt to be confused.* Moreover, conscientious children usually do better in school, are less stressed, are more successful and healthier later in life[3] and live longer.[4]

Fourth, look for ways to help your children feel proud and accepted. Joining extracurricular activities such as a sports team or a club is a way to do this. Just as there are many types of athletic teams, there are many types of clubs. There are clubs for art, music, politics, scientific pursuits, hobbies, volunteering, and other things. They will gain prestige and confidence as they grow more skilled and accepted by the squad or club. Urge your children to find their niche and watch their mood improve.

Fifth, encourage your children to imagine doing well in school and extra-curricular endeavors before going to bed every night. Explain that top athletes are taught to imagine achieving a new or improved skill to gain confidence and talent. Those who apply this approach are rewarded whether the issue is athletic, academic, artistic, or something else. When you say goodnight, double-check to make sure that they have remembered to do this. Going to bed with happy thoughts can quicken their sleep, too.

Sixth, your child can benefit from reading either a fiction or nonfiction text on how to cope with divorce. Your librarian or a bookstore can quickly point you to a good, age-appropriate selection. Magination Press, a division of the American Psychological Association, publishes some of the best choices for younger children. Their authors are child experts. These books include two sections: half for you to read to your child and half just for you. The second portion will help you understand your child and how to support her.

Other texts are for older children, who can read and benefit on their own. Even if your children are handling your divorce relatively well, they can learn more effective ways to deal with their situation.

As a final remedy, especially for those who rarely see their father or mother, consider a Big Brother/Big Sister program or shore up your child's relationship with another relative. A "big brother or sister" from this organization can give your minor a chance to form a stable family-like relationship. A close tie with another relative will do the same. Many see an older sibling, aunt, uncle, or grandparent as a second parent and are emotionally buoyed and protected by this link.

Twelve Tips for Your Children
- Tell your children you love them daily!
- Parent checks child's homework for completion and understanding.
- Tutoring for children.
- Child joins a sports team or an academic club.
- Child increases daily exercise.
- Child and parents become more conscientious—organized, reliable, and timely.
- Instill a gratitude habit for children and parents.
- Every day the child imagines doing better in school and happier times.
- Child reads a fiction or nonfiction book demonstrating divorce solutions.
- Child spends more fun time with parents or supplemental parents.
- Child joins a local Big Brother/Big Sister program.
- Counseling for children.
- Parents improve your well-being. The sooner parents recover, the sooner most children recover.
- Parents take parenting classes.

GRADES BACK UP

Academic problems are a red flag that your child needs help. In some courses, like math, learning is cumulative. When your child doesn't learn these subjects as assigned, he will fall further and further behind. If so, he may stop trying to learn and start getting into trouble. Respond quickly. See if the school can provide extra help with his studies.

Consider private lessons. Just a few sessions with a tutor could make a difference in your child's academic skills. To emphasize the point, a fourth grader, who can't read at grade level, can usually learn to do so in less than 40 hours with individual instruction.

To prevent your child from falling behind, check to make sure his homework is completed and understood. Remember the saying "a stitch in time saves nine." Tell your child that education is important and that you know he can do well in school if he keeps up with his work. Education and hard work are two keys to success. Adults with divorced parents tend to lag in education and, as a result, lag in financial and marital success. Don't let your child be part of these statistics.

> ***Help Your Children in Multiple Ways***
> Try as many suggested ways as possible to help your children. Different children benefit from different approaches. Which approach will you try first?

THINGS TO REMEMBER ABOUT CHILDREN:
- Your children's reactions to your divorce depend on your response and on your child's birth family, age, and gender.
- Most first-union children will do better during your second split than they did during your first. Some are thrilled or relieved.
- Typically, second-marriage children have a negative reaction to a redivorce. Your school-aged ones will have the most intense response.
- Sons are more likely to report lowered self-esteem, scholastic difficulties, and anger issues, while daughters are more likely to become demanding, embarrassed, act too grown up, and grow closer to or withdraw from you.

CHAPTER 16

Project Design

This book integrates the findings of the first four studies in an ongoing investigation started in 1989. The project reports information from 722 men and women, most of whom are exiting a remarriage. Almost everyone in this study was in an opposite-sex marriage, because my research began prior to the legalization of same-sex marriages.

In the first three studies, I randomly selected adults who had been divorced for less than a year from the Connecticut Health Department Divorce Records, who met each study's other criteria. These public records had the couple's names and addresses, basic demographic information, and marital data for each spouse, such as the number of prior divorces; marriage, separation, and divorce dates; and the number of children.

In the first investigation, 286 twice-married men and women joined my research. About half had once-married ex-spouses, while the remaining had twice-married ones. The survey focused on complaints, the breakup process, adjustment, family-of-origin, and personality. Three years later, 108 completed a follow-up inquiring about their recovery, relations to ex-spouses and children, social life, and children's reactions to the split.

In the second study, 191 once-divorced and 2 twice-divorced men and women returned a survey almost identical to the one used in the first phase. About half had a twice-married ex-spouse and the others had a once-married ex-spouse. Two adults joined, who were mislabeled on the decrees and were redivorcers.

The third study collected questionnaires from 143 once- and twice-divorced men and women. Roughly half of each group had a once-wed ex-spouse, while the other half had a twice-wed ex-spouse. This third survey included most of the topics in the first two studies including questions about their children's reactions, as well as new items. As such, this phase replicated and extended many of the findings from the earlier research.

Out of 1,800 invitations, 622 individuals contributed to the Connecticut evaluations. Of these, approximately 9%, or 165 men and women, were unreachable; they either died or moved without leaving a forwarding address. Overall, the 622 men and women represented about a 34% response rate, or a 38% response rate correcting for the undelivered requests.

In the fourth inquiry, Survey Monkey collected information from 100 adults, most of whom had only one failed union. They were exiting traditional-first marriages (75%), as well as mono-remarriages (10%), uni-remarriages (5%), and bi-remarriages (10%). Topics in this last segment came from earlier waves and included re-partnering details, self and ex's personalities, and love style. Parents described their oldest and youngest child's responses to the split.

In sum, participants gave three divorce perspectives. Two— the second-timer and the hybrid-first views are the focus of this paper. The third outlook from the more typical first-timer with a once-wed ex is used from time to time as a control or comparison to highlight the uniqueness of the remarriage breakup path.

APPENDIX

Progressive Muscle Relaxation (PMR) (Modified version Norelli et al., 2023; designed originally by Jacobson, 1929)

Jacobson originally designed progressive muscle relaxation (PMR) in the 1920's. Since then, behavior therapists have used PMR to reduce anxiety and distress. The procedure starts by sitting or reclining in a comfortable position. Then one by one, you tense and then release each of the 7 muscle groups going from your head to your toes or vice versa. Emphasis is placed on the release of each muscle to maximize calm.

1. **FACE:** Tense muscles of your FACE, including squeezing your eyes shut for a count of 5 seconds, then slowly release for the next 10 seconds, focusing on your relaxation experience.
2. **SHOULDERS:** Tense the muscles in your SHOULDERS for a count of 5 seconds, then slowly release for the next 10 seconds, focusing on your relaxation experience.
3. **STOMACH AND CHEST:** Tense the muscles in your STOMACH AND CHEST for a count of 5 seconds, then slowly release for the next 10, seconds focusing on your relaxation experience.
4. **HANDS:** Tense the muscles in your HANDS, making a fist for a count of 5 seconds, then slowly release for the next 10 seconds, focusing on your relaxation experience.

5. **HIPS AND BUTTOCKS**: Tense the muscles in your HIPS AND BUTTOCKS for a count of 5 seconds, then slowly release for the next 10 seconds, focusing on your relaxation experience.
6. **LOWER LEGS**: Tense the muscles in your LOWER LEGS for a count of 5 seconds, then slowly release for the next 10 seconds, focusing on your relaxation experience.
7. **FEET**: Tense the muscles in your FEET for a count of 5 seconds, then slowly release for the next 10 seconds, focusing on your relaxation experience.

Notes

CHAPTER 1: YOUR DIVORCE GUIDE
1. Mayol-Garcia et al., 2021.

CHAPTER 2: HOW ARE REMARRIAGES DIFFERENT?
1. Vultaggio, 2015.
2. Bramlett, & Mosher, 2002.
3. Kreider & Ellis, 2011.
4. Francis-Tan & Mialon, 2014.
5. Shattuck & Kreider, 2013.
6. Asselmann & Specht, 2020.
7. Ceglian, & Gardner, 1999.

CHAPTER 3: HOW ARE REMARRIAGE DIVORCES DIFFERENT?
1. Taibbi, 1979.

CHAPTER 4: MONO-REMARRIAGE PITFALLS
1. Barash, 2000.
2. Ahrons, 2004.

CHAPTER 5: UNI-REMARRIAGE PITFALLS
1. Weir, 2019.

CHAPTER 7: BI-REMARRIAGE PITFALLS
1. Herman, June 21, 2006.
2. Stoner, 2024.
3. Affifi & McManus, 2010.
4. Stahl, 2011.
5. Woodhouse & Fethering, 2020.

Chapter 8: Uprooted
1. Taraborrelli, 2006.
2. Norelli et al., 2023.
3. Doskow, 2024.

Chapter 9: Weathering the Storm
1. Chen et al., 2016.
2. Luks & Payne, 200.
3. Borkovec, 1983
4. Norelli, et al., 2023.
5. Moser et al., 2017.
6. Schaan, et al., 2019.
7. Amato & Gilbreth, 1999.
8. Cohen & Sherman, 2014.
9. Jacobs, 1998.
10. Whitton et al., 2008.

Chapter 10: First Year Postdivorce Transition
1. Modified attachment style question from Bartholomew & Horowitz, 1991.
2. Chen, et. al., 2016.
3. Lourey, 2017.
4. Jain et al., 2007.
5. Gortner et al., 2006.
6. Bain, 1928.
7. Shallcross & Simpson 2012.

Chapter 15: How Will my Children React?
1. Doskow, 2024.
2. Luks & Payne, 2001.
3. Hampson, et al., 2007.
4. Hill et al., 2011.

Glossary

Bi-redivorce: A divorce between two remarried individuals.

Bi-remarriage: A union between two remarried individuals.

Blended family: A remarriage family with minor children from both the wife's previous marriage and the husband's previous marriage.

Collaborative divorce: An expanded version of divorce mediation. Instead of one neutral professional, the facilitator, you have a team to assist you and your spouse to achieve a cooperative agreement that meets the needs and interests of everyone in your family. Specialists include a separate lawyer for each spouse as well as neutral experts such as a facilitator, financial advisor, and real estate appraiser.

Composite case: A group model, which profiles a type of individual. The illustration describes the major characteristics of this type of person, such as his or her typical age, gender, background, traits, and behavior.

Conscientiousness: A trait marked by such characteristics as responsibility, orderliness, respectfulness, and hard work.

Deep breathing: In deep breathing, you regulate your breathing using your diaphragm to increase the inflow and outflow of air and, at the same time, slow down your breathing rate. Deep breathing is an ancient method used to improve health and reduce stress.

Dismissive attachment/ Dismissive lover: One of the four adult love relationship styles and an insecure form. Typically, an individual with this approach has good self-esteem, but a negative view of others.

Disunion: is a divorce or legal dissolution of a marriage.

Divorce mediation: To avoid litigation, a neutral professional helps a divorcing couple resolve disputes and develop an agreement covering child custody, visitation, and finances.

Early postdecree: The first year after the decree issuance.

Egocentrism: Until about age seven, children think everyone sees and thinks the same way they do. Dr. Jean Piaget called this egocentrism.

Extrovert: An outgoing and talkative individual. The opposite of extrovert is introvert.

Family-of-origin: is the adoptive or birth kin group in which an individual grew up.

Fearful attachment/ Fearful lover: One of the four adult love relationship styles and an insecure type. An individual with this perspective has low respect for both himself or herself and others.

First-marriage family or couple: A family or couple in which both the husband and wife are in their first and only marriage.

Guided imagery: Either sitting or lying down comfortably, imagine a calming scene from memory or make one up. Increase calm by using all five senses (vision, hearing, smell, taste, and touch).

Hybrid first-timer: First-timer who is or has been married to a remarried person.

Introvert: In social situations, an introvert is reserved, quiet, and uneasy. The opposite of introvert is extrovert.

Mono-redivorce: A legal breakup between a remarried man and a once-married woman. The prefix mono- is derived from a Greek term meaning one; here it refers to one redivorced partner, who is the husband.

Mono-remarriage: A union between a remarried man and a once-married woman.

Postdecree or postdivorce: is the period after the divorce decree.
Predivorce: The stage before the divorce decree.
Preoccupied attachment/ Preoccupied lover: One of the four adult love relationship styles and an insecure subtype. Those with this viewpoint have low self-esteem, but high respect for others.
Progressive muscle relaxation (PMR). In this method, the individual tenses and then relaxes each muscle group in the body, one by one, starting with either the toes and working to the head or vice versa. Focus is put on the muscle release or relaxation phase for each muscle. (see Appendix for protocol).
Recoupled: A new partnership—going steady, engaged, partnered, or remarried.
Redivorced: Divorced two or more times.
Redivorcers: Individuals who have divorced two or more times.
Secure attachment/ Secure lover: The love style, which promotes the best interpersonal relationships of the four approaches. Secure lovers have excellent self-esteem and high respect for others.
Social investigation: A study conducted by a mental health professional to help the court determine a parenting plan, including child custody and visitation schedules.
Statistically significant difference: The likelihood that two or more sets are the same is very unlikely. A .05 or .01 statistical difference suggests that there is a 95% or 99% chance, respectively, that the sets are different on some measure. Our confidence in this conclusion increases as the level goes from .05 to .01, to .001, to .000.
Traditional first-marriage: A union between two partners who are in their first marriage. This is also known as a first-marriage or a double-first family.
Transition year. The first year after the divorce is called the (first) transition year.

Triangle breathing. A form of deep breathing with three steps: inhale for 4, hold for 4, and exhale for 4. Repeat the cycle until you are calm.

Uni-redivorce: A divorce between a remarried woman and a once-married man. Uni- a Latin prefix meaning one, is used here to mean one redivorced partner, the wife.

References

Affifi, T. D., & McManus, T. (2010). Divorce disclosures and adolescents' physical and mental health and parental relationships. *Journal of Divorce and Remarriage*, 51(2), 83–107. https://doi.org/ 10.1080/10502550903455141

Ahrons, C. R. (2004). *We're still family*. HarperCollins.

Amato, P., & Gilbreth, J. (1999). Nonresident father and children's well-being: A meta-analysis. *Journal of Marriage and the Family*, 61, 557-573. doi: 10.2307/353560

Asselmann, E., & Specht, S. (2020). Taking the ups and downs at the rollercoaster of love: Associations between major life events in the domain of romantic relationships and the big five personality traits, *Developmental Psychology*, 56(9), 1803–1816, https://dx.doi.org/10.1037/dev0001047

Bain, J.A. (1928). *Thought control in everyday life*. Funk & Wagnalls.

Barash, S. (2000). *Second wives*. New Horizon Press.

Barnet, H. S. (1990). Divorce stress and adjustment model: Locus of control and demographic predictors. *Journal of Divorce*, 13(3), 93–109. https://doi.org/10.1300/J279v13n03_08

Bartholomew, K. & Horowitz, L. M. (1991). Attachment styles among young adults: A test of a 4- category model. *Journal of Personality and Social Psychology*, 61(2), 226–244. https:// doi.org/10.1037/0022-3514.61.2.226

Benjamin, M., & Irving H. H. (1990). Comparison of the experience of satisfied and dissatisfied shared parents. *Journal of Divorce & Remarriage*, 14(1), 43–61. https://doi.org /10.1300/J087v14 n01_05

Booth, A. & Edwards, J.N. (1992). Starting over: Why remarriages are more unstable. *Journal of Family Issues*, 13, 179–194.110.117710_9251392013002004

Borkovec, T.D., Wilkinson, L., Folensbee, R., & Lerman, C. (1983). Stimulus control applications to the treatment of worry. *Behavior Research Therapy.* 21(3):247-51. doi: 10.1016/0005-7967(83)90206-1. PMID: 6615390.

Bramlett, B. D., & Mosher, W. D. (2002). Cohabitation, marriage, divorce, and remarriage in the United States. *National Center for Health Statistics,* 23 (22) 1–93.

Brown, S. L., & Lin I. F. (2012). The gray divorce revolution: Rising divorce among middle-aged and older adults, 1990-2010. *The Journals of Gerontology Series B: Psychological Sciences and Social Sciences,* 67 (6). 731–741. https://doi.org/10.1093/geronb/gbs089

Brown, S.L. & Lin, I.F. (2022). The graying of divorce: A half century of change, *The Journals of Gerontology: Series B,* Volume 77, Issue 9, 1710–1720, https://doi.org/10.1093/geronb/gbac057

Cargan, L., & Whitehurst, R. (1990). Adjustment differences in the divorced and redivorced. *Journal of Divorce and Remarriage,* 14(2), 49–78. https://doi.org/10.1111/j.1758-0854.2010.01045.x

Ceglian, C. P., & Gardner, S. (1999). Attachment style: A risk for multiple marriages? *Journal of Divorce & Remarriage,* 31(1-2),125–139. https://doi.org/10.1300/J087v31n01_02

Chen, Y., Mark, G., & Ali, S. (2016). Promoting positive affect through smartphone photography. *Psychology of Wellbeing.* 6, 8, https//:doi.org/10.1186/s13612-016-0044-4

Chiriboga, D. A., & Cutler, L. (1977). Stress responses among divorcing men and women. *Journal of Divorce,* 1(2), 95–106. https://doi.org/10.1300/J279v01n02_01

Clarke-Stewart, A. & Brentano, C., (2006). *Divorce cause and consequences,* Yale University Press

Cleek, M., & Pearson, T. (1985). Perceived causes of divorce: An analysis of interrelationships. *Journal of Marriage and the Family,* 4(1), 179–183. https://doi.org/10.2307/352080

Cohen G.L. & Sherman D.K. (2014). The psychology of change: self-affirmation and social psychological intervention. Annual Review of Psychology, 65, 333-371. Doi.org/10.1146/annurev-psych-010213-115137

Doodson, L. J. (2014) Understanding the factors related to stepmother anxiety: A qualitative approach, *Journal of Divorce & Remarriage*, 55(8), 645–667, https://doi.org/10.1080/10502556.2014.959111

Doskow, E. (2024). *Nolo's essential guide to divorce*. Nolo.

Eckharet, R. (September 9, 2012). Courts seeing more do-it-yourself divorces, *Downloaded from http://www.heraldtribune.com / article/20120909/ ARTICLE/ 120909620 on February 28, 2016.*

Francis-Tan, A., & Mialon, H.M. (2014). "A diamond is forever" and other fairy tales: The relationship between wedding expenses and marriage duration. *Economic Inquiry*, 53(4), 1919– 1930. https://doi.org/10.1111/ecin.12206

Gaunt, R. (2006). Couple similarity and marital satisfaction: Are similar spouses happier? *Journal of Personality*, 74(5), 1401–1420. https://doi.org/ 10.1111/j.1467_6494.2006.00414.x

Gortner, E., Rude, S.S., & Pennebaker, J.W. (2006). Benefits of expressive writing in lowering rumination and depressive symptoms. *Behavior Therapy*, 37, 3, 292–303

Gray, J. (2012). *Men are from Mars, Women are from Venus*. HarperCollins.

Hampson, S. E., Goldberg, L. R., Vogt, T. M., & Dubanoski, J. P. (2007). Mechanisms by which childhood personality traits influence adult health status: Educational attainment and healthy behavior. *Health Psychology*, 26(1), 121–125. https://doi.org/110.1037/0278_6133.26.1.121

Herman, M. (June 21, 2006). Pro se statistics, Downloaded from https://www.nacmnet.org / sites/default/ files/04Greacen_ProSeStatisticsSummary.pdf, February 28, 2016.

Hetherington, E. M., Stanley-Hagan, M. & Anderson, E. R. (1989).

Marital transitions: A child's perspective. *American Psychologist*, 44(2), 303–312. https://doi.org/10.1037/0003-066x.44.2.303

Hill, P.L., Turiano, N.A., Hurd, M.D., Mroczek, D.K., & Roberts, B.W. (2011). Conscientiousness, and longevity: An examination of possible mediators. *Health Psychology*, 30(5) 536–541. https://doi.org/10.1037/a0023859

Jacobs, G.D. (1998). *Say good night to insomnia*, Holt.

Jacobson, E. (1929). *Progressive muscle relaxation: A physiological and clinical investigation of muscular states and their significance in psychological and medical practices.* University of Chicago Press.

Jain S, Shapiro S.L., Swanick S., Roesch S.C., Mills P.J., Bell I., & Schwartz G.E. (2007, Feb) A randomized controlled trial of mindfulness meditation versus relaxation training: Effects on distress, positive states of mind, rumination, and distraction. *Annual Behavioral Medicine.* 33(1):11-21. doi: 10.1207/s15324796abm3301_2. PMID: 17291166

Kerry, N., Chhabra, R., & Clifton, J.D.W. (2023). Being thankful for what you have: A systematic review of evidence for the effect of gratitude on life satisfaction, *Psychology of Research and Behavior Management,* 16, 4799-4816. https://doi.org/10.2147/PRBM.S372432

Kirshenbaum, M. (1997). *Too good to leave, too bad to stay*. Plume.

Knox, D., & Zusman, M. E. (2001). Marrying a man with "baggage": Implications for second wives. *Journal of Divorce & Remarriage*, 35(3-4), 67–79. https://doi.org/10.1300/J087v35n03_04

Kreider, R. M., & Ellis, R. (2011). Number, timing, and duration of marriages and divorces: 2009. *Current Population Reports*, 70–125. US Census Bureau.

Lewis, J. M., & Kreider, R. M. (2015). *Remarriage in the United States, American Community Survey Reports*, ACS-30, U.S. Census Bureau.

Little, M.A. (1992). The impact of the custody plan on the family:

A five-year follow-up: Executive summary. *Family and Conciliation Courts Review*, 30, 243–251. Cited in Clarke-Stewart, A. & Brentano, C., (2006). *Divorce cause and consequences*, Yale University Press.

Livingston, G. (2014). *Four-in-ten couples are saying I do again*. Pew Research Center.

Lourey, J.A. (2017). *Rewrite your life: Discover your truth through the healing power of fiction*. Conari Press.

Luks, A., & Payne, P. (2001). *The power of doing good*. IUniverse Publications.

Mahindru, A., Patil, P., & Agrawal, V. (2023). Role of physical activity on mental health and well-being: A review. *Cureus*, 15 (1): e33475. doi:10.7759/cureus.33475

Martin, D.J., Garske, J.P., & Davis, M.K. (2000). Relation of therapeutic alliance with outcome and other variables: A meta-analytic review. *Journal of Consulting and Clinical Psychology*, 68 (3), 438–450. https://doi.org//10.1037/0022-006x.68.3.438

Mayol-Garcia, Y., Gurrentz, B., & Kreider, R. M. (2021). Number, timing, and duration of marriages and divorces:2016, *Current Population Reports*, 70–167, U.S. Census Bureau.

McMullen, J. G., & Oswald, D. (2010). Why do we need a lawyer? An empirical study of divorce cases. *Journal of Law & Family Studies*, Vol. 12, p. 57; Marquette Law School Legal Studies Paper No. 10-16. Available at SSRN: https://ssrn.com/abstract=1580243

Moser J.S., Dougherty, A., Mattson, W.I., Katz, B., Moran, T.P., Guevarra, D., Shablack, H., Ayduk O., Jonides, J., Berman, M.G., & Kross, E. (2017). Third-person self-talk facilitates emotion regulation without engaging cognitive control: Converging evidence from ERP and fMRI. *Sci Rep*. 2017 Jul 3;7(1):4519. doi: 10.1038/s41598-017-04047-3. PMID: 28674404; PMCID: PMC5495792.

Naparstek, B. (1994). *Staying well with guided imagery.* Warner Books.

Nielsen, L. (1999). Stepmothers: Why so much stress? A review of the research. *Journal of Divorce & Remarriage,* 30(1-2), 115–148. https://doi.org/ 10.1300/J087v30n01_08

Norelli S.K., Long A., & Krepps J.M. (2023). Relaxation Techniques. In: "StatPearls" [Internet]. Treasure Island (FL): StatPearls Publishing; 2024 Jan. https://www.ncbi.nlm.nih.gov/ books/ NBK513238/

Rabinor, J. R. (2012). *Befriending Your Ex After Divorce,* New Harbinger.

Roper, S.W., Fife, S.T., & Seedall, R.B. (2020). The intergenerational effects of parental divorce on young adult relationships, *Journal of Divorce and Remarriage,* 61(4), 249–266. https://doi: 10.1080/10502556. St.1 699372

Rowen, J., & Emery, R. (2014). Examining parental denigration behaviors of co–parents as reported by young adults and their association with parent–child closeness. *Couple and Family Psychology: Research and Practice,* 3(3), 165–177. https://doi.org/10.1037/cfp0000026

Schaan, V.K., Schulz, A., Schachinger, H., & Vogele, C. (2019). Parental divorce is associated with an increased risk to develop mental disorders in women, *Journal of Affective disorders,* 257, 91–99, doi.org/10.1016/j.jad.2019.06.071

Shallcross, S. L., & Simpson, J. A. (2012). Trust and responsiveness in strain-test situations: A dyadic perspective. *Journal of Personality and Social Psychology,*102(5), 1031–1044. https://10.1037/ 00026829

Shattuck, R. M., & Kreider, R. M. (2013). Social and economic characteristics of currently unmarried women with a recent birth: 2011. *American Community Survey Report,* U. S. Census Bureau.

Simpson, J. A., Collins, W. A., Tran, S., & Haydon, K. C. (2007).

Attachment and the experience and expression of emotions in romantic relationships: A developmental perspective. *Journal of Personality and Social Psychology,* 92(2), 355–367. https://10.1037/0022-3514.922.355

Sin, N.L. & Lyubomirsky, S. (2009). Enhancing well-being and alleviating depressive symptoms with positive psychology interventions: A practice-friendly meta-analysis. *Journal of Clinical Psychology.* 65 (5), 467–487, https://10.1002/jclp.20593

Sprecher, S. & Fermlee, D. (1992). The influence of parents and friends on the quality and stability of romantic relationships: A three-wave longitudinal investigations. *Journal of Marriage and the Family,* 54, 4, 888–900, http://doi.org/ 10.2307/353170

Stahl, P.M. (2011). *Conducting child custody evaluations: From Basic to complex issues,* Sage, https://doi.org/10.4135/9781452275222

Stoner, K. (2024). *Divorce without court: A guide to mediation and collaborative divorce.* Berkley, CA: Nolo.

Strack, S. (1991). *Manual for the Personality Adjective Check List (PACL).* South Pasadena, CA: 21st Century Assessment.

Tabbi, R. (1979). Transitional relationships after divorce. *Journal of Divorce,* 2(3), 263–269. https://doi.org/10.1300/J279v02n03_04

Taraborrelli, J. R. (2006). *Elizabeth.* Rose Books.

Varvogli, L., & Darvini, C. (2011). Stress management techniques: Evidence-based procedures that reduce stress and promote health. *Health Science Journal,* 5(2), 74–89

Vaux, A. (1985). Variations in social support associated with gender, ethnicity, and age. *Journal of Social Issues,* 41(1), 89–110. https://doi.org/10.1111/j.1540-4560.1985.tb01118.x

Vultaggio, M. (2015). Jackie Kennedy Onassis quotes: 10 things she said to remember the former first lady on the anniversary of her death. *International Business Times,* downloaded https://www.ibtimes.com/jackie-kennedy-onassis-quotes-10-things-she-said-remember-former-first-lady-1924689 3/10/2017

Weir, K. (2019). Sex therapy for the 21st century: Five emerging directions. *Monitor on Psychology*, APA.

Whitton, S.W., Rhoades, G.K., Stanley, S.M., & Markman, H.J. (2008) Effects of parental divorce on marital commitment and confidence. *Journal of Family Psychology*, 22(5):789-793. doi: 10.1037/a0012800. PMID: 18855515; PMCID: PMC2704052.

Woodhouse, A. V., & Fethering, D. (2020). *Divorce & money: How to make the best decisions during divorce.* 13th edition. Nolo.

Yu, T., & Adler-Baeder, F. (2007). The intergenerational transmission of relationship quality. *Journal of Divorce & Remarriage*, 47(3-4), 87–102. https://doi.org/10.1300/J087v47n03_05

Zagrean, I., Russo, C., Di Fabio, M., Danioni, F., & Barni, D. (2020). Forgiveness and family functioning among young adults from divorced and married families, *Journal of Divorce & Remarriage*, 61(8), 543–555. https://doi.org/10.1080/10502556.2020.1799307

Topic Index

Abuse
    Emotional (psychological) abuse 57, 109
    Physical abuse 63, 64, 77, 81, 102, 103, 115, 128-129, 253, 255
Adjustment 27-31, 37, 54, 78, 100, 113, 123, 144, 145, 153-242, 258-260, 274, 279
Anger 27, 36, 74, 80, 84, 100, 104, 114, 118, 128-132, 138, 142, 144, 145, 148, 158, 200, 202, 204, 236, 262, 272-274, 278
Attachment love style 17, 152, 172-173
Attitude toward ex-spouse 163-165
Children
    Academic problems 252, 254, 255, 265, 269, 275-278
    Age differences 257-273
    Divorce causes 62
    Emotional issues 251-277
    First versus second marriage 251-257
    Parent-child relationship changes 259
    Sons versus daughters 273-274
Communication 74, 75, 79, 99-100, 114-115, 154, 155, 189, 249
Confidence 22, 23, 28, 55, 108, 119, 169-173, 177, 183, 185, 195, 221
Counseling choices 73-78
Dating/romantic relationships 159-164, 191-194
Decision time/ divorce initiation 200, 203, 212, 217, 232, 235
Depression (adult) 119-122
Divorce complaints 32-67, 114, 202, 243, 253
Emotional problems (adult) 16, 18, 56-57, 202
Erased marriages 20-25, 31
Ex-spouse relationship 188-190
Failure/remorse 112, 117, 135-137, 148

Financial difficulties 40-41, 87-95, 181-183
Happiness 37, 56, 109, 121, 123, 148, 154-158, 162, 177, 181-186,195, 235, 254, 268
Health 23, 94, 120-122, 125, 128, 137-148, 155, 180-187
In-law friction 24, 29, 36, 39, 40, 42-44, 52, 63, 110-112, 199
Infidelity 42-47, 53-54, 58, 84, 99-100, 104-106, 109, 135, 174, 198-199, 210-211, 216
Insomnia 23, 27, 93, 137-141, 148, 155, 182, 202, 208, 235-236, 240,
Legal divorce settlement methods 78-82
Life Satisfaction 178-188
Loneliness 43, 44, 109, 110, 129-134, 142, 144, 145, 148, 182, 202, 243
Marital review 27, 153, 165-169, 176, 177
Parental divorce (adults) 15, 42-43, 54-55, 133, 142
Redivorce differences 19-32
Relief 108, 129, 144-148
Relocating 86, 112-115
Remarriage—desire 191-195
Remarriage traits 8-18
Sexual problems 54-58, 216
Social difficulties 99-112, 183-185
Social investigation 87
Spousal problems 72, 97-104, 114-115
Stress
    Comparative 22-31, 203-207, 220-223, 233-236
    Patterns 123-125, 154-156
    Reducers 125-128
Substance abuse 53-54, 143
Stepchildren 111-112, 115
Trust 27-31, 36, 39, 52, 54, 81, 97, 129-130, 134,148, 153-154, 172-177, 193, 194, 207, 216, 223, 237, 238, 243, 250
Violence 102-104
Work problems 137, 143-145

Acknowledgments

Over the years, many individuals contributed to this inquiry. More than fifty of my students at several universities helped with the data collection. Sacred Heart University and Western Connecticut State University endorsed the investigation and provided financial assistance for the earliest survey materials and mailings.

In addition, colleagues both in and outside of these sponsoring Connecticut universities provided stimulating questions and remarks. Neighbors, relatives, and far-flung friends added to the initial readership and feedback pool. My husband Stephen Barnet helped with the data collection during the onset of this investigation. My son Bradford Barnet, M.A., a friend, Felicity Hyde, and eight psychologists—Michael Antoni, Ph.D., Demarra Bennett, Psy.D., Cyntha Gonzalez, M.Sc., Katherine Den Houter, Ph.D., Andrew Dobo, Psy.D., Peggy Hollen, Ph.D., Teresa Nellans, M.A., and Carol Oseroff, Ph.D., as well as the Writer's WindowPane Critique Group in Vero Beach, FL gave helpful advice. A special thank you goes to the Connecticut Public Health Department for providing repeated access to their marital dissolution records. Survey Monkey collected the information for the fourth survey.

Most importantly, I appreciate the participation of the many individuals who joined this project. Despite their own concerns, these men and women took time out from their busy lives to discuss their recent divorces. Opening up their lives to me, a stranger, was an act of trust, generosity, and concern for others, who will wrestle with the same issues. By sharing these experiences and knowledge, they not only made this project possible, but also hopefully will contribute to the well-being of future divorcing adults and their families.

About the Author

Dr. Helen Barnet has investigated divorce for more than 30 years. In 1990, she published one of the first studies on adult divorce stress and adjustment in the *Journal of Divorce and Remarriage*. Over the years, she has researched the breakup of over 700 marriages, most of which were re-weds. Her self-help book, *Divorcing Again?* is based on her groundbreaking work on remarriage splits. As a psychologist, she has dealt with family transitions in multiple clinical settings as well as taught psychology at Connecticut College, Sacred Heart University, Western Connecticut State College, and the University of Connecticut.

Dr. Barnet has three psychology degree starting with a B.A. from Smith College. The other two include a M.A. (University of Vermont) and a Ph.D. (New School for Social Research, NYC). In addition, she has a Sixth Year Certificate in School Psychology (Southern Connecticut State University). Helen is a member of the American Psychological Association (APA), Florida Psychological Association (FPA), and Southeastern Psychological Association (SEPA). Dr. Barnet is a Past President and Continuing Education (CE) Chair of Brevard/Indian River Chapter of FPA.

For fun, Dr. Barnet enjoys aquatic sports and floral arranging. With her late husband, Stephen, she has one son Bradford. Bradford and his wife, Brianna, have two children, Cooper and Oliver.

www.ingramcontent.com/pod-product-compliance
Lightning Source LLC
Chambersburg PA
CBHW071110160426
43196CB00013B/2523